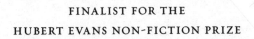
Praise for
Mexican Hooker #1

FINALIST FOR THE
HUBERT EVANS NON-FICTION PRIZE

"This is a book that draws tears. . . . *Mexican Hooker #1* is more than brave—it is dauntless, and Aguirre's telling of it, even in its devastating moments, accomplishes what she set out to do: integrate it all in order to bare her true self." *National Post*

"An engaging, terrific read. . . . Stylistically the book is raw and vibrant, bursting with energy. Sex and love are examined candidly. Aguirre doesn't cut herself any slack and is utterly fearless. . . . *Mexican Hooker #1* works on many engaging levels." *Vancouver Sun*

"A deep, soul-searching book. . . . [Aguirre's] writing is fluid, funny and vibrantly alive. . . . By its conclusion, it may bring you to tears." *The Georgia Straight*

"Effortless, enthralling prose. . . . *Mexican Hooker #1* is a memoir about identities and escape. . . . An incredibly effective and beautiful memoir." *Room*

"Bold, brave and beautiful, this book might break your heart, but it will also bring you joy and hope." *Richmond News*

"*Mexican Hooker #1* is open and raw, like Aguirre's life. Once started, I could not put it down." Laurie Glenn Norris, *Quill & Quire*

"This is extraordinary and, often unexpectedly, beautiful reading." Noah Richler, author of *This Is My Country, What's Yours? A Literary Atlas of Canada*

"What a bold, brave, and wise artist Carmen Aguirre is. Despite some soul-crushing experiences in her past, she's written a memoir that's life-affirming, awe-inspiring, and even wickedly funny in parts." Neil Smith, author of *Boo*

"This book roars with a kind of courage one rarely witnesses in this world. It is a harrowing read, horrific yet unexpectedly—almost impossibly—tender. Carmen Aguirre will show you what compassion truly looks like. And the final few pages will leave you gobsmacked." Alison Wearing, author of *Confessions of a Fairy's Daughter*

"How many shocks can the body and mind endure? Carmen Aguirre has a courage and love of life that feeds her writing. Each valuable day is of interest to her. But again, how much pain can be absorbed without the mind detaching? I read all Aguirre's work with fascination and a kind of awe, but *Mexican Hooker #1* takes us further inside. The shocks are hitting us as we read." Heather Mallick

Carmen Aguirre

Mexican Hooker #1

Art, Love and Forgiveness After Trauma

Vintage Canada

VINTAGE CANADA EDITION, 2017

Copyright © 2016 Carmen Aguirre

Published by Vintage Canada, a division of Penguin Random House Canada Limited, in 2017. Originally published in hardcover by Random House Canada, a division of Penguin Random House Canada Limited, in 2016. Distributed in Canada by Penguin Random House Canada Limited, Toronto.

Vintage Canada with colophon is a registered trademark.

www.penguinrandomhouse.ca

Library and Archives Canada Cataloguing in Publication

Aguirre, Carmen, 1967–, author
    Mexican hooker #1 : art, love and forgiveness after trauma / Carmen Aguirre.

ISBN 978-0-345-81385-5
eBook ISBN 978-0-345-81386-2

    I. Aguirre, Carmen, 1967– . 2. Dramatists, Canadian (English)—21st century—Biography. 3. Rape victims—Canada—Biography. I. Title.

PS8601.G86Z85 2017   C812'.6   C2015-905924-0

Book design by Leah Springate

Front cover photo: Alejandra Aguirre. Back cover images: (wall background) © RoyStudio.eu / Shutterstock.com; (flowers) © Irina Mishina / iStockphoto.com

Printed and bound in the United States of America

2 4 6 8 9 7 5 3 1

Penguin
Random
House

VINTAGE CANADA

For my parents

I do not know where I am going, where I have come from is disappearing. I am unwelcome and my beauty is not beauty here. My body is burning with the shame of not belonging, my body is longing. I am the sin of memory and the absence of memory.

—WARSAN SHIRE

excerpt from the poem
"Conversations About Home (at the Deportation Centre)"

ONE

I t all went down in the church basement on Forty-Ninth Avenue, South Vancouver, after the voice teacher instructed me to drop my back ribs. It had been a month since I'd started theatre school and learned the importance of that particular set of bones, and maybe a week since I'd begun trying to grasp the concept of succumbing to the floor. As I lay there, I imagined carrying my ribs in a bag, upturning the contents.

"Let your hip sockets go," she intoned.

Which made sense, this being a church and all. Fingers placed on my solar plexus, she instructed me to exhale.

Hip sockets. Before Labour Day, I'd never heard the term and envisioned electrical sockets whenever it came up, numerous times a day.

"Drop, let go, drop, let go, drop, let go," I repeated to myself, reaching for breath over and over again, pushing my back down, willing the electrons coursing through my body to somehow plug or unplug into the alleged sockets.

I knew I was doing it all wrong. You weren't supposed to push the breath, you were supposed to let it be. The Beatles song popped into my mind.

"Focus, you idiot," I thought.

I was twenty-two years old, this was voice class 101, I had three years to go, and I planned on acing theatre school, landing on the honour roll, like I had in high school.

My classmates sat cross-legged in a circle around me, the sacrificial lamb splayed belly up. The instructions continued.

"Take a risk."

Take a risk. I had taken many risks in my life thus far, most notably while being in the Chilean resistance a mere eighteen months earlier, but I was to take another kind of risk, and I had no way to measure, weigh, or determine what it looked like. Deaf, dumb, and blind, I groped my way through the forest, grasping for a new definition of a concept so familiar to me in another hemisphere, south of the equator, a world where the constellations were different and spring had just begun.

"What is the worst thing that can happen if you just let go?" she asked.

I knew the right answer. Nothing. 'Cause the floor is there to catch you. The floor as open arms. Not as dispenser of bruises, breaker of bones. My hip sockets gripped. Instead of releasing. They clung to my pelvic bone, and I started to shake, a leaf at the mercy of an electrical storm. My body leapt up, hit by a bolt of lightning, and landed back down again. I wondered if my hair had gone wild like Medusa's. Keeping my eyes shut, I surrendered to the surge, battered white flag flapping in the air. Completely pathetic. Out of control. Right. That's what was required. Loss of control. Right.

"Let it out on sound," she ordered. "Open your mouth. Out on sound," she repeated forcefully.

There was only one sound we were to use in voice class 101, and it was the sound we'd uttered when we were expelled from the womb and took our first breath.

"Aaaaahhh."

The *aaaahhh* escaped my mouth, tears poured down the sides of my face, and the shaking grew worse.

I had only been back in Canada for six months, after four harrowing years in Argentina, where my sole reason to live was the Cause. I had made many incursions into Pinochet's Chile during that time, on buses, in cars, and on planes, sometimes flown by my then-husband Alejandro and me. Border runs, they were called. We carried goods for the underground and harboured resistance members in our home in Neuquén, Argentina. I had returned to Vancouver to go to acting school and planned to go back to South America as soon as I graduated to pursue a career in the theatre. Canada, where I'd grown up in exile after the coup in Chile, had not felt like home since I was a child, and there was too much going on in the South for me to miss out on. Although I spoke perfect English and was bicultural to the core, my heart ached for home, and I was not sure how I would survive the next three years away from that Southern Cone, the towering Andes Mountains a seam, the long country of my birth lying stoically in wait for the explosive Pacific to swallow it whole.

"Keep your back on the floor."

But I couldn't. The shaking intensified.

"What's going on?" she demanded.

"He's got a gun," I answered through chattering teeth.

"How old are you?"

"Thirteen," I replied, impressed at her ability to decipher that I was having a childhood flashback.

Fuelled by adrenalin, I ran through the coniferous forest, oblivious to the branches whipping my face, the underbrush drawing beads of blood from my shins. Shafts of light penetrated the tops of the towering rainforest trees as I tore my way through the dense greenery, carrying my sandals in my trembling hand, the soles of my bare feet pounding the pine needle–covered ground. A plane flew overhead, a jogger panted on a trail nearby, the sounds of traffic grew louder.

"What's happening now?" the teacher asked, my inhalations wind in the sails of my undoing.

"We're alive!" I yelled back. "We're alive."

I could hear my cousin Macarena, twelve years old, covered in bits of moss, twigs in her tangled hair, right behind me. The woods spit us out onto University Boulevard, on Vancouver's west side, cars racing past. Her face was smeared with dirt, snot, and tears. Tears flowed from my eyes as well, and I was shaking too hard to put my sandals back on.

"Stop!" I yelled at the cars. "Stop!"

But nobody would.

Macarena and I broke into a run again.

The exorcising electrocution in the church basement went on for the rest of the class. By the time my back ribs were fossilized onto the crust of the earth and I had the flexible hip sockets of a marionette, two hours had passed. My classmates witnessed in silence. Coached up to sitting, I opened my eyes and met the steady gaze of my peers, the circle of them breathing together like a great furry beast. I held eye contact with each and every one of them, as the teacher instructed.

4

Released from class, I skipped down Forty-Ninth Avenue, woo-hooing at the top of my lungs, arms outstretched, head thrown back, taking in the Indian summer sky. It was September 1990, and Laura Ashley baby doll dresses worn with black tights were all the rage. My beat-up Sally Ann combat boots, however, were most incongruous with my *Sound-of-Music* behaviour.

Not only did I feel a million pounds lighter, I had mastered the concept of giving in to the floor and would no doubt get an A in voice class 101.

As for the childhood rape that had come to the surface, always present, never dealt with, it was clear as day that it was now cast out from my body, never to come back and bother me again, the way an unruly drunk is unceremoniously thrown onto a sidewalk from a nightclub door. The way an insurrection brings an oppressive system to its knees, expelling the culprit from a country, a continent, an entire hemisphere, or, in this case, a body: mine.

Nine months earlier, in December 1989, my mother and I had joined a crowd of ten thousand people on Buenos Aires's Avenida de Mayo to hear Tomás Borge, founding member of the Sandinistas, former political prisoner, and minister of the interior for Sandinista Nicaragua, speak to the Argentinian left. Two elections loomed that night: the Nicaraguan, to be held in February 1990, and the Chilean, days away.

In 1970, Chile had become one of the first countries in the world to elect a Marxist president, Salvador Allende. He had gone on to implement socialist change through agrarian reform, literacy campaigns, land takeovers by Indigenous peasants, and nationalization of the world's biggest copper mine. The last had prompted Nixon and Kissinger to mastermind the coup, along with the Chilean bourgeoisie. On September 11, 1973, the new, Allende-appointed commander-in-chief of the armed forces, Augusto Pinochet, headed the overthrow. The air force bombed the presidential palace, Allende died, and thousands ended up being murdered, imprisoned, tortured, disappeared, or were exiled.

Now, after seventeen years, Pinochet was about to step down, but the revolutionary change we had struggled for was not to be. Pinochet's neo-liberal system would remain intact and Chile would be idolized on the world stage as a "democratic" nation where deregulated capitalism had not only overthrown socialism but done away with every last vestige of it. University education, once superb and publicly funded, had been privatized, social programmes demolished, and the country's state-owned resources sold to multinationals. As for the resistance, it had pretty much dissolved in the year leading up to the December 1989 election. The revolution had been lost. We had fought through the eighties not only to topple Pinochet's infamous dictatorship, known around the globe for its gross violations of human rights, but also to pick up where Allende had left off. The difference being that this time socialism would happen through armed struggle, as the coup and its aftermath had proven that the peaceful way to build and defend a socialist society was not yet viable.

As Mami and I awaited Tomás Borge's appearance at that Buenos Aires rally, I chewed on the fact that the struggle was lost in the macro, as it was in the micro. The indisputable, mortifying evidence of my own monumental failing as a revolutionary was allowing myself to be swallowed whole by the mainstream persona so carefully cultivated as a cover during my years in the underground. When the resistance disintegrated, shortly after my separation from Alejandro, I kept my permed, highlighted hair and my cutting-edge-of-eighties-fashion wardrobe, and threw myself into the lifestyle of a super-privileged, apolitical Argentinian youth. There was no more double life. All was lost. None of it was meant to be. So I laid down my arms and surrendered to the role of mainstream basketball girlfriend to my new boyfriend Estéban, a player in the professional league. I moved from Neuquén, the capital city of a province that bordered Chile, where I'd led my double life of petit bourgeois English teacher and classless underground worker, to Santa Fe, Estéban's hometown in northeastern Argentina. There, I'd capitulated to the shiny veneer of basketball games, high-end discos, and conversations that centred around the latest celebrity gossip, crash diets, and Hollywood blockbuster films.

Ultimately, though, my succumbing to what I saw as a superficial, meaningless existence was a total bust, because it left me feeling hollow, lonely, and disconnected from my true self. Not only was I a failed revolutionary, I was now also an abysmal basketball girlfriend, weeping incessantly due to my intense grief, causing Estéban great frustration, stress, and anguish. He didn't understand why I couldn't just be happy following *his* dreams, like the rest of the wives and girlfriends were.

After my year of failing to find fulfillment as a basketball girlfriend, to my great relief my mother swooped in and saved me from that life, if only for a short while. Together, we wound up standing on the cobblestone Buenos Aires avenue, surrounded by throngs of activists waving banners that covered the broad spectrum of the left, from the Communist Party to the Teachers' Union to the Mothers of the Plaza de Mayo in their white scarves, dedicated to looking for Argentina's thirty thousand disappeared.

Sweat poured down my face on that muggy night. I was wearing a Fiorucci white, stretch-denim micro-miniskirt, cork platform heels, door-knocker earrings, full makeup, and huge hair. To say I stood out was an understatement, as many of those present had come from the shantytowns, and the middle-class activists wore hippie attire. Mami stood next to me looking very much like a refined señora, in a prim white skirt with matching shoes and purse. We had carefully chosen our spot, at the very back of the throng, on the outskirts of the masses, and taken note of all the possible getaway points if and when the repression began, including a couple of cafés a few feet away that we could slip into.

It was my first time participating in a rally in the South. The last time my mother had been to one in this hemisphere, it was the marches in support of Allende, before the coup in Chile. It had been two years since we'd seen each other, back when it seemed like revolutionary change was still possible, before I'd met Estéban, when I'd been operating the safe house in Neuquén and doing border runs with Alejandro. Over the last year of self-imposed exile, I'd had minimal contact with her and the rest of my family. When I'd seen her disembark from the plane at Santa Fe airport a week earlier, the turbines whipping her hair, I'd run across the tarmac once she reached the bottom of the airplane stairs and fallen into her outstretched arms, the way I had when I was a preschooler after my first day at day-care. The sweltering, humid Santa Fe summer had her instantly wiping beads of perspiration from her brow, and our damp embrace was long and hard, my nostrils flaring with the familiar scent of Mami. We'd made our way hand in hand to Estéban's waiting Fiat, where we began catching up on all the family gossip and the political state of the world—Nicaragua was hanging on despite the Contras, the final offensive in El Salvador could triumph, Gorbachev was spearheading necessary, overdue change in the Soviet Union seemingly without compromising socialism, the Palestinians' intifada was an inspiration to oppressed people all over the world, South Africa's apartheid state was becoming more and more isolated due to the international boycott—before boarding a bus to Buenos Aires, where we continued our session during the six-hour ride. Best girlfriends, we had always shared our thoughts, questions, dreams, opinions, and given each other advice. Nothing was off limits, except the rape. That was the one thing we didn't speak of.

I kept my arms crossed and face perfectly still as the crowd chanted its slogans around me. It was a given that members of Argentina's former underground guerrilla movements, the Montoneros and Revolutionary People's Army, were at the rally, but they'd be hoping to go unnoticed and wouldn't be caught dead waving a flag. Beating on drums, jumping up and down, the crowd hushed when Tomás Borge finally appeared. He arrived on the makeshift stage wearing his green fatigues, the uniform of the Sandinista government. As Nicaraguan minister of the interior, he was commander of the war against the US-backed Contras, which had already claimed thirty thousand lives. During the Somoza dictatorship, he'd been severely tortured and made to witness the rape and murder of his wife, Yelba Mayorga. In his youth he'd gone to law school, and credited John Steinbeck's writings, among others, for forming his revolutionary consciousness. A friend of Che Guevara, he'd fought in the mountains of Nicaragua and contracted leprosy, like many of the guerrilla fighters. He was a prolific and respected writer, and in one of his most famous poems, "My Personal Revenge," he told his torturers that instead of jail, he hoped a socialist society with schools for all and streets free of beggars would shake the sorrow from their eyes.

When he opened his mouth that day, his message was so clear that a stunned silence fell over the crowd:

"Unite. The great lesson of the twentieth century for the left is this: Unite. Right now."

Murmurs and shouts rippled their way through the multitude and a new chant erupted:

"*El pueblo unido jamas sera vencido!*" (The people united will never be defeated.)

It was a simultaneously heartbreaking and joyous moment, to hear that rallying cry, born during Allende's Chile, here, in Buenos Aires. We were about to enter the last decade of the twentieth century, the century that had proven neo-colonialism and capitalism could be defeated, as had been the case in Cuba, Nicaragua, and much of Europe, Asia, and Africa—even in Chile for a short while. The chant, a tsunami surging over the crowd now, was both tribute to a dream and eulogy for a loss.

Camera crews were everywhere, recording the event. It was an out-of-body experience, to stand there openly, surrounded by like-minded people—dared I say comrades?—to be a part of what I'd ached for during my years of total isolation in the underground followed by my Santa Fe escape. Even though I was still an outsider—standing on the margins in an outfit beyond ridiculous for the occasion, hair going limp, makeup melting off, not chanting, not holding a banner, not standing in the first row clapping, whistling, and cheering at every word Borge uttered—my jaw trembled with emotion. The chant reached its crescendo. Men with cameras took our picture and we let them. Who knew if there was anything to lose anymore, after so much had already been lost? Who knew if those pictures would come back to haunt Mami and me? Who cared anymore? We didn't seem to. Argentina was falling, falling hard, into the worst economic crisis in its history, Chile would remain staunchly neoliberal, Panama was about to be invaded by the USA—which would murder thousands of poor civilians and test chemical weapons they would use a year later on Iraqis during the Gulf War—but Nicaragua was still hanging on. Little did we know on that night that the image of ten thousand leftists chanting "El pueblo unido jamas sera vencido!" would become the symbol of a bygone era. The Sandinistas would lose the elections and within two years the Soviet bloc would fall, the overarching triumph of deregulated capitalism ushering in the 1990s.

I thought of Estéban, with his centrist politics, back in Santa Fe, oblivious to my presence at this rally. I was to spend the Christmas holidays with my mother, her partner Bill, my little brother Lalito, my uncle Boris (my mother's brother), his wife Magdalena, and their daughter, my little cousin Sarita. While Mami had come to pluck me from Santa Fe, they'd all gone to Chile from Canada, like thousands of fellow exiles from around the globe returning for the election. After it was over, she and I would fly into Santiago.

Mami and I were boycotting the election. Although Pinochet would step down as dictator and undoubtedly many human rights abuses would cease, he would continue as commander-in-chief of the armed forces and a lifelong senator, his constitution would remain in place, and there would be no trials for crimes against humanity.

Two young men, roughly my age, were standing next to us. I clocked them through my peripheral vision and whispered, "Chilean." What with their dark skin, almond eyes, full lips, Mapuche woven bags, and leather handmade sandals, everything about them would scream "Chilean leftist" from a mile away. Keeping her head stock-still, my mother darted her eyes in their direction. Every time a camera pointed their way, they hung their heads, ensuring their faces were not in the shot.

"They're in deep shit," I commented in English under my breath.

The Chilean left had several strands, and I knew right away that these two belonged to ours, the MIR—Movement of the Revolutionary Left. Mami and I pricked up our ears so as to hear the young men talking in hushed tones. Their accents were Chilean. Accents I hadn't heard in so long, a lump formed in my throat. A couple of minutes passed, and my mother began a conversation with them. This would have been unheard of in the recent past, when if you were to detect a fellow MIRista in your vicinity, you would vanish as quickly and effectively as Jeannie the genie when she was in trouble with the Major. A MIR comrade had the high probability of "bringing a tail," as we called being followed by the secret police. But again, our struggle was over, and none of us had the slightest clue as to what the new rules were, so we made them up as we went along.

"So. You're Chilean," she offered.

"Yes. Yes," the older and darker one nodded.

"We are too," Mami said in an effort to connect.

Neither of us had ever before spoken these words out loud to absolute strangers in the South. Words that not only pointed to our dangling roots, but grabbed them by the fistful and planted them back in that long, skinny country over the Andes we'd had to leave so many lifetimes ago.

"Oh! Are you from Santiago?" the younger, lighter-skinned one asked.

"Yes," I answered, swallowing hard.

"But I live in Canada," Mami clarified.

"Oh. Do you know Nubia Villanueva, also known as La Huasa?" the older one asked.

My mother and I glanced at each other. They had just named one of the leaders of the MIR in Canada, one of the ones who had been in charge of the Return Plan ten years earlier, when many Chilean exiles, including us, had quietly left Canada to join the underground. Not only was La Huasa a leader, she had been one of Mami's best friends and an aunt to me before she too had slipped out of Vancouver to come back south, leaving no forwarding address.

"Yes," my mother answered.

It was an electrical shock, witnessing her reply in the affirmative to a question that such a short time ago would have been suicidal to ask or respond to.

"She's our aunt," the younger one stated.

My mother, stone-faced, brought her index finger to her mouth. We all stared forward, as the throngs moved on to another chant now, and the cameras continued to shoot and roll.

"Go now. In exactly thirty minutes we will meet at the café on the corner one block east of here," she ordered.

The young men didn't miss a beat. They dissolved into the crowd and Mami and I looked at each other, the sweat pouring down our faces as the sun set on that rally. When darkness set in, raucousness would follow. At any moment, we knew, all hell could break loose.

Their names were Miguel and Manuel. Miguel, the darker one, was eighteen, Manuel seventeen. The United Nations was putting them up at a boarding house while they awaited a response from the Canadian government regarding their refugee claims. A few months earlier, they had crossed the Andes on foot, leaving Chile behind for the first time in their lives. They hailed from Estación Central, a Santiago neighbourhood with the city's train station at its core. When their cell, comprising four teenagers, was discovered and the other two had fallen into the secret police's hands, Miguel and Manuel had had to escape with only the clothes on their backs. Comrades and helpers had got them through the Andes, including a toothless old man who took them through a treacherous stretch on his mule, and they'd managed to make it to Mendoza, Argentina. From there, they'd taken a bus to Buenos Aires.

"I knew I was in Argentina when I saw them eat half a cow for lunch, speak on humongous orange public telephones instead of regular-sized grey ones, and drive on avenues with nine lanes on each side as if it were the most normal thing in the world!" exclaimed an awed Manuel before taking a long sip of his café au lait, ignoring the accompanying croissant.

Santiago was also scorching in the summer, I thought, but not muggy. People there were mostly dark-skinned, as opposed to Argentinian fair, and drank black tea rather than café au lait, taken with avocado-covered homemade bread, not croissants.

We sat in the café for hours that boiling Buenos Aires night, the drumming, whistling, and cheering of the rally just outside the window. The crowds, now chanting *"Viva Nicaragua Sandinista! No pasaran!"* almost drowned out our voices as we huddled and Miguel and Manuel spoke. Shell-shocked, they were coming to terms with the fact that they would probably never be able to go back to Chile, for they'd been accused of ambushing an infamous torturer on the street and shooting him in the head.

Listening to them, I was overcome with emotion. There was empathy for them, for the life of exile that awaited them, with its torturous longing, but there was also grief for all that I had lost. Until recently, they had lived the life I'd always dreamed of, the life of a Santiaguina in a graffiti-covered, working-class neighbourhood, packs of wild dogs roaming its streets, groups of teenagers talking, laughing, and making out on its corners, participating to the fullest in the mass movements to topple the dictatorship and re-establish a socialist Chile. That they had materialized at that rally, physically unscathed, was an act of sheer magic as far as I was concerned. I took a bite of my croissant and leaned in further to hear their delicious Chilean singsong.

For the next few days, we spent every waking hour with them. We were staying in the heart of Buenos Aires, three blocks from the Plaza de Mayo, at the Gran Hotel Hispano, right next to the Café Tortoni, one of the oldest in the city. Some of the country's most acclaimed writers, such as Jorge Luis Borges and Alfonsina Storni, had gathered around its marble-topped tables. Miguel and Manuel's boarding house was not far from us. We walked up and down Corrientes, Santa Fe, 9 de Julio, Lavalle, and La Florida together, talking into the wee hours. They told us how sometimes, upon hearing their Chilean accents, bus drivers would order them off the bus or kiosk vendors would refuse to sell them cigarettes. In those days, being Chilean meant one of two things: either you were filthy rich and over for a weekend shopping spree, prompting bowing sales clerks to fall all over you, or, more often than not, you were poor, brown, undocumented, and on the run, despised by some almost as much as the gypsies. I did all the talking when it came to dealing with others. My impeccable Argentinian accent, acquired through my years of living there, and middle-class attire ensured all doors remained wide open.

On December 14, 1989, as millions of Chileans took to the streets in celebration when the Concertación, a coalition of seventeen parties that opposed the dictatorship, won with 55 percent of the vote, Mami and I sat in a Buenos Aires café with Miguel and Manuel. Although the young men also saw the election as a loss, the fact that they were not on the Alameda jumping for joy with their friends and neighbours caused them physical pain. Doubled over, faces pale and blank, they were speechless with homesickness. Mami and I recognized that yearning, for it was all too familiar for us. The four of us simply took each other in and, after sitting in silence, walked the foreign streets of Buenos Aires in a daze until the sun came up.

On our last night, we took Miguel and Manuel to an intimate concert in the courtyard of a colonial building in Caballito. Everyone sang along as León Gieco, legendary Argentinian folksinger, played his hits, and Miguel and Manuel couldn't wait to shake his hand afterwards. When he wholeheartedly embraced their Chileanness, they beamed with pride for the first time since I'd met them.

The following morning, we had breakfast together at the Tortoni. Then the four of us stood on the sidewalk, delaying the final goodbye. We finally flagged down a cab. After they helped us put our luggage in the trunk, we hugged Miguel and Manuel for a good long while. When the taxi pulled away, they chased us down Avenida de Mayo. I looked back and waved as they ran and ran, shimmering like a mirage, as if by running they could materialize in their beloved Santiago with us, and not be left behind in a city that did not see them, did not value them, kept them at arm's length.

We hadn't exchanged last names or other personal details. They understood we were exiles and comrades, we knew they were comrades on the run, and that was all the recognition needed to establish an unbreakable bond. No coordinates were given. They dissolved in the heat, and for a moment I wondered if they'd been an optical illusion, a beacon of water in the desert, their presence a phenomenon manifested by my parched soul at the end of a year spent in basketball limbo, in disguise. Real or hallucinatory, they had passed through my life to remind me of all that I was, all that I had given, and all that had been lost. Miguel and Manuel, who spent their destitute, empty days rambling around Buenos Aires, waiting to see who would take them in, embodied the thousands who would now retreat into corners, licking their wounds, wondering if the giving of life and limb for a cause much greater than our individual lives had been worth it. Only history could answer that question, and in that moment, it told us our defeat was complete. Mami took my hand, and together we cried.

TWO

Santiago was overcome with post-election euphoria, a frenzy that would continue for months. After a few days in the capital, we returning exiles spent Christmas with my grandma Carmen in her town of Limache, 125 kilometres west of Santiago, before piling into a rented Citroën and driving to coastal Valparaíso to ring in the New Year with old family friends. Just shy of midnight, the *barrio* of Cerro Bellavista spilled out onto the cobblestone streets to watch the city's "world-famous" fireworks usher in 1990.

The carnival atmosphere was overwhelming. I stood at a railing overlooking the bay below, surrounded by people who looked and sounded like me, holding my breath, for if I exhaled, I feared I would faint from the emotion. After seventeen years of lockdown, the dictatorship was finally over. In this working-class port and naval base, resistance had been strong. As had repression. And now the streets flooded with revellers: women with babies in their arms, couples, scores of children, old people who in spite of their lousy backs and failing organs had come out to celebrate, mischievous toddlers, necking teenagers.

The cheering reached a dull roar at the stroke of midnight, when the first explosion lit up the bay, the Southern Cross sky, the beaming faces of those around me. There was no more need to chant "And he will fall!" because Pinochet had fallen, the year in which he would step down now palpably here. As people dove into each other's embrace, "1990" fell from every mouth. On some lips it was a whisper, barely audible, as if the speaker didn't want to jinx what the new year represented by saying it too loud. The younger, adolescent voices yelled it full blast at the firmament, a challenge to the gods. New calendars could now be pinned on walls, this tiny act momentous in its denoting of a "before" and "after." From this year on, almost two decades of darkness would enter the past, remembered or forgotten, distorted, downplayed, or denied, but no longer an omnipresent, irrefutable reality.

The "before" was an entire existence for the young people and children who surrounded me that night. A whole life lived in exile for me, half a life for my mother and her brother, Uncle Boris. His gaze was fixed on that horizon imprinted on his retina. He'd spun tops and played soccer with his band of boys on this very street in the 1940s and '50s, running home for tea in the late afternoons, when the orange sun danced on the ocean below and hundreds of fishermen made their way out in their yellow wooden boats, the barrio of bright-coloured houses, murals, graffiti, monuments, statues, and unexpected nooks and crannies at every turn of its labyrinthine streets a glowing jewel in the dusk. My mother stood next to him, siblings back on their childhood turf. As for the matriarch, my *abuelita* Carmen, she stood straight and tall, eyes shining like the candles on the altars that lined the streets of this city, the shrines for the disappeared, always accompanied by the placard that demanded to know:

Donde estan? (Where are they?)

My uncle Boris had been fired from his banking job and arrested here after the coup. My abuelita Carmen and abuelito Armando had spent seven sleepless days and nights besieging every police station in town, demanding to know their son's whereabouts, while his first wife, my aunt Tita, and children, my cousins Macarena and Gonzalo, stayed put in case he turned up at the door of the house they all shared. When he was released, it was with strict orders to "leave the country or else." It struck me now that I knew nothing about his time in jail. Although he was a boisterous storyteller, the week in which he'd disappeared from all our lives was only mentioned in passing to state that his conscience had been born in prison, and that he would be forever thankful to the comrades there who had steered him onto the correct political path.

After he'd been freed, he suffered from insomnia and spent his nights chain-smoking and studying the bay with binoculars from the front windows of the house. He noticed that several navy ships would make trips out into the ocean and come back at the crack of dawn. Years later, it would come to light that prisoners were held and tortured on these ships. Some had their feet placed in wet cement; once it was dry, they were pushed overboard. Uncle Boris liked to say that he proved to himself and to others that he was willing to risk it all for his new-found politics on the night his binocular vigil was interrupted by the military chasing a group of people during curfew. Shots rang out amidst the shouts. The household rose from its slumber and everyone except my abuelito Armando and Uncle Boris took shelter lying prostrate on the bathroom floor. My abuelito, shotgun in hand, said: "If anybody comes pounding on our windows or doors, we shoot." My uncle responded, "No. If the military comes, we shoot. If anyone else does, we let them in." No one was more surprised than he at this declaration, because until then he had always identified as apolitical. Once he arrived in Canada, he joined the MIR in exile.

I looked back, taking in the crowds behind me, and saw that at the top of the next hill—for Valparaíso is made up of hills—a modest house suddenly caught fire. A gasp escaped my mouth. Jaw slack, I looked around and saw that others from Cerro Bellavista were also beholding the blaze. Time stood still in our newborn 1990, and for an eternal collection of moments the centre of our altered universe was not that great big ball of fire around which our planet spun, but the flames that devoured that humble dwelling. Although we were impotent to stop it, there was nothing passive in our bearing witness. Spellbound, we observed those ruthless flames licking the ebony sky, consuming the little wooden house until only a mound of ashes remained. Suspended in the aftermath, we swallowed down our sorrow as we contemplated the cold, swift, and brutal destruction that seemed like a message from the many ghosts that inhabited this old port city.

Someone on our street had put their speakers on a windowsill. The classic cumbia "Colegiala" served as a portal, transporting us back from our hypnotic state. The sound waves tickled our ears and seduced our hips before travelling to our feet. In spite of—or because of—the big, smoking black hole, which to the innocent eye might look as if a meteorite had landed in the neighbouring barrio, the dancing got under way. Down at the port, a twenty-four-piece cumbia band in gold-sequined blazers played to a crowd of thousands.

A few days later, my mother, her partner Bill, my little brother Lalito, my uncle Boris, his wife Magdalena, my cousin Sarita, and I piled into the Citroën and began the long drive to Puerto Montt, in the south of Chile. My uncle Carlos, Mami and Boris's older brother, waited there with his family.

En route, we spent a night in Concepción, where the Cousin, Carlos's eldest, was attending law school. When we'd phoned from Limache to tell him we'd be stopping to see him, his landlady had offered us, free of charge, the vacant rooms at the boarding house left by students gone home for the holidays. The Cousin had stayed to spend the summer with his girlfriend.

I'd fallen head over heels in love with my cousin at the age of twelve, during my first trip back to Chile, and had only seen him once since then. Although we'd made out on both those visits, we had yet to consummate our decade-old love.

At five in the morning, just as I was falling asleep, he appeared at the narrow cot I was sharing with eight-year-old Sarita.

"Exiled Cousin," he whispered in my ear.

Drunk, he was still standing—or in this case, kneeling—after an all-night bender with Uncle Boris.

"Let me into the bed, baby. It's now or never."

I contemplated his assertion. Concluding that it was probably true, I surveyed how best to make it happen, for there was no way he was coming into the cot with Sarita and me.

"Okay," I whispered back. "But we have to go to your bed."

"We can't. The whole house will wake up," he murmured through his pisco-sour breath.

This was true. The house had the creakiest floors I'd ever heard, due to the effects of the great earthquake of 1985. The building had been spared, but ever since that terrifying day, it leaned alarmingly to one side. When you walked, you had to bend your knee and cock your head in order to feel parallel to the floor.

"Just let me in. She's on the fifth dream by now," the Cousin insisted.

After I convinced him that sealing the deal in a squeaky cot with our little cousin in it was far from optional after a ten-year-long wait, we made our way to his room. Our family slept nearby, and the walls shook with Uncle Boris's snoring. The Cousin was hammered, and I was stifling a laughing fit. We hugged the hallway walls on tiptoe, the floor a minefield of creaks to avoid. It was critical that nobody wake up. First, there was the scandal of us being first cousins, and second, there was the fidelity issue. I was with Estéban, and although the Cousin's illegitimate children could be found scattered from Limache's central region to the tip of Patagonia, for absolutely no one could resist his charms, it was imperative that his girlfriend remain in the dark, as it were, about his affairs.

When we finally reached his bed (the final stretch of the journey done on all fours), we tore each other's clothes off, the Cousin jumped on top of me, and, before anything could happen, he passed out cold. A minute later, the light of dawn brought the room into sharper focus. Uncle Boris's alarm clock went off, as we were to continue our voyage as soon as the sun came up, and a minute after that he was stumbling into the shower. Heart pounding like a *bombo* drum, I managed to extricate myself from beneath the dead weight of the Cousin, throw my nightgown back on, and creep my way back to the cot, just in time for my uncle's entrance, announcing that the bathroom was now unoccupied and that the house boasted no hot water.

In Puerto Montt, copious amounts of wine and pisco were imbibed, laughter abounded, story upon story was told, and I only wished my cousins Macarena and Gonzalo, who had yet to make a trip back to Chile, and my sister Ale could have been there too. It was the first time my mother and her brothers had been back together inside Chile since the times of Allende, because Mami and Boris had been blacklisted by the Chilean consul in Vancouver for their solidarity work and forbidden to return for the entire dictatorship. They'd even been denied a special permit to go bury their father, Armando, when he died in 1985. Hence the all-night sessions recollecting their childhood, as well as life under Pinochet and anecdotes of exile. They told stories of the 1960 Valdivia earthquake, the worst in recorded history, which all three had lived through. "Remember how the earth actually rolled and split and the mountains moved, and that ship was catapulted through the air and landed in the middle of the valley?!" Then there were all the times my cousins had broken curfew and their parents hadn't known whether to slap them or congratulate them. "Was he fucking one of his many girlfriends or blowing up a tower for the resistance?! I'll never know!" exclaimed my uncle Carlos. And Uncle Boris's countless tragicomic Vancouver janitor stories. "This gringo spends fifteen minutes explaining how to use the supersonic vacuum cleaner, but I don't know how to tell him that I don't speak English, so it takes me the whole shift to figure out how to turn the fucking thing on, for fuck's sake!" He'd been an accountant in Chile; Canada had de-skilled him and reinvented him as a cleaner.

There were stories that were not shared, such as the rape. The Chilean part of the clan didn't know about it and the exiles never spoke of it.

Day after day, dawn caught us around the table, the odd silence coming over us as we realized that, from now on, anything was possible. The unspoken question of our longed-for, definitive return hovered in the loaded air, for it was too soon to speak of our family being an inseparable clan again, like most Chilean families. We had been torn apart, half remaining where our roots lay in the southernmost reaches of the Americas, the other half flung so far north that social signals were the opposite of everything we'd ever known. Touching was welcomed in the South, in the North it was shunned; lingering eye contact with strangers was friendly in the South, in the North it aroused suspicion; flirting with strangers was a compliment in the South, in the North it was unacceptable and verged on harassment; pleasure was far more important than work in the South, in the Protestant North work was a surefire way to heaven, hence held in higher regard than almost anything else.

Now that the dictatorship was virtually over (elected president Patricio Aylwin would take charge in March), the lives of the exiled family hung in limbo, the future less like the light at the end of a seventeen-year tunnel and more like a black hole. The long-awaited return was no longer a pipe dream but a here-and-now reality within our reach, yet exile's end tasted surprisingly bittersweet. Little did we know that what awaited us was a long process of de-exile. Ironically, it would inflict a dull pain not unlike the torment of exile itself.

At the end of the visit, my mother and the rest of the no-longer-exiled-but-still-feeling-disoriented-and-rootless family returned to Canada, and I to Santa Fe, Argentina, and my bas-ketball-girlfriend persona, where my year of extended nervous breakdown—there was no other way to label my daily sobbing sessions—would reach fever pitch. Now there was no excuse: I could go back to Chile and be master of my own destiny in the country of my birth, the country that was imprinted in the deepest layer of my being, the country that I'd flown all my flags for, that we'd fled from and now offered a tentative hand, where my flailing roots could be planted again and a new Chilean me, the one I had always wanted to meet and be, could be born and promenade down those streets. And yet I couldn't shake the feeling that returning would be less like setting down roots and more like walking on quicksand and grasping at straws. Even though its doors were now open, Chile was far from free, and, with its unbridled neo-liberalism, hyper-consumerism, and fer-vent, powerful right wing, the opposite of revolutionary. The dream that Allende had spoken of in his last speech, of march-ing on Santiago's great liberated avenues alongside millions of comrades, the dream of living in the Chile I had fought for with all my being, was not meant to be.

So what could going back possibly look like? I was at a loss to know, for I had only ever allowed myself to imagine a tri-umphant, glorious return, waving a red flag, left fist pumping the air. I had never expected exile to end with no pomp and circumstance, for it to dwindle and disappear imperceptibly, sand between my fingers. Just as no map had been provided to help us find our way through the trials of exile, I was completely unprepared for the crossroads I now found myself at. Either I became an immigrant, a label implying that uprootedness was not only a choice but a welcome one at that, and yet the only label available if I were to stay outside Chile's borders, or I returned to a homeland where my sacrifice would not be celebrated, revered, or respected. On the contrary, my revolutionary activity would be not only something to hide but something to be ashamed of, that some comrades would apologize for in order to be embraced by the new, "free" Chile, now referring to itself as the Tiger of the South.

Back in Santa Fe, the boiling hot 1990 Southern Cone summer reached temperatures as high as fifty-two degrees Celsius with the humidex, causing several people to die. I swam daily in the chocolate-brown Paraná River, passing *palometa* fish nipping at my skin, a weeping willow on Piedras Blancas beach providing refuge when the afternoon sun was too much to bear.

I contemplated my immigrant future. I loved Estéban, and wondered how I could stay in Santa Fe playing the part of basketball girlfriend and eventual wife. In order to be happy there, I knew I had to let go of the persona and just be myself, but I had no idea how to do that. There was just too much to be undone. For starters, I'd have to tell his circle that I was a Chilean who'd grown up in exile and then explain why I'd kept this key part of my identity from them. My entire existence in Argentina had consisted of living a double life, and I had no idea how I was to insert my integrated, non-compartmentalized self into mainstream society. In the underground, I'd had two confidants who knew it all: my ex-husband Alejandro, whom I'd lost all contact with when I'd left Neuquén a year earlier, and my loyal friend and resistance helper Luisa. She had also moved from Neuquén, back to her hometown of Paraná. Thankfully, it was just across the river, an hour away from Santa Fe. It was this soul sister who got me through my year of post-loss-of-revolution exile. As for Estéban, he was at his wits' end as to what to do with the crying fits, which only grew worse after my return from Chile. As did my violent outbursts, for it was not unheard of for me to pound on his chest during an argument.

I had met Estéban in Neuquén in 1988, when I was twenty years old. I was still in the resistance, and married to Alejandro, a man whom I loved but with whom I hadn't been sexually involved for a year. He was a husband, a brother, my best friend and soulmate, a comrade whom I had married at eighteen at the MIR's request so I could get my Argentinian residency papers. He was everything to me, except a lover. The thought of making love with him had become repulsive to me, and when he would raise the rape as the possible culprit, I would stare at him blankly. I secretly blamed the fear that had taken over my visceral brain—no doubt it did have something to do with my frigidity—and now occupied my pleasure centres. I lived in fear of being arrested, tortured, and murdered for my underground activities, and had concluded that the Terror had not only shut down my stomach (I was dangerously thin from not eating) but had rendered me asexual and had me playing dead in bed with the man I was married to. It had got so bad that I wouldn't go to bed at all, "I have to study these documents" my go-to excuse, magnifying glass held to the tiny print on the top-secret MIR correspondence, only retiring at six in the morning, when he got up to go to work. Although I had grappled with leaving him, as we were both equally unhappy with our lack of sexual intimacy, the thought of being alone was scary, so I had made peace with what I was sure would be a lifetime without sex.

Until I went to a basketball game.

It all started when Alejandro and I visited the phone company's office—the only place in town for long-distance calls—to make a resistance call. "We'll take the presents to Aunt Lili's house on the surprise date," code for something else entirely, of course, was the line we were rehearsing in our heads while we waited for our booth. A seven-foot-tall black man with a high-top haircut, fake nerd glasses, and gold chains with diamond-encrusted charms in the shapes of the letters M and A around his neck walked into the joint. Standing in the biggest black and red Jordan Nikes I'd ever seen, he drawled, "New York," to the man behind the counter.

"I'm sorry, Señor, I have no idea what you're saying," responded the clerk, mouth hanging open.

Apparently, he'd never seen a black man before, much less a towering one, and neither had the rest of the customers. A dead silence overtook the room. Some of the booths opened and heads popped out to get a good look. People walking by came in to gaze at him too. Impressively unfazed by the blatant stares, he repeated, "New York." The clerk stammered again that he had no idea what the man was saying. I stepped up and translated. From that day on, Martin, also known as Miles Away because of his height, clung to me like a koala.

Miles Away, who explained we could call him M for short, was twenty like me, hailed from Brooklyn, and had only been in Neuquén a month when we met him on that fateful day. To say that he was an alien in that small Patagonian city would be an understatement. First there was the fact of his seemingly being the only black man in town. Add to that his height, the bling, the high-top haircut, and his puckered-lip, rhythmic, head-back-and-forth gait reminiscent of Weird Harold from *Fat Albert*, and it was fair to say that M came from another planet. The citizens of Neuquén had of course seen men like M countless times on the big and small screens, just not in person. For M, New York was the centre of the universe—an opinion admittedly difficult to argue with—and the Neuquinos were the aliens.

"Do the women have asses here?" he'd often ask in semi-earnest shock and dismay at the lack of big round booty.

Alejandro and I started to refer to M as our adopted son, as he went everywhere with us and pretty much moved into our apartment the very night we met, going home only to sleep. His services as a player had been bought by the local basketball team, and from one day to the next he had gone from playing for his Brooklyn college to battling gale force winds and tumbleweeds in Patagonia. Meeting M catapulted me into the centre of mainstream Neuquén society, for everywhere we went, doors were flung open and drinks, coffees, and sometimes even entire meals were on the house. I now understood that the stares were not only because he was black, but because he was famous.

On the next home-game day, Alejandro and I were M's guests, seated in the VIP section, dressed in our best, cheering at the top of our lungs along with the team's wives and girlfriends. The gym was a carnival, fans pounding on drums, blowing on horns, and singing non-stop. It was packed and many stood outside, listening to every play on radios held to their ears while jumping up and down.

In an analogous universe, Alejandro and I were preparing for a high-stakes moment of our own. We were planning a flight into Chile, carrying goods for the MIR in a Cessna to be flown low through the Andes, in order to duck the radar. On the whole, 1988 was shaping up to be a critical year. In a few months, Chileans would be asked to vote Yes or No in a plebiscite that posed the following question: Do you want Pinochet to stay? If the No side won, elections would be called. As exciting as it was to be front-row centre at the game, surrounded by a gymnasium of exuberant fans, it was impossible to forget my life-or-death situation. If our plane was intercepted, we'd have to crash it into the side of a mountain and go up in smoke with it. The Terror, like a gun to the back of the head, was master of my thoughts and movements day and night. No matter how much fun I was having, it made sure my alternate reality always clawed at my door.

Although I wanted my resistance life to seem like a dream, thus perhaps weakening the Terror's hold on me, the opposite was true. It was as if my day-to-day existence, including my presence at that basketball game, was an illusion, a mere hologram, a physics experiment designed to trick the eye into believing that the three-dimensional image of myself cheering at that match was real, when for all intents and purposes the underground me was the truer reality. In physics terms, the all-encompassing Cause was the complex object. Despite the terrifying consequences if I was ever caught, the Cause was the one thing that gave immense meaning to all I did. It was the centre from which I operated, from which laser beams rebounded, scattering light in all directions, creating virtual, insubstantial images that didn't stand a chance against the promise the Cause held.

The game ended with a foul. A Neuquén player was to shoot three times at the basket. A gorgeous, curly-haired, quintessential Italian-Argentinian was chosen. The fans held their collective breath as he shot, taking his time between throws, breathing deeply and deliberately, landing the ball in the basket all three times. He was relaxed and focused, exuding complete confidence when he went in for the kill, not unlike a feline ready to pounce on its target. By the third shot, the Terror that stalked me like a starving predator, that had colonized my body and consumed me around the clock, surrendered to a different sensation. My stomach did a double flip. Not from fear, from ecstasy. An insurrection happened. Not in Chile, inside me. It banished the Terror from my nervous system that night. Estéban's appearance on that court blew my compartmentalized life to pieces. My spirit, a shadow hovering next to me for so long, now claimed its rightful place: the core of my body. From there, it beamed, and together we soared.

Jubilation filled the gym when our team won. The festival atmosphere reached its crescendo, mirroring my inner life. Fans stormed the court and mobbed the players, bombarding them with hugs, kisses, and slaps on the back. As Alejandro and I smiled at M from the edge of the court, my peripheral vision, hyper-operational since I'd joined the resistance, now monitored the curly-haired team member's every move.

Released from the fans' grip, the drenched players disappeared into the changing rooms. When a freshly showered M emerged, he was accompanied by the object of my desire.

"This is Estéban," he said by way of introduction.

After shaking Alejandro's hand, Estéban kissed my cheek and said:

"M has been talking non-stop about you guys. We're all so happy he met you."

Looking right into my eyes, he continued,

"I hear you're from Canada. My brother went on a student exchange there. We should all have coffee sometime."

As I stared up at his face, a foot away from him, I knew I was on a roller coaster that had arrived at its summit and was about to drop at a ninety-degree angle. There was a moment of suspension, and my stomach flipped again. I had to bite my lip to prevent a delirious shriek from leaving my mouth.

After every game, a barbecue happened on site for the players and their wives. We joined the festivities as M's guests. M was elated—he'd played his best game yet, he told us—hugging Alejandro and me over and over again, proposing toast after toast. As for Estéban, my radar's waves bounced off him all night, detecting his every move, determining his location. It was impossible to tell whether I was on his radar too, but there was no wife or girlfriend in sight and this filled me with expectation. He had arrived to show me that my erotic self was a force to be reckoned with, that I was a sexual person after all, and that no matter how hard I tried to suppress that key part of myself in order to stay married to a man I was no longer attracted to, my body was now telling me self-repression was not an option anymore. I had lacked the courage to end the marriage, as had Alejandro, but now that my sexuality had burst forth and expelled the Terror for a night, there was another undeniable truth to be faced: the marriage was over.

Within a month, Alejandro and I were separated. We both cried long and hard, and mourned by immediately seeking solace in others' arms. I hoped my infatuation with Estéban would become mutual, and Alejandro started dating a skydiver he'd met at the Flying Club. She would become his second wife and they would have a son together.

M morphed from adopted son to long-lost brother and self-appointed personal stylist. Although during my marriage I'd possessed a decent array of mainstream eighties outfits, once I was single again, M, who was making a killing by Argentinian standards, announced he'd be overhauling my wardrobe after fattening me up. Huge plates of gnocchi were ordered, and for the first time in over a year I ate heartily and watched my face and body fill out again. The Terror was still ever-present, but slumber, with apocalyptic, epic dreams, came back too. At the most expensive boutiques in town, he yayed and nayed each outfit I paraded in. "That hard!" was his stamp of approval. According to M, walking lessons were imperative. "Shake that ass, woman!" he would yell as we strutted down Avenida Argentina, Neuquén's main thoroughfare. A visit to the hair salon was in order, to get my hair permed and highlighted. When he was satisfied with the results (unbeknownst to him, he had also invested in a now-impeccable petit bourgeois cover for my ongoing MIR activities, still carried out with Alejandro), he instructed me on the ways of men. Or, specifically, the ways of Estéban, the team member M was closest to, as Estéban spoke a little English.

"All he does is brag in the change room about how he can have any girl he wants."

"So what should I do?"

"Ignore him completely. Don't even look at him. Never acknowledge his existence."

"For how long?"

"For as long as I tell you."

"But isn't that rude?"

"Woman, do you want this guy or not?"

"Very much so."

"Then do everything I say."

And so, for every home-game night, I'd don an outfit that had been assembled, green-lit, and financed by M and make my way down to the gymnasium with Luisa. She was a janitor at the cathedral and could give a rat's ass about her appearance. Her uniform consisted of filthy acid-washed jeans, an unflattering T-shirt, and falling-apart espadrilles, dirty hair in a messy bun.

Luisa was a free spirit, who despite being penniless travelled to Argentina's four cardinal points with nothing but a small pack and her thumb to take her wherever she wanted. Like her mother back in Paraná, she was a clairvoyant able to read people's intentions before she got in a car, or feel the energy in a shantytown before she walked its dirt roads in the middle of the night. She possessed nerves of steel and fed herself through a thoroughly rehearsed shoplifting method that involved a large woven bag and targeted only chain supermarkets.

"I am an ethical thief and will never steal from a small business, although sometimes I'll borrow a magazine from a kiosk and then return it."

As for shelter, she lived at a female students' boarding house funded by the local chapter of the Catholic Church in exchange for janitorial work. Meals were taken every day at my apartment, where she would show up with vegetables or a kilo of stolen meat, and she did any odd job that was offered to her, including now being M's cleaning lady. The three of us went everywhere together—cafés, bars, discos. I'd met Luisa at the Comahue National University when she'd taken my conversational English classes at the Tourism Department. When I recruited her as a resistance helper, she'd immediately pickpocketed Argentinian ID cards for comrades who needed to get out of Chile as soon as possible. A true adventurer at heart, she was always game for anything, including the systematic seduction of Estéban. As for her romantic life, she was in an open relationship with a sexy, intense, recovering heroin addict who had supported his habit by prostituting himself on the streets of Buenos Aires and now lectured on the evils of drugs and prostitution at local high schools. Omar was clean, but still so wild that a night out with him and Luisa provided legends as opposed to mere stories.

Weeks passed and I followed M's instructions to a T, obedient student that I was. At the post-game meals, I conversed with everyone but Estéban, avoided all eye contact, and moved to a different part of the room if he came within ten feet of me. Adoquin, the most chic disco in town, was the preferred destination after the barbecues, where groupies were the bees that buzzed around Estéban, the honeycomb. Once there, I was not to dance with him or ever look his way. "Remember, he doesn't exist."

Just as I was about to throw in the towel by professing my love to him—treating like a leper this man for whom my toes curled was torture—the modus operandi started to work. Luisa—tickled by the goings-on that were as alien to her as taking tea at Buckingham Palace, for it would never cross her mind to invest any amount of time, energy, or money in entrapping a man, her preferred style being simply to go up to an object of her affection and declare, "I want you"—reported that she had caught Estéban's eyes unequivocally lingering on me numerous times, most notably when I was cutting a rug to Whitney Houston's "I Wanna Dance with Somebody" in my pumps, satin leggings, and butterfly belt buckle.

"Told ya," M bragged as he applied lotion to himself before our next outing. M was the most convincing moisturizer I'd ever met, his boudoir stocked with face serums, hand creams, hair oils, and body butters. "Now keep doing what I say."

Omar accompanied us to the game and Adoquin that night. The Luisa–Omar combo being what it was, something for the history books was bound to happen. When we were all leaning up against the bar and Estéban made his way over, M said: "Stay here tonight."

In laying the groundwork for that week's game, he had bought me a floor-length denim Calvin Klein jacket with enormous shoulder pads, underneath which I wore thigh-high black lace stockings, a black knit micro-miniskirt that clung like a sleeve, and a crocheted black top with gold thread woven through it.

"Don't talk to him and don't look at him, but don't leave either. Keep your eyes on the dance floor and gyrate to the music a bit."

When "Time of My Life" from the *Dirty Dancing* movie began to play, rather than awaiting further instructions, I turned to Estéban and said, "Wanna dance?"

"Uh. Yeah."

I grabbed him by the hand, took him to the dance floor, nailed him with my smoky eyes, and got down with my moves. I had no idea what had hit me, for this was definitely not part of the plan, to go from avoiding him like the plague to dry humping his leg with no transition, but there it was. Possessed, I laughed and woo-hooed, and Estéban took me in with a smile. As for M, he was grinding with a voluptuous groupie and gave me a high-five. Then the music stopped and a scrawny, whiskered teenager, microphone in hand, materialized under the disco ball.

"Good evening, everyone. Thanks for coming. Don't know if you know this, but half the cover charge tonight is going to the Industrial High School's fundraising efforts for our graduation trip to Córdoba. So yeah. Thanks for that. And we're gonna be having a little kissing contest now as part of the evening. So in three minutes the dance floor will be cleared and we'll be holding the contest for the longest, saliviest, juiciest kiss. The winning couple will receive a special prize. So yeah, let's finish dancing while those interested couples get organized."

Before either of us could say a word, Luisa came running up to me.

"Help me look for Omar. I've gotta do this contest with him."

Found necking with a high school student and told about the contest by Luisa, who could care less about his exploits, Omar didn't skip a beat: "Yes!"

While Michael Jackson's "The Way You Make Me Feel" played out, Luisa ran to the bathroom. Pale as a ghost on her return, she pulled me aside and told me she'd just shit her pants.

"What do you mean you shit your pants?" I asked.

"I shit my pants. That's all. I was nervous and I shit my pants."

To be more precise, she'd only managed to get her pants halfway down before the shit hit the fan, as it were. Since Argentinian bathrooms didn't provide toilet paper or paper towels, she was screwed. So she pulled her pants up, shit and all, and ran out to tell me about it. In charge of damage control, I retrieved her fire-engine red, knee-length corduroy coat made by her mother from the coat check, and she threw it on to cover her nether regions and pulled Omar onto the stage just in time for the contest to begin. I whispered the story to Estéban, and together we laughed until tears poured down our faces.

A plump, pimply, bespectacled teenager monitored each couple, making sure their lips never lost contact. As for Luisa and Omar, the urgency of their kissing made one think of a desert traveller coming across his first drop of water in days, although every time Omar's hands went anywhere near her ass, she would gently yet unmistakably guide them away. Meanwhile, Estéban and I had to lean on each other so as not to fall over from laughter.

Luisa and Omar won the contest and were awarded a life-sized poster of a lion-maned Tina Turner in a minidress for their efforts. They promptly disappeared, poster tucked under their arms. Estéban and I found ourselves alone against the bar, wiping the tears from our eyes, hands resting on our thighs as we tried to get our breath back from the laughing fit.

"What do you want to do now?" he asked.

"Make love to you," I said.

His jaw literally dropped.

"Make love to you. Right now. At your house." I drove the point home, reducing him to rubble with my eyes.

He floored his Ford Taurus convertible to the top of Neuquén's only hill, where he shared the penthouse suite of the city's tallest high-rise with the team doctor, an equally renowned Casanova. Once there, he took me by the hand and walked me

down the hall. I shook with nerves and excitement while he bedded me like the expert he was. From that day on, we were inseparable.

Luisa showed up at my apartment the next day with a stolen baguette and a block of Gouda cheese. We devoured it as she shared the outcome of her shitty night. Omar had driven her to lover's lane, a bluff near the university that overlooked the city, and they'd made out in his Peugeot 504. Somehow, she'd managed to keep his hands away from her ass. Then they'd waited in line at Loving Moments, one of the local pay-by-the-hour motels. Once in the room, he threw her on the bed, stuck his hand down her pants, pulled it back out covered in shit, didn't bat an eyelash, and declared, "This explains why you stink. Ya shit yourself," before going to the washroom to wash up. When asked why he'd been so nonchalant about the whole thing, he'd responded with:

"Honey, I sucked dick and got fucked on the streets of Buenos Aires for three years. You think a little shit's gonna turn me off? Uh-uh."

We almost died laughing, I told her all about Estéban, and then we lay down for siesta.

THREE

In early 1989, six months after the No side won the plebiscite in Chile and elections were called for December of that year, Estéban was traded to a Santa Fe team. I moved with him.

The MIR ceased its activities; Alejandro and I were no longer needed. I was free to do with my future what I would. There was no one left to answer to and no dream to struggle for. Cut loose, I escaped into my new identity, following a man who had always put himself first and believed only in pursuing an individual goal, as opposed to fighting for a greater cause. The new existence he offered was a lifesaver, and I grabbed it before the alternative—staying in Neuquén and facing the MIR's colossal loss alone—led me to suicide. I pushed the grief down and went numb. Alejandro stayed and became a commercial airline pilot. For years, he struggled with debilitating depression.

Neuquén, with its dry, windy terrain, was exchanged for Santa Fe, the oldest city in the country, on the shores of the Paraná River. It was so humid there that houses actually broke into a sweat. Drops trickled down the walls, sometimes streams, all resulting in the spread of fungi. If housekeeping in Neuquén had consisted of endless sweeping, wiping, and dusting of the dirt that the howling wind blew in through every crack, crevice, and opening, in Santa Fe it was all about battling the mildew that seeped through the walls' pores on an hourly basis. Litres of bleach seemed to have no effect on the black, green, and pink affliction that spread with the same predictability as the earth spinning full circle on its axis every twenty-four hours.

I followed Estéban to this wet basin of a city. In one swift motion, I swept the cause to which I had given body and soul under the carpet and plowed forward, a racehorse with blinders on, eyes fixed on the horizon, hoping to obliterate all that had come before.

Although I told Estéban I'd been in the Chilean Movement of the Revolutionary Left, no details of my militancy were disclosed. His only words when I told him were:

"Do you ever plan on joining a resistance movement again?"

Knowing full well what he wanted to hear, I answered without pause.

"Of course not."

It wasn't that he disagreed with revolutionary politics. It was that he understood that being in a resistance movement required one to give one's life, and he was not looking to hook up with a guerrilla, but rather to settle down with someone who would follow wherever the whims of professional sports took him.

The basketball-girlfriend lifestyle certainly had its moments of fun. Touring with a professional sports team was all about excess, and although I never drank a drop of alcohol, as I had always been a teetotaller, I relished the all-night parties and danced till the sun came up. Within a couple of months my frozen-smile exterior began to thaw, and the grief over all that I'd lost came up in the form of non-stop crying. Estéban, who had only known the don't-worry-be-happy, party-girl me, was flummoxed.

I cried for hours on a daily basis, usually in a heap on the floor, often while walking down the street, sometimes while sitting at an outdoor table at Las Cuartetas restaurant, which was strategically placed at a busy downtown intersection for one to see and be seen. A bawling fit even overtook me at Danes, the hottest club in town, while I danced in the strobe lights to the Fine Young Cannibals' "She Drives Me Crazy." Then there were the long-distance bus rides with the basketball team. Curled against the window, I'd weep like a widow at her husband's grave. It was chronic. And Estéban, who knew what I was mourning—I had explained it as the loss of a dream, of a war, of a revolution, and he had nodded, trying to understand the bigger picture I had described while not giving away the details of my MIR tasks—was at a loss.

As for me, I knew my well of sadness was bottomless, I understood that this would probably go on forever, and I was okay with that. Anguish had been a constant companion since the day of the coup, when I was five years old and tears poured down my parents' faces during Allende's last speech. Exile had followed swiftly and mercilessly, and triggers were everywhere. Being at the home of Estéban's parents, an operatic Italian clan, reminded me of the extended family in Chile I was not with; walking the boulevards of Santa Fe, as opposed to Santiago's "great liberated avenues" that Allende had referred to on the day of his death, smashed my heart to smithereens.

In short, being immersed in my new identity, without the outlet for my beliefs that my MIR activities and comrades had provided, destroyed me. Not to mention the fact that giving my life to a revolutionary cause had all apparently been in vain. And the knowledge that I had not only survived but landed in the lap of luxury, while many others had died, had disappeared, or were perishing in jail, filled me with guilt and shame. But my escape and attempt at a mainstream life after the defeat of our dream had the exact opposite of the desired effect. I had hoped to wipe away the past and be happy in the present. Instead, my Santa Fe exile shone a spotlight on my losses and produced a pain so primal that it hurt to touch my chest.

And yet the naked eye would tell you that I was unscathed. I'd never been captured, arrested, tortured, or even threatened. It never occurred to me to try to get help, for there was none to be had. What was I supposed to do? Go to a counsellor and say: "Hi. I was in the Chilean resistance and it was fucking rough on my body, soul, psyche, and life because I lived in a state of chronic terror for years, and even though nothing ever happened to me, I think I may have PTSD, which I know is presumptuous, pathetic, and weak, considering there are thirty thousand disappeared people in this country and tens of thousands of torture survivors walking the streets, going to work, paying their bills, and raising children. By the way, we lost the revolution, and even though elections have been called for later this year, don't be fooled, we really did lose the revolution. Can you help?"

Not only did I believe that so much torment was unearned, I also felt undeserving of professional care. Who was I to seek help when I knew there were comrades living on the streets? Not to mention that the prospect was far too dangerous, what with the political climate in Argentina. After several tries by the military, people feared that the next coup attempt would be successful. Many were burning their compromising books and address lists. The economy was collapsing due to unpayable foreign debt, austerity measures, and corruption, and the starving shantytown dwellers who raided supermarkets and ate on the spot were being fiercely repressed. A few had been shot dead at a supermarket a few blocks from our house. Then there was Operation Condor, a Kissinger-conceived plan that saw the secret police forces of several South American countries working together to track down resistance members and do away with them through torture and murder. Considering that 179 Chilean resistance members had disappeared in Argentina, spilling the beans to a counsellor was out of the question.

As for the rape, it was like a satellite orbiting my life, part of my northern narrative, far enough away that we didn't share the same air, but visible on a clear day or night. Gravity didn't threaten to pull it through the atmosphere and crash it into me, hence it was not on my radar as a trauma to look at, but merely as a phenomenon to observe from afar.

Months passed and my self-loathing intensified. I had made the unequivocally un-revolutionary and un-feminist decision to be a woman whose identity could be summed up as "basketball girlfriend," and I started lashing out at Estéban. When not conducting a full-frontal attack, I could be found engaging in passive-aggressive behaviour, such as lying next to him in bed pompously reading Marta Harnecker's The Social Revolution while he flipped through Clarín newspaper. It was the only book

I had saved from my underground days, and it had always lived in a hiding place back in Neuquén. Now that I could read it openly, I did so, just to clarify that, although I was no longer involved in a leftist organization, I still believed in revolutionary change. Estéban was a whip-smart news junkie with centre politics who held a degree in journalism. Debating was one of our favourite pastimes, and it never took long for an argument to start.

Our relationship could be summed up with two F-words: *fucking* and *fighting*. We fought not only about politics but about everything. He wanted me to do all the housework because he was the main breadwinner (I tutored English and taught at a private institute), while I wanted to share it; he wanted to hire a maid and pay her the going rate to resolve the issue, I would refuse to exploit a shantytown woman; he wanted to get married, I didn't believe in marriage and reminded him that I had only married Alejandro at the MIR's request; he wanted to have children, I spouted imperial feminist dribble passed down from my mother about how the maternal instinct was a patriarchal construct that didn't exist. Our fighting, also triggered when, in my blind jealousy, I would accuse him of fucking groupies despite there being no evidence of this, would usually end up with me pounding on him to no effect. He was two hundred pounds of muscle, a six-foot-three professional athlete, and I was close to a foot shorter than him and weighed almost half what he did. He'd grab my forearms and stare into my face as my mouth, now a submachine gun, spit out the filthiest swear words in the Spanish language. Finally, after I'd exhausted every possible configuration of the Southern Cone's most popular insult, "Go back to your mother's cunt," I'd stare back at him in silence, out of breath, covered in sweat, nostrils flaring. Within moments we'd be fucking each other's brains out. And thus the vicious cycle would continue.

It was the polar opposite of my marriage to Alejandro, a model of diplomacy, respect, tenderness, and like-mindedness. Our fights over the four and a half years of our relationship could be counted on the fingers of one hand.

The fiery connection with Estéban provoked great fury in me, but it also sparked a great furor, for he reminded me what it was to be fully alive, engine firing on all cylinders. He was funny, intelligent, and so sexy my knees still buckled every time I looked at him. And he put up with me. He loved me, and I was mad about him.

There were times I would disappear from his life after a particularly brutal fight, slipping out of the house when he was asleep and taking the bus to Paraná, where I would hole up at Luisa's for a few days. Once, I recruited her to take me to Buenos Aires. Penniless, we snuck onto an all-night train and spent the entire ride avoiding the conductor. We divined that the train was crawling with thieves, our antennas up in the dark, and, it being the dead of winter, we almost froze to death because the windowpanes were broken. When we reached Buenos Aires at the crack of dawn, we knocked on Luisa's cousin's door, shaking from the frigid train ride. He was an economics student and shared his studio apartment with a classmate. We all slept on the floor after debating for hours about neo-liberalism. They were pro, we were against. The argument, unresolved, continued in the dark as we lay on the floor.

"Oh! I'm coming! I'm masturbating to Fidel Castro and I'm coming, 'cause I'm a Communist!" yelled the cousin's friend.

"Che Guevara's the hot one, you fucking imbecile," was Luisa's response. And then we both faked loud orgasms while yelling out, "Oh, Che!"

After a few days of aimless roaming around Buenos Aires, we snuck on a train back to Santa Fe, where I knew Estéban would be worried sick. I had fled without a plan, but while on the run Luisa and I had attended a showing of *Romeo and Juliet* at the Buenos Aires University Theatre Department. All their plays were free to the public, and every show was sold out. This particular version of Shakespeare's classic reimagined Romeo and Juliet as an old, sour, bitter couple who did nothing but bicker. The students had spent a semester developing it, devising an alternative ending to the original wherein the star-crossed lovers instead fled their families and grew old together. It was brilliant, and those students pumped my blood full of life with their joie de vivre.

On the voyage back to Santa Fe, eyes still shining from the performance, for the first time since I was a child I started to wonder about a possible future as an actor. I'd put on plays at social gatherings throughout my childhood, been part of theatre troupes in my teenage years, and had a starring role in my high school play the year I graduated. The theatre had seduced me at a tender age, and had been my one true love ever since. I had sacrificed that love for an even bigger one: revolutionary love. But now that was lost. And perhaps the future, which as far as I had always been concerned was going to consist of a socialist Chile where I would do whatever job was required of me, could now involve a life onstage. Who knew where, how, or when? For it was still difficult to fathom anything other than the dream I had fought so hard for, the crushed dream of so many.

⌒

The year came to an end and things got progressively worse between Estéban and me. Mami came to fetch me from Santa Fe and we ushered in 1990 in Valparaíso. During our time together, I told her about the Buenos Aires play and my long-lost dream of being an actor, and she urged me to follow that path no matter what, insisted that staying in Santa Fe would kill me and that the theatre would save my life. Mami came from a line of women who had never had the opportunity to follow a calling. Her maternal grandmother had raised thirteen children while being beaten regularly by her husband. Due to malnutrition and disease, only five of her offspring had made it to adulthood. Her paternal grandmother, a seamstress who had also raised a brood of thirteen, only three of whom made it past adolescence (one of them, my abuelito Armando, had become a teacher and subsequently a high school principal), had suc-cumbed to tuberculosis at the age of thirty-five. Her mother, my abuelita Carmen, had fled her violent family home at age sixteen, pregnant with my abuelito's child, my uncle Carlos. My mother was the first to go to university, because it was free of charge. I could be the first to follow a calling.

Shortly after my return from Chile, I bit Estéban's chest during a bad fight, drawing blood and leaving a scar. Much to my amazement, no matter how much I aimed my anger at him, he stayed put, never kicking me out or giving me an ultima-tum. Admittedly, many would have seen Estéban as the culprit in this particular fight. He had returned from an out-of-town basketball game with a crab-infested pubic area (no matter that I too had just nearly cheated on him with the Cousin). I had known the second I saw him that he'd slept with some-one else. If anything, being in the resistance had sharpened my instincts to such a point that one glance was all it took to read a person like a book. Pulling down his pants and seeing the crabs crawling on his belly and inner thighs had provided tangible evidence of the infidelity I'd always suspected him of. He denied it, of course, blaming dirty sheets in the hotel room he'd stayed in.

After the crab-induced chest-biting incident, my year of nervous breakdown reached its peak. I cried for a few days straight. Night and day. He did the best he could, although, being a young, super-privileged guy who'd never seen overt trauma up close, he had no skills to deal with me. All I wanted was to be held and reassured; all he could do was throw his hands up in the air in exasperation and walk away, shaking his head. Sure, the VD situation had sent me over the edge, proving to me that I was indeed alone in the universe, but the roots of my suffering went much deeper than being deceived by Estéban. I couldn't let him know what was wrong, no matter how much he asked, because I had no words to express what it felt like to be in a state of post-exile, post-revolutionary inertia. As for the rape, it was the furthest thing from my mind, as I was convinced that the basis of our relationship—sex—had proven that the rape was not an issue in my life.

"I'm going to theatre school in Canada," I announced a few weeks later.

The way out of inertia was to apply a force to it, I had learned from my father, a physics professor, so I decided that following my calling surrounded by the exiled part of my clan in the land that had taken us in might dry my endless stream of tears.

I'd been chewing over Mami's inspiring words, no longer taking stock only of all that was lost but also of all that could be. Even though Pinochet was about to step down, I was afraid that going to theatre school in Santiago would be too painful to bear in the immediate aftermath of our defeat, so it made sense to end my Santa Fe banishment by following my childhood dream back to Vancouver. I could study theatre and upon graduation return to Argentina or Chile and be an actor.

As a professional athlete, Estéban understood the power of a calling, so he supported me in my plans. I would go to Vancouver for the audition, and he would follow three months later, abandoning the basketball season midway. Within three years my schooling would be done, and we'd return to the South, probably to Buenos Aires and its thriving, world-renowned theatre scene and basketball teams he could try out for. During my summer breaks from theatre school, we would visit Argentina.

On a warm Buenos Aires day in March 1990, I waved goodbye to Estéban from the escalator taking me to my Canada-bound flight at Ezeiza International Airport. I wore the same Calvin Klein, floor-length, gigantic-shoulder-padded denim coat M had bought me many lifetimes before, when I was a twenty-year-old, on-fire divorcee. Although that had been only two years earlier, a revolution had been lost since then and my adventuresome little group had scattered. M had returned to Brooklyn and I'd lost all touch with him, Luisa now lived in her hometown of Paraná, and Estéban had been traded to Santa Fe. Neuquén, where I had spent my first years of adulthood, seemed like a faraway dream, with its underground life and many secret excursions into Chile, that imagined country with its promise of imminent socialist triumph. Looking down from the escalator at that loyal, if not entirely faithful, man, I put on a brave face and bid farewell to the Southern Cone, the place where I'd given my life to a cause so much bigger than myself. Rudderless since that colossal loss, no one was more surprised than me when my compass pointed north.

I'd known acting was my calling since the age of three, when my parents had taken me to the circus in Valdivia and I'd watched a bikini-clad lady stand on one leg on a galloping white horse. I also knew that acting had little to do with talent and much to do with skill—I'd taken acting classes since the age of eight—hence my decision, to my parents' delight, to try out for one of the top classical theatre conservatories in Canada, located in the basement of a South Vancouver college. An Emmy-nominated American TV actor prepared me for the audition. He'd coach me late at night, after he returned from twelve-hour stints on set, where he played a detective on a Vancouver-shot Hollywood cop show. I met him when he hired me to be his Spanish wife's English tutor, and the three of us became fast friends. They lived in a penthouse suite on Beach Avenue, overlooking the Burrard Inlet, and he was kind enough to help me work through a comedic monologue about a harried waitress and a dramatic monologue about a girl who'd lost her mother to cancer. A white girl. A middle-class girl with a name like Sandy.

His patience and persistence paid off: I was accepted into the acting programme at the conservatory, along with fifteen other people. Hundreds from across the country had auditioned for sixteen slots, eight for men and eight for women. Of those original sixteen, only five would graduate. The rest would bow out of their own accord or be asked to leave within the first year—par for the course at this theatre school.

I think it was my rendition of "Happy Birthday" in Spanish that tipped the scales in my favour. The audition, two hours long, had ended with a request for a song. My jaw dropped. The mailed instructions had only required two contrasting monologues; no mention of singing had been made. But then again, movement exercises, icebreakers, ensemble builders, improv, cold readings, and group games with names like Let's Do It! hadn't been alluded to either. So I sang "Happy Birthday" to the director, giving it my all, a Broadway belter beaming at the centre of a spotlight. Thankfully, my friend Lucho, a fellow Chilean exile about to graduate from the school, had advised me to wear tights, a loose T-shirt, hair in a bun, and zero makeup. It was clear that the others had not had the privilege of inside information. Some of the women were in pointy shoes and denim miniskirts, blond perms on full display, Bordeaux lips contrasting with their powdered faces. None of those made it in.

Now that I was in theatre school, I was beginning to realize that I had been wrong in my assumption that acting was about acquiring the skills to pretend convincingly—in effect, to be a bald-faced, superlative liar. It was mid-October 1990, I was halfway through my first term, and so far I had learned that I was an absolute disaster as an actor, that indeed it was foolhardy ever to have thought I could grace the stage. Coming to this conclusion wasn't difficult. First of all, there was the question of vulnerability, the fact that in order to be an actor one must be willing to open one's heart and expose oneself to an audience of strangers who had paid money to see you do that. I had no idea what vulnerability in the professional realm was—what it felt like, how it manifested itself. Although I had just spent an entire year in the fetal position sobbing inconsolably on a daily basis, I was clueless as to how one went about accessing one's emotional life on demand.

"The answer lies in the text," my teacher affirmed. "Now get onto your voice and speak on the breath."

Voice class was helpful. We had lessons on how to get out of one's head, drop into one's guts, and strengthen and trust one's back so that one could let the front of one's body relax and open. Still, no matter how hard I cried in voice class, once I got to acting class, where I was required to relinquish control and lay myself bare while interpreting a script, I shut off, any access to my emotional well sealed like an adamant clam at the bottom of the sea.

When I grasped that acting was about honesty as opposed to masterful posturing, my awe and respect grew exponentially for the actors and plays that had changed my life. The most searing of these had been in 1986, in civil war–ridden Lima, Peru, the day after I'd taken the MIR oath at the age of eighteen (Lima was the MIR's South American headquarters-in-exile). I was walking around downtown, weeping under my mirrored sunglasses, gripped by the Terror, when Alejandro pointed out a scribbled sign on a telephone pole advertising a play that was to start after curfew. The scrawled note taunted: *Come if you dare.*

Being young and stupid, Alejandro and I broke all the rules of the oath we'd taken twenty-four hours earlier, which included never being seen at any alternative, much less illegal, events, and we dared to go to the play.

We arrived just before curfew at the mentioned location, a rundown school. There were a couple of dozen people there, of all ages and mixed social classes. We all nodded at each other and then stared at the ground as Lima prepared for curfew, last stragglers running home, packed buses speeding down the street, the first military helicopters hovering in the sky. I cried quietly, the Terror not giving an inch. Finally, an Indigenous man in bare feet and white pants came out and gestured to us to enter the building.

We were taken to a classroom. The chairs had been arranged in a circle. After we took our seats, the man disappeared. Time passed, the score of curfew becoming more prominent: silence, except for the intermittent hum of helicopters and military vehicles, an order being barked out, a bomb exploding here and there, and the odd shot ringing through the night. These sounds became our walk-in music. I wondered if there were secret-police members in the audience. More tears sprouted at the thought. Un-revolutionarily.

All of a sudden a guitar played and a man came in, a troubadour, also in bare feet and white pants. He sang a song with no lyrics, just haunting vocals. He was followed by a woman and two other men, all in bare feet and white attire. The last was the man who'd let us in. For the next two hours they told us the history of Peru from the Spanish Conquest until that very moment in time: May 1986, the civil war. They told the story with their bodies. No text was spoken. They created image upon image, and a soundscape with their voices and breath, periodically punctuated by the hums, shouts, shots, and explosions of curfew. The images were of genocide, rape, slavery, starvation, and, ultimately, resistance. A celebration of life. The history of that country from the point of view of the oppressed, now freedom fighters. They finished their play by dancing cumbia as they sang the only text:

"We may be fucked, but we're happy."

That performance, and the circumstances I saw it in, would be embedded in my brain forever. I had been willing to break all the rules and risk everything to have a story told to me, and it had paid off. The play gave me the inspiration to continue. It contextualized why I had chosen to join a movement that sought to liberate my continent from the very oppression it depicted. It brought the Terror to its knees and filled me with joy, expanding my tiny universe of paranoia and letting in the light. It reminded me not to take myself so seriously, that the story was much larger than my own personal narrative, that I had put myself in a terrifying situation in order to serve a sweeping epic in which I was a mere player. And it showed me that that was worth doing. Those highly skilled storytellers had been able to articulate my own defining story, conjuring meaning out of raw experience. They took us into the dark and transcended the pain, reminding us that our stories mattered, their fierce commitment to social and artistic transformation exhilarating and life-affirming. I had known when I witnessed this play that if I hadn't chosen to give my life to a cause, I would have dedicated it to the art of telling these kinds of stories.

Now here I was in Vancouver following my calling, overwhelmed at the realization that terror, failure, and risk were a key part of actor training. I had been convinced that the artistry behind superlative storytelling was about feigning persuasively. Now I was finding out that a well-told story was most effective when there was no pretence at all, that a story affects us when the storyteller unmasks herself and seeks the truth in every moment. That truth seeking is by its very nature risk taking, and that risk taking can lead to failure. That often failure happens in front of an audience, and that a successful artist is simply someone who insists on doing her work, in spite of the failure and the public humiliation that comes with it. All of this was almost as frightening as taking the resistance oath and surrendering my life to the underground. I wondered, would I ever be able to do any of it?

Halfway through the term, I was called into the school director's office for a chat with her, the associate director, and the voice instructor. Everybody in the programme had a mid-term session to discuss and evaluate their progress. During my talk, it was mentioned that I was entering a racist business where more often than not I would be offered Mexican hooker and Puerto Rican maid roles. Was I sure that I wanted to continue?

Incredibly, this came as a shock to me. Like many young, naive acting students, I had thought the theatre was a utopia free of racism, sexism, homophobia, classism, ageism. It had never crossed my mind that the theatre was just like every other place in society. Moreover, I had assumed that I was an invisible minority to my all-white instructors, not a visible one, possibly because I was one of only three students of colour in the entire conservatory, made up of fifty mostly middle- and upper-middle-class white kids. But now my colour was being directly addressed, when I thought it had been washed out by all that whiteness. At least, that was the way I always felt until I left the confines of the conservatory, because the college was located in South Vancouver's Little India. Whenever I climbed the stairs to the cafeteria and passed hundreds of other students dashing to class, half of whom were Asian and South Asian, I let out a sigh of relief and recognition and smiled at the passing faces.

As for my fellow Latinos, they could be found in the form of a Guatemalan family, acquaintances from community events, mopping the college's floors. The sight of them was always a jolt to me. It reminded me of my own 1970s Vancouver childhood, when my family would all pile into a beater and do the janitorial work together, sometimes late into the night. The sight of the Guatemalan family brought me back to who I really was, where I actually came from, and how far all of that was from my whitewashed Shakespearean acting life in the building's basement. It was beyond me how I'd ever merge the two. Because it was beginning to dawn on me that if I was ever to succeed at risking vulnerability in front of paying strangers, that if I was ever to stage the stories I wanted to tell, compartmentalization (all I'd ever known, in both the North and the South) would have to go by the wayside. I would have to find a way to desegregate my life, to become whole and integrate it all in order to bare my true self.

My teachers had meant to be helpful with their verbal reality check of hooker and maid roles. But I flew into a rage that lasted for my remaining three years at school. It was exhausting to be infuriated at my superiors all the time, convenient as it was. I could just blame them and their remarks on racism for my not being able to take a risk and be vulnerable onstage. No matter that that was wholly the actor's responsibility, the blame could still be put on their white, middle-class privilege.

So I wore a button on my Le Château red dungarees that proclaimed *Token Minority* and joined the college's People of Colour Alliance, in a minuscule room adjacent to the Student Union's building where brown students would congregate. The continent of Africa was painted on its door, and posters of Malcolm X ("If you have no critics, you'll likely have no success"), Muhammad Ali ("He who is not courageous enough to take risks will accomplish nothing in life"), and Assata Shakur ("No one is going to give you the education you need to overthrow them") graced the walls. A couple of futons were provided for reading the many biographies of Nelson Mandela, Che Guevara, and Ho Chi Minh that were stacked on the shelves, but they were mostly used for making out on while Public Enemy played on the ghetto blaster.

A Salvadoran nephew of a Farabundo Martí National Liberation Front (FMLN) leader ran the joint. He wore a black leather baseball cap with a white X stitched on it, tiny silver hoops in his ears, and a necklace with a leather pendant in the shape of the African continent. Ernesto Cardenal's collection *Zero Hour and Other Documentary Poems* lived under his arm, and he skateboarded all over the city. His girlfriend was a Filipina-Canadian activist who wore long cotton skirts, mukluks, and a red beret.

The one rule of the People of Colour Alliance was that no whites were allowed in. You could only cross the threshold if you identified as a person of colour. So as my classmates lined up for their cappuccinos, I would nonchalantly announce that I was going to the People of Colour Alliance. Usually there wasn't a soul in the room, but at times I would come across the Filipina-Canadian activist power-napping, a pool of drool forming on the futon, "Fight the Power" blasting from the boom box. I'd raise my left fist to the posters on the wall while I sang along to the lyrics. Then I'd take a deep breath and run back to the land of reciting lines from the writings of dead white European men.

As well as the racism of the business, another equally delicate matter had been raised during that mid-term session with my instructors:

"We highly recommend that you go to therapy if you want to make it through the programme."

They were referring to my being seized by the memory of the rape in the now-legendary voice class. The rape was so taboo in my family that even Macarena and I hadn't talked about it since my return to Canada. The staff mentioned post-traumatic stress disorder, and I froze. As far as they knew, the only trauma present in my body was that of the rape. They knew nothing of my MIR life of chronic terror, and they never would. I had taken the oath a mere four years earlier in Lima. In it, I had promised never to speak of the MIR to anybody. Not only that, I was no naïf when it came to the Canadian Security Intelligence Service and the Royal Canadian Mounted Police. My family's phones had been tapped since the 1970s, we'd found a bug on the back of one of our shelves, and we knew that the secret police was the same everywhere; they had probably infiltrated the Chilean community in exile, and therefore nothing of great importance or detail was spoken of in our public events. Our private gatherings were on lockdown too; nobody shared any information there either.

The Chileans who had returned south to join the armed resistance in the late seventies and early eighties, whether it was the MIR or the Manuel Rodríguez Patriotic Front, had left quietly, like us, vanishing from Vancouver without a trace. Those who had stayed behind in the North, holding down the solidarity fort, were sworn to secrecy as to exactly whom the solidarity funds had gone to, and although there was an innate intimacy and understanding amongst us all, nobody asked questions and everyone looked the other way, even though the odd sound bite about resistance activity might be dropped at a cumbia dance party since the dictatorship had ended. Despite the struggle being over, and especially because we had lost, the unbreakable rule was still followed religiously: the less you know, the better. And you will take anything you do know to the grave. Period.

I started to see a therapist near the campus. She was a middle-aged white lesbian in Birkenstocks to whom I unloaded the entire story of the rape in our first session. That's what I was there for, so I figured I'd dive right in. She'd conclude that I was completely over it when she saw that I had no problem talking about it, my account littered with graphic detail. Instead, she said: "You just relived the experience as you told it. It's as if it happened a moment ago. We have a lot of work to do."

The rape, until now confined to its solitary outer-space existence, crashed through the atmosphere, the force of gravity pulling it right to my core, where it left a gaping, burning hole, not unlike the one left by the fire on the Valparaíso hill on New Year's Eve earlier that year, when exile had come to an end and the rape had been relegated to my northern identity, a satellite orbiting around that hemisphere's constellations. Now it fell in flames from the sky and landed in the centre of my life. Resistance was futile. For the next two years, almost the entirety of my remaining time at theatre school, I didn't menstruate.

FOUR

True to his word, Estéban had arrived in June 1990, three months after I'd left Argentina. Now it was December of that year, I was about to complete my first term, and he was still in deep culture shock. In the early 1990s, the Latino community was one of the poorest immigrant demographics in the city. When we went to a party, cumbia, considered low class in Argentina, was danced, and often recent refugees from other continents were invited. Most of the community were labourers, working as janitors, construction workers, mechanics, and dishwashers. Unlike most Latinos in 1990 Vancouver, Estéban was a Euro-Latino. Not only that, he came from the upper middle class, had centre, not left, politics, was not a refugee, and had never held down a regular job. He came from the Argentinian elite and hadn't been aware of it, not unlike some of my peers at theatre school. Now he found himself being referred to as a minority, being told that he came from a Third World country ("What the fuck are these idiots talking about?!"), barely able to communicate due to his rudimentary English, driving a rusty second-hand car for his job as delivery man for a popular Indian restaurant on Kingsway, and hanging out with a politicized Latino community made up of mestizo and Indigenous members of resistance movements from all over the South. Many were survivors of concentration camps and mass killings, such as those from Guatemala, where over two hundred thousand Mayan people had been murdered by the right-wing, US-backed regime.

The upper-crust lifestyle that was a given to Estéban seemed so far away, it was as if it hadn't even taken place on the same land mass, much less only months before. Evidently, he was on a different planet altogether, where not only were the social signals of mainstream Canada the opposite of those in Argentina ("Why do these people jump when you touch them?"), whenever he did hang out with fellow Latinos, they came from a domain that had been invisible to him back home—the realm of political involvement. He was now immersed in stories that he'd read about in the papers in Argentina, even though in that country thirty thousand people had just disappeared. As for being surrounded by brown, working-class Latinos, it made him appreciate the maids in his parents' house. On an outing to Gastown, Vancouver's historic tourist quarter, the first thing he bought were T-shirts for them. For the first time in his life, he laboured. Not only was he a delivery man, he also painted houses and bussed dishes at a popular west-side bistro. As an undocumented worker, he worried he'd be caught and deported. Although the shock to his body and ego was intense, it expanded his world view and made him appreciate the work of the women who'd always been a blur to him, toiling in the background of his childhood home. Now they came into sharp, foreground focus.

I spent at least twelve hours a day at school. First there were classes, from early morning until dinnertime. Then there was a short meal break, followed by crew calls. One made costumes, props, and posters, built and painted sets, and hung lights for the school's productions. Sometimes the calls would go until two or three in the morning, until the work was done. Lying on the floor with a glue gun, pasting bead by bead to the bottom of a set piece at one in the morning, hair covered in glue, wrist shaking from exhaustion, dust in one's eyes, knowing there were still hours to go, understanding that one would have to sneak into the costume room and sleep on an Elizabethan gown covered in mouse droppings before morning class without getting caught by the night security guard (a disenchanted Sri Lankan immigrant who had been a brain surgeon back home)—all of this was matter of course. After a certain point, going home was futile if one wanted to get at least a few hours' sleep before the 8 a.m. theatre history class, and besides, there were no more buses and one was hanging by the thread of one's meagre student loan and could not afford a cab. Complaining was out of the question; our conservatory was renowned not only for its "know thyself" motto, but also for being a boot camp of sorts, and one could be kicked out for having an attitude problem. Mondays were the one day off, spent doing homework, housework, laundry, and in my case therapy, where I avoided the now flashing-in-neon-lights-in-front-of-me, period-stopping rape and talked about my family history instead.

The theatre was slavery, pure and simple, and our acting school was there to drive the point home ("If you're not *obsessed* with the work, you're not *doing* the work!" barked our mask instructor). It would take only a couple of terms to find out if it was indeed your calling or if you'd been attracted to the supposed glamour of the thing. In spite of the fatigue and fury the school engendered in me, I adored being a slave to the theatre. Whenever I walked onto the stage, even if it was to mop it before the show, my skin tingled. The thought of actually gracing the boards as an actor once I reached the higher terms made me euphoric, despite my being warned that roles would be limited and stereotypical once I graduated into the real world of professional theatre. In the meantime, I had to figure out a way to risk vulnerability every night while interpreting a playwright's text in front of paying strangers. The risk I was being asked to take was so daunting, I had yet to find the edge of the cliff in order to jump from it.

Going home covered in paint and plaster to shell-shocked Estéban, pontificating on the importance of alignment, spine rolls, vocal resonators, loose jaws, contact improvisation, verbing, Labanotation, authentic movement, Grotowski exercises, connecting to one's sacral floor, the voice and body as sole instrument available to the actor, the deconstruction of scenes into objectives, tactics, units, and beats while he stared blankly at MuchMusic was akin to talking to a man who had just landed on the moon and was trying to figure out how to plant his flag on its strange surface. Not only did we rarely see each other, when we did, we were both so fatigued and dumbfounded for completely different reasons that it was virtually impossible to connect. My exhaustion and stupefaction was balanced by a feeling of elation; his was simply bone- and soul-crushing. I knew his experience and sympathized completely. He understood mine, because his calling had been basketball and he'd given his life to train and acquire the skills that had got him into the professional leagues.

Our fighting continued, even though my sobbing fits were now confined to voice class, where they at least happened in the context of accessing the bottomless swamp of emotion that was required to be an actor. At the end of the term, I pounded on him so badly that in his effort to restrain me we ended up falling into the bathtub together and I got a concussion. Right after Christmas, he went back to Argentina. Despite our relationship being a train wreck, splitting up was not on the table. We professed our undying love for each other and decided that once my second term was over, in May, I would go to Santa Fe to spend my summer holidays with him. We agreed that we would do this for the next three years. It was doubtful that he'd return to Vancouver.

A month after Estéban left, in January 1991, I broke up with him over the phone. Blindsided, he demanded to know what was going on. All I could muster was something along the lines of fear, telling him that fear had overshadowed love when it came to him, that my fear of him was greater than my love for him. It was impossible for me to admit—to myself, much less to him— that the violence in our relationship had always come from me. Being raised as a radical feminist, I had interpreted that ideology to mean that the patriarchy was to blame for everything, that I could basically beat a man and still be considered the victim. I conveniently cast him as the villain, and talked myself into believing that I was afraid of him because the bathtub incident had given me a concussion, failing to examine what had come before, what had led us there, convincing myself of the theory that I was afraid of Estéban, that big, bad, sexist man. And I told him as much. He was devastated.

Twenty-five years would pass before I saw him again and could apologize for the violence I'd felt entitled to take out on him.

Every term there was a student-run evening called Performance Lab. The rules were basic; there were none. Students were invited to experiment as much as possible, to take things too far in a safe environment where no critics or paying audience were present. The audience would be made up of the school's student body, and the staff would be invited to attend. Performance Lab was legendary. Plays that achieved success in the professional world had begun as five-minute seeds there. Students had found their voice, their guts, their confidence while trying something out on the Performance Lab stage. People sobbed, raged, took off all their clothes, or just stared out into the audience in absolute silence and stillness. Anything went. Most numbers were embarrassingly self-indulgent and hence crashed and burned. And that was all right. Because that was the point: to make a buffoon of yourself in a safe environment. Pushing boundaries was how you grew, how you learned.

During my first term, I decided to present a ten-minute skit on the day of the coup in Chile. I didn't write anything down. I knew what I wanted to say and what I wanted to play: myself at the age of five. I recruited my friend Lucho, my fellow Chilean exile who was about to graduate, to take on the smaller roles. Standing onstage, I relived the day of the coup in front of my peers and superiors. I described my dirt road in my Valdivia neighbourhood, the southern city we'd been living in when the

coup happened. I spoke of my parents, my sister, the radio playing Allende's final speech. My father, head of the physics department at the same college where the conservatory was, managed
to run down to the performance. Knowing he was there, both
of us aware that I was exposing a part of myself no one at school
had any inkling of, brought tears to my eyes. They poured down
my face. I was vulnerable in front of a warm, safe audience who
wanted me to succeed in whatever I was experimenting with,
people who had never experienced political violence witnessing
my first step in the long journey of desegregating my life in order
to be an artist. A step symbolized not only by the story I was
telling but by whom I was telling it with: my childhood friend
who had hidden his Chilean-exile identity and was only letting
the school know about it now, on the cusp of his exit. My explo-
ration was straightforward: How do I unmask myself, my *true*
self, in front of an audience of mainstream Canadians? How do
I become vulnerable as an artist? How do I tell a story so foreign
to this audience and still have them identify with the character?

I thought I succeeded that day. But when I checked with my
voice teacher, she was clear:

"That wasn't performance. That was therapy. It was too
personal."

She wasn't referring to the content. She meant the delivery. I
had been working my shit out onstage, and that was not entertainment. Instead of telling the story to affect the listeners, I
had told the story to see what effect it had on me. When it produced tears, I congratulated myself, as opposed to keeping my
focus outward, on the audience, the most important character
in a play. I began to understand what my teachers had been
saying all along. Give It Away. Always Just Give It Away. I had

been self-indulgent because I hadn't actually included the audience by releasing the story. Doing so would have transformed it into a symbol that the whole room owned, making it art.

Defeat overtook the thrill of Performance Lab. Little did I know then that there was so much more to it than learning how to be vulnerable and open without being too personal, that this was the tip of the skill-acquiring iceberg, that the further I dove into my schooling, the more I would discover that the tools available to a storyteller were endless, seemingly impossible to acquire in one lifetime. According to my instructors, it was all about process. But surely a product must lie at the end of the creation tunnel? No. Product was also to be viewed as process. I decided that they were wrong, that they were only referring to the training itself, that once I graduated I would have learned how to create art in a certain, reliable way, positive results guaranteed one hundred percent of the time, like a formula of sorts. That surely art was not unlike the exact sciences, an equation to be solved, as opposed to an ever-elusive, fleeting practice whose success was so subjective and ephemeral as to render it possibly pointless every time.

Meanwhile, well into my second term at theatre school in 1991, the demand to continue to shed all veils, pull out my demons, and examine them one by one grew exponentially.

"You're afraid to be ugly," my teachers asserted.

One of my male classmates had been told to cut off his long hair, which he presumably wore as a mask. He had felt butt-naked after doing so. I tried to embrace grunge, all the rage, wearing ripped flannels, fire-engine red Doc Martens, and distressed cut-off denim shorts over flowered tights. I cut my long hair to my chin. But instead of ugly being synonymous with vulnerable, grunge just made me hard. Torrents of tears continued to fall down my face in voice class, but as soon as I had to play Lady Macbeth in acting class, the walls came up and my work was so flat and boring I might as well have been reciting the contents of the telephone book. Conversely, I overacted like an amateur, not trusting in either case that I was enough ("There is nothing more compelling than *you* when you are courageous enough to show us your heart," my mentors taught). I cut off all access to my emotional and creative well when I had to interpret a character in a written scene.

Then there was my weight. I had stopped eating again, which gave me the illusion of having control over my life. I became so light there were times I had to hold on to the walls to get down the school halls.

It was similar to when I'd been in the MIR and the Terror, self-starvation, sleeplessness, and a sexless marriage would bring on a near fainting fit in the street and force me to hang on to buildings.

Although that period had ended only three years earlier, it belonged to a reality so far removed from anything in theatre school that I was still at a loss as to how to integrate it into my work. I fluctuated between extremes, being too personal during Performance Lab and detached while playing Lady Macbeth. If being an actor meant having the ability to serve as a conduit for others' text, then I was a colossal failure. The story of Macbeth was probably much more familiar to me than it was to my classmates, because Chilean politics was as Shakespearean as you could get. Macbeth was Pinochet, King Duncan Allende. I knew the story in my bones. And yet I didn't know how to inhabit it.

"The problem is the English language," was my voice teacher's assessment.

My command of English was that of a native speaker, all my elementary schooling having taken place in North America, but it was confined to my head. Spanish was in my heart, guts, and soul. How to make English move to the nether regions? Who knew? It was all too discouraging to contemplate.

It wasn't just language. It was dissociation, she said. The concept was new to me, though not the sensation. I had left my body and unplugged my heart many times to survive traumatic moments. Much of my MIR time had been spent in a state of dissociation, I now realized. Apparently my spirit stood next to me while I was acting too, only entering on the rare occasions when it found a chink in my armour, before being expelled once more. Dissociation had saved me from irreversible damage time after time. I feared it would be impossible to talk myself—body, psyche, and soul—into dropping my guard and letting my spirit inhabit its temple while onstage. I wondered if I was still dissociating in my everyday life as well.

The Terror, that constant underground companion, had retreated back into the shadows since my return to Canada. The threats during the Terror had been concrete: torture, murder. Easy to put a finger on, easy to put a face to. The military, the cops, the dreaded secret police. I did not feel that kind of fear anymore, yet it was clear that fear kept me from renouncing dissociation. I wanted to let my guts shine in a play, but no matter how far I was willing to go for my calling, I knew in my heart that I wasn't ready to drop my shields and invite my spirit in to stay so I could do that. I felt certain that if I bared the ugliness my teachers had spoken of—as well as the beauty—with an embodied spirit onstage, I would die of pain, sorrow, and shame. This new fear took hold of me and wouldn't let go, my animal brain convinced that the vulnerability required of an actor equalled being at the mercy of torturers and murderers. Or a rapist.

In the spirit of looking at one's demons and hence one's fears, I decided to examine the first time I remembered dissociating. Although I had dissociated before the age of thirteen, the rape was a good place to start, as it had come up almost immediately in my training and was the sole reason I had started therapy. Since landing downstage centre of my life in that first session, it stared me in the face, even though I'd never spoken of it again with my ever-patient therapist. But lifting up and turning over the rock labelled "rape" and studying its underbelly was not unlike peering into a kaleidoscope. Images collapsed into each other, as did sensations. At its nucleus lived a pain so sharp and unfamiliar, so unfathomable, that my spirit had escaped to the crowns of the rainforest trees, where it bore witness to a man on top of me, my face covered by my white shirt, tied in a knot behind my head.

Tops of trees had always been my saviours, one in particular. Other kids had pets, I had Cedar. I could survey the entire neighbourhood unseen when I reached Cedar's pinnacle and sat on one of his branches. He became my tree in 1974, when I was six years old and my family had just moved to student housing at the University of British Columbia, on Vancouver's west side. My parents were still together, and both were revalidating their degrees. No matter that my father had been the head of the physics department and my mother the head of the English department at Austral University in Valdivia, not to mention both being adult educators during Allende's literacy campaign, their "Third World" education and experience seemed to have little value in English Canada. They found themselves back at school, never complaining, always grateful for the chance to start over. Papi washed cars, delivered newspapers, and tended gardens to pay the bills. Mami was a teaching assistant. Both got janitor jobs that were shared with the other Chilean refugee families, and for years we'd all go en masse to clean downtown buildings at night and on weekends. We kids were in charge of collecting the garbage and other menial tasks, and showing the adults how to use the vacuum cleaners. We also served as translators when Mami (the only adult who spoke English, learned at the age of sixteen when she'd spent a year in Salt Lake City on a student exchange) was too busy scrubbing toilets; we'd interpret the instructions on the various bottles of cleaner.

Our favourite place to work was a luxury men's hair salon on the fancy part of Hastings Street, just west of the Downtown Eastside. While the adults immersed themselves in the chore of getting rid of every last hair that graced the shiny tiled floor, we practised the hustle as we Windexed the mirrors. Once our jobs were done, we'd head east, to Pigeon Park, where all the winos hung out. We'd come back super rich, because the melancholy drunks would give us all their money. "You're just like my kid. Here. Take this quarter and buy yourself a Revello," they would offer, rummaging through their coat pockets, change rolling around on the ground, glistening in the puddles. We'd dive for the coins and the occasional dollar bill, and run back to the salon before the adults missed us too much. There we'd play dumb, arranging the magazines, captivated by the bushes on full display in the *Penthouse* centrefolds.

Student housing at UBC consisted of five cul-de-sacs referred to as "the courts." The houses were all identical: two-bedroom, two-storey white stucco with diagonal roofs for the chronic rain. Designed as they were for families, children could be found at every address. We lived in Salmo Court, the twelve homes in our cul-de-sac inhabited by families from Germany, Bermuda, Sweden, Iran, England, and the rest of Canada. On the day we arrived, I went for a walk to get the lay of the land while five-year-old Ale made a dash for the playground. I had seen that our sliding glass living room door gave way to a forest, and I would certainly check that out. But first, I decided to exit the front door and saunter by all the other houses, hoping to get a glimpse of the worldly children who lived there.

As soon as I emerged, I heard a witch cackle. I pricked up my ears and heard it again. Without a shadow of a doubt, a witch was cackling. Turning my head in every direction, including up to the sky to see if the witch was passing by on a broom, I decided I had to find this witch to see if she could show me her potions. Two potions would be good: one for love and the other to kill Pinochet. Boys would go crazy for me, and Pinochet would be dead and we could all go back to Chile. Just then, the witch rounded the corner across the way, wearing a long black dress and a cone-shaped black hat, carrying her broom in both hands. A green mask covered her face, with its pointy nose and hideous, oversized black mole. The witch was about eight, two years older than me; that was clear from her height. A group of laughing children followed her as she cackled away, head thrown back, long light-brown hair cascading down her back. I crossed the centre of the court, which also served as a parking lot, with a space in front of every house, and took up the rear. The witch led the kids around the laundromat building and I broke into a run, not wanting to lose sight of them.

As I rounded the corner, I crashed right into a girl coming in the opposite direction. My age, she had enormous brown eyes, her baby-blond hair in pigtails. She held a sandwich in her hand, intact despite the collision. I was taken by her beauty, elegance, and femininity; she wore a satiny dress, white knee socks, and impeccable white shoes. Ribbons adorned her hair, and a gold chain with a cross hung around her neck. A sharp pang hit me, right in the gut, forcing me to swallow the knot that formed in my throat, for she took me back, right back to the dirt lane of my yellow wooden house in Huacho Copihue, my Valdivia barrio, where little girls dressed like this, where I myself had once worn patent-leather white shoes on the day I'd declared my love to the boy across the way.

There was fury in this girl's eyes, and her glare soon landed me back in Salmo Court, the exile land, where my braids were falling apart and I donned barf-coloured corduroy floods, a brown T-shirt with a fading decal on it of hugging squirrels with the caption *Best Friends*, and beige stained waffle runners, all donations from a church group that helped refugees. The witch long gone, I smiled at this girl instead, for there was nothing to do but dive into the deep end. New, friendless—in short, fresh off the boat—I knew I needed to act if I was to put a dent in my state of exile.

She didn't smile back. She just stared at her sandwich as if it was made of shit and piss. I approached, fingers interlocked behind me, swinging my leg a little bit, whistling softly as I looked at the ground, trying to appear as nonchalant and non-threatening as possible. The girl spoke to me in rapid-fire sentences. Mystified as to what she was saying, I just nodded and smiled. Keeping eye contact, I broke into a sweat on that warm, mid-August afternoon. She spoke again, this time with even more urgency, her eyebrows knitted together. I nodded and smiled again. Then she thrust the sandwich into my face, her words pleading. I looked at the sandwich. Then I looked at her. She rammed it against my mouth, her tone indisputably one of life and death. I opened my trap and she fed me the sandwich.

It was the strangest thing I'd ever tasted, as far as sandwiches went: peanut butter and banana on Wonder bread. My taste buds imploded, unable to decipher what this combination of tastes and textures was, but I continued to smile and nod as I chewed and swallowed, chewed and swallowed, chewed and swallowed. At long last the sandwich was eaten, all evidence of its existence gone. The girl sighed with relief and took off around the corner in a blur like the Road Runner, ponytails bouncing. Standing motionless, I decided that seeing a witch and then getting fed a free sandwich wasn't a bad way to start my new life in Salmo Court.

I started ambling again, past the laundromat and up a little grassy knoll. I came across another patch of forest and wandered through it, past ferns, salal, and huckleberry bushes, stepping over ancient fallen trees into rugs of moss, ducking spiderwebs. I reached a stump and sat on it. As I looked up, I noticed that if I stood on the stump and got on my tippytoes, I was able to reach the lowest branch of this tall, tall tree. Shafts of light led the way, and I climbed to its top. Surveying the land for any sight of the witch, her gaggle of children, or the beautiful sandwich feeder, I saw sets of swings, little playgrounds, more forest, the tops of the houses in adjacent courts, and a plane crossing the sky. I leaned my head against the trunk of my new tree, put my arms around it, and kissed Cedar.

FIVE

Unlike the other Chileans who'd arrived in Vancouver via air, we'd come by land, my father at the wheel of a 1970 baby-blue, two-door Chevrolet Malibu bought for seventy dollars in San Diego, California. Crossing the border into Canada in the early summer of 1974, we'd driven down Oak Street on a clear blue day, the north shore mountains a beacon in the distance.

We'd left Chile in December 1973, just three months after the coup. My mother had been fired and fingered as an MIRista (she was) to the military by the right-wing dean of Austral University. MIRistas were amongst the most wanted, because during Allende's government the MIR was the only organization that had openly called for arming the people in order to defend socialism. Formed in 1965 in the universities, the MIR had stood for revolutionary change since its inception. Within months of Pinochet's takeover, most of its central committee was imprisoned, had been disappeared, or were dead. A year later, its secretary general, Miguel Enríquez, would be murdered in a shootout, and most of the MIR's membership, made up of students of all social classes, teachers, factory workers, miners, peasants, homemakers, artists, soldiers, liberation theology clergy, and more, were in jail, exiled, or in deep hiding. If it hadn't been for Giovanna, my mother's best friend, Mami would probably have been dead or in a concentration camp.

Giovanna was an Italian American from San Francisco who had moved to Chile in 1970, just before Allende's win. Her Chilean husband, a diamond smuggler wanted in Europe, had brought her there, and it wasn't long before she became politicized. Many other foreigners arrived at that time, not following a spouse but in order to witness Allende's peaceful road to socialism and, more importantly, to offer their solidarity work. Giovanna's marriage didn't last. When it ended, she decided to stay on and be a part of history in the making: revolutionary socialist change without the armed revolution. She taught alongside my mother in the English department of the university in Valdivia. They became fast friends, and many evenings were spent in a large wooden house on the shores of the Calle-Calle River, where their colleague James, a British professor from Oxford University who had come to support Allende, lived with his wife and children.

A revolutionary Swede lived in their attic, and he spent copious amounts of time pounding away on a typewriter. When the coup happened, James's house was raided and the military, led by plain-clothed secret policemen, tore the attic apart. But the Swede was nowhere to be found. They even combed the river, where they discovered the famous typewriter lying under the currents. The evening before the raid, Giovanna and James had had the presence of mind to let themselves into the attic and burn every last document found in boxes upon boxes belonging to the Swede, who they assumed was in hiding somewhere. As they incinerated the papers through the night, they skimmed over the writing. The documents made it clear that the Swede was unequivocally in the MIR, had extensive military schooling, and was one of those in charge of arming and training the Mapuche people in the nearby Indigenous community of Neltume. The documents stated in no uncertain terms that the coup had been planned far in advance, and even correctly predicted its date. It was evident that the MIR had infiltrators in the highest echelons of the Chilean military, because the documents went into minute detail about said preparations, and named CIA members who had come from the United States for the purpose of overseeing the coup.

Reading the contents of those documents before setting them ablaze cracked Giovanna's mind wide open. She had been an apolitical jet-setter when she'd arrived only three years earlier at the age of twenty-three, had quickly fallen in love with Allende's socialist project, and now found herself reading the top-secret documents of the most-wanted revolutionary organization in Chile.

It was later said by exiled MIRistas that the Swede managed to cross the Andes into Argentina after keeping the military at bay for days in Neltume. Once on the other side of the border, he joined the Revolutionary People's Army. Three years later, in 1976, he was arrested by the Argentinian secret police. He remains disappeared.

On the day of the raid in 1973, James and Giovanna were thrown into the back of a secret-police car while James's wife and daughters looked on. INTERPOL had taken over the military offices in downtown Valdivia, and Giovanna and James were driven there in order to sign a book. All foreigners had to sign on a daily basis from then on, so their movements could be tracked; not doing so was breaking the law. After they signed, James and Giovanna were informed that they were now under arrest. Giovanna had eighty-six charges laid against her, James ninety-seven. They ranged from marching to "talking politics" to signing petitions. The INTERPOL offices, now a makeshift jail, held every leftist foreigner in Valdivia. Giovanna was the only American there. The wife of the head of the secret police, obsessed with American pop culture, would visit her every day in an exquisite lamb-leather jumpsuit and get Giovanna to regale her with tales of life in the United States.

A week after their arrest, James was transferred to the Valdivia jail. He spent months there, his family paying daily visits, until his release and their expulsion to England, with orders never to come back. Giovanna was given the choice of voluntary departure with a promise never to return to Chile or military trial. She chose the former and was transferred to the Santiago Women's Prison. There, she shared a cell with two terrified Bolivian teenagers while she awaited the airplane ticket from her father, a powerful right-wing Bay Area lawyer. Knowing it was only a matter of time before Mami fell too, Giovanna made a promise before she left:

"I will not rest until I get you guys to San Francisco."

And she kept her word. In December 1973, four days after Giovanna managed to bring us to the States, the spot where my mother would have been hiding was raided by the military.

For some reason, every time I heard the words *San Francisco*, I imagined an enormous red rose. "San Francisco" fell from everyone's lips, more often than not in conspiratorial whispers. It was the place we were going to, and I just kept thinking, "We'll arrive onto a petal and then just kind of work our way around this huge red rose." Who knows where, why, or how I fastened on to that image, but these were the ruminations of a six-year-old who had only ever lived in Chile, spending summers in Valparaíso and my father's hometown of Paihuano in the Elqui Valley. We belonged to Chile. Our Spanish and Basque blood had been there for centuries, and our Indigenous blood since time immemorial. So when it was mentioned in hushed tones that we would be going to San Francisco, a city not only in another country but in another hemisphere where everyone spoke English, not just my mother and her university friends, all I could come up with was the image of a velvety red rose. It was clear that this San Francisco place was somehow safer for us than our current geographical location, so perhaps my mind conjured the image of a rose because when our house had been raided a few weeks before our departure by a dozen armed soldiers, and Ale and I had been banished to the front yard, it was our pink rose bush that had provided comfort. My spirit that time hadn't fled to the crowns of cedars, firs, and cottonwood trees, as there were none in the vicinity of our yellow Huacho Copihue house, but had instead taken only one step out of my body to the rose bush, diving so far into the centre of its buds that the overpowering scent of those flowers had managed to provide some light in what was undeniably the darkest hour of my tender young life.

When we arrived in San Francisco, Giovanna awaited us with her brother Giancarlo. This airport was like a blasé afternoon at the plaza compared with the one in Santiago. It had been teeming with military men wielding submachine guns, and one could barely move due to the hundreds of families present, most of them in states of despair, as few were there by choice. There was so much crying and embracing going on at Santiago airport, it had seemed like a funeral. I could tell that my parents almost died of a coronary when some military men had taken us aside and forced us to put our luggage in a circle so they could count it.

"That seems like a lot of baggage. Are you moving away forever? Why do you want to leave Chile? Don't you like our new General?"

Mami and Papi had bowed their heads, shuffled, and stuttered, and my heart had broken for the millionth time since the coup, for nothing hurt more than seeing them denigrated. They'd just shown the authorities the letter that would get us out, an invitation by the dean of Stanford University to teach there for a semester. It was a fake, of course, because although the letter had been written by the dean, there was no invitation. Upon arriving in San Francisco, Giovanna had gone to Stanford and told the dean about our situation. Needing little prompting, he had written the letter and Giovanna's father had loaned her the money for our airplane tickets, which she never let my parents pay back. We had managed to get tourist visas to the States. The plan was to come back to Chile within six months, because Pinochet would only ever last that long, according to my parents (they would have scoffed at the notion of him staying in power for seventeen years), and when a provisional government was set up, we would return to the yellow wooden house in Huacho Copihue. We were *visiting* San Francisco while things sorted themselves out in Chile. *Exile*, a word that only existed in literary, abstract settings, such as Shakespeare's plays, was not part of our vocabulary.

As we made our way to Giancarlo's Russian Hill bachelor suite on Lombard, the crookedest street in the world, I realized that San Francisco really wasn't a large rose. Oddly, it was a city whose citizens did not walk on its streets, where the few people you saw seemed to have a bubble around them, where there were no signs of life. A cold feeling seized my gut and I swallowed hard.

Not only was Giancarlo putting Giovanna up in his tiny apartment, now he was also housing a family of four. Many nights were spent around his table with Bay Area leftists. We were the first Chileans to arrive after the coup, and my parents were like celebrities. For Christmas, Joan Baez invited us over to her house, and my parents were introduced to Ginette Sagan, the regional president of Amnesty International, an Italian woman who had been in the resistance during the Nazi occupation. After that, much time was spent with her, going over names of the disappeared, the arrested, the dead.

"Give me all the names of prisoners you know of German descent. I may be able to pressure the German government. Same with Chileans of French and Italian descent. Let's try and look at every angle here."

Lists were drawn up at her house while Ale, Joan Baez's son—Gabriel, and I ran up and down the long, gleaming hallways, and Mami tried to avoid having a nervous breakdown every time the Ming dynasty vases shook as we dashed by.

As for Ale and me, within a week we were enrolled in school, where she adapted to kindergarten with flying colours, making fast friends and communicating without a problem, and I was known as Deaf-Mute Pee-Pee Girl in my grade one class. It wasn't just the culture shock, lack of English, lingering trauma from the coup, friends being imprisoned, murdered, or forced to flee, or our own tenuous circumstances that made me pee my pants numerous times a day; it was also the unfortunate reality of the buses. The night before our first day of school ("It'll be so much fun!" my mother had promised while jumping up and down and clapping her hands with forced glee), we'd been watching the evening news. Boston images of black and Latino kids cowering on yellow school buses as white people threw stones at them, breaking windows and denting the vehicles, dominated the TV screen. Mami explained that a thing called the "civil rights movement" had taken place in the United States, and that it was very very good. In fact, right here in the Bay Area there was a group called the Black Panthers that had taken up arms in order to defend themselves from police brutality. On top of that, they provided free breakfasts for Oakland kids.

"Isn't that great?" Mami asked.

As a result of this civil rights movement, another thing called "affirmative action" had been set in motion. What this meant for us was that a yellow bus just like the one on TV would pick us up and, along with other Latino and black kids, take us to an upper-class neighbourhood where white kids went to school. Evidently, we brown and black kids were the first to attend this white school.

My head was reeling.

First of all, I had never heard the word *Latino* until I got to San Francisco, which was looking to me more and more like the thorns of a rose rather than the petally part. Apparently I was a Latino, but I had no clue what that was. Then there was the part about ducking rocks. I hoped I'd be able to get out of the way of the onslaught and not be hit on the head and pass the rest of my life as a vegetable, saliva dribbling down my chin. There had been a kid like that in Huacho Copihue, and also a couple of kids with polio, who walked with their collapsed legs in braces. At least my legs would probably be spared in the rock attack.

In any case, my day began with my peeing my pants on the way to school, while the bus stopped at the ghettos and picked up the brown and black kids and then made its way to the wealthy white neighbourhood, where, in spite of having lost control of my bladder, I was stolidly prepared for the angry white people waiting with rocks. Luckily, this never happened. While at school, I peed my pants repeatedly, mainly because I didn't know how to ask where the bathroom was, and also because I was too shy to leave my desk and have everybody see that I'd peed my pants. A vicious circle it was; a Catch-22 situation.

Ale would skip into her classroom and disappear until the end of the day, arriving home dry as a bone, licking a lollipop given to her by her new friends, chattering away about the jungle gym and tube slide in the playground, unlike anything she'd ever seen before. I'd be soaking wet and reeking of rancid pee, only to find Mario, my current crush, Giovanna and Giancarlo's twenty-year-old brother, sitting at the table listening to yet another story about how many children had disappeared in Chile or how Kissinger had ordered another ten union leaders to be shot in the firing squad of Chacabuco concentration camp.

Mario was a garbageman and I found that supremely sexy. So I drew a picture of him throwing garbage into a truck and gave it to him. It was my first love letter. But not my first declaration of love. That had been in Huacho Copihue two years earlier, when I was four and, fortunately, not drenched and stinking of stale piss, but rather of Coral cologne dabbed on my wrists. I had donned my white patent-leather shoes, white knee socks, pink frilly dress with white lace accents given to me by my great-aunt Charo, and the necklace my abuelita Carmen had helped me make with the buttons from her formidable sewing kit—really more of a treasure chest—with its bottomless arsenal of porcelain, wooden, mother-of-pearl, and bejewelled buttons.

My first love was called Manuel and he was a full ten years older than me. But age was just a number and I knew deep down that he loved me. He just needed to see me first. Really really see me. At fourteen, Manuel was already a man, getting up early and going to work at the market, where he sold kitchenwares. He left the house across the way at the crack of dawn, loaded down with pots, pans, and kettles that hung from his body on ropes, just like Ekeko, the Aymara god of abundance. He clinked and clanked his way along the dirt road, holes in the elbows of his lambswool sweater, the knees of his burlap pants worn to a shine. Thick jet-black hair combed to the side, his copper skin glowed in the pouring rain, the downpour cascading from his prominent cheekbones, for Valdivia was smack in the middle of the Chilean temperate rainforest, and rain was the order of almost every other winter day.

Manuel had proven himself to be a god many times over. First, there was the fact that he was a kitchenware vendor at the market. And then there was the bike. My man worked so hard that he had been able to buy himself a vehicle. It was the first bicycle in Huacho Copihue, and its introduction was a coup—in the good sense of the word, like the miniskirt being the fashion coup of the sixties. I'd read all about that in *Paula*, Chile's most popular women's magazine, which featured, among other things, a satirical column by Isabel Allende called "How to Civilize Your Troglodyte." To top things off, Manuel actually knew how to manoeuvre the bike, and if the butterflies in my stomach weren't already out of control, then witnessing him mount his new vehicle and ride it in a little circle around the dirt road made me almost shit my pants with excitement. I watched him from my bedroom window as every kid in the lane ran around shrieking and pointing, demanding to have a turn. He was the biggest kid on the block, although he of course was no child, providing for his family at the tender age of fourteen, being the god of abundance—abundance of pots, pans, and kettles, abundance of beauty, and now abundance of organizational skills. A union leader in the making!

Just as I thought he couldn't get any sexier, my beloved outdid himself: he lined the kids up and let each of them have a turn, helping them keep their balance.

"That's good! You can do it, Jana! You can do it!" he called encouragement in his tenor, a twinkle in his tender, almond-shaped eyes.

This was it. Spurred on by his kindness, I'd declare my love in front of all the children, even the mothers and grandmothers who hung out of their windows and leaned lethargically in their doorways, brooms in hands, aprons around waists, the odd gold tooth flashing in their smiles as they looked on at the bicycle miracle, the one performed by Manuel, the god of everything.

The outfit I modelled had never been worn, only to be turned out on special occasions and solely with my mother's permission. If declaring one's love to the love of one's life didn't count as a special occasion, then I was at a loss to know what did.

I emerged from my house, Aphrodite floating on my shell, on tiptoe, arms slightly raised, a *Swan Lake* prima ballerina. Floating my way to the centre of the universe, I was led by chirping chucao birds, rainbows, and winged cupids strumming golden harps, fireworks lighting up the sky above. Manuel came into sharp focus, and everything else—the kids, the leaning women, the dirt road, the brightly coloured houses and grey sky—dissolved into the background, washed out by his overpowering light, the children's shouts reduced to static in the presence of Manuel's tummy-tickling voice. I landed next to the bike. His obsidian eyes found mine.

Crouching, he rested his hand on my shoulder and asked, "Carmencita, do you want a turn?"

His palm had the force of a lightning bolt that turned me into stone. Motionless, unable to nod or shake my head, tongue-tied too, I was a statue, my pounding heart in my ears the only sign I was still alive. I ordered my mouth to open and proclaim the rehearsed words, "I love you," so that he could answer that he loved me too, that he had always loved me but hadn't been able to appreciate me in all my stupendous goddess glory until that moment. But stubborn as a mule my mouth was, and my lips remained clamped tighter than a clam. Never fear, I thought, as his eyes continued to probe mine, the words will come out and it will be like a surprise wedding, what with the women and children of the barrio bearing witness and me in my white lace undies. A bouquet will be improvised and I'll throw it and perhaps Jana, my best friend, will catch it and she'll get married next.

"Do you want a turn, Carmencita?" Manuel, the god of lightning bolts, repeated.

I nodded, my tongue a useless old shoe. His hand moved down to my waist. The other followed. The god of abundance of lightning bolts and winged creatures he was; the butterflies in my stomach went wild, multiplying to millions in moments, the cupids' wings fluttered, the strumming of their harps invading the chambers of my galloping heart, and I was seized by a distinct, pleasurable new sensation similar to peeing. He lifted me up, the brown muscles in his forearms flexing, and placed me ever so gingerly on the seat, while my heart exploded in my chest and my insides liquefied.

"Carmencita shit her pants!"

The voices, machine-gun fire, snapped me back to reality. Huge and distorted like reflections in a warped amusement park mirror, the kids' faces jutted into mine. Fingers pointing, the whole lane chanted now.

"Car-men-ci-ta shit her pants!"

I looked down. There was diarrhea running down my thighs. It had already stained my socks. Manuel's nostrils flared at the stench, his hands still gripping my waist. He lifted me up, revealing the shit-covered bike seat. More poo ran down my legs, fresh drops landing on the tops of my white shoes, the spell that had made them glass slippers moments earlier now broken. This was no spontaneous wedding, this was spontaneous combustion. Holding me as far away from himself as possible, Manuel walked me to my front door, breathing through his mouth, his benevolent eyes on my horrified, down-turned face. He placed me on my front step, knelt down, and lifted my chin.

"Carmencita," he asked, "are you in love with me?"

I met his encouraging eyes, paused for a moment, and jumped off the cliff. I nodded, smiled a little bit, looked back down at my now-brown white shoes, and shuffled. Caressing the back of my head, he kissed me on the cheek, while the kids ran around laughing in the background, still chanting, some of them holding their noses and crotches. Hands held to their mouths, the women, static moments earlier, giggled too, shoulders heaving in the frames of their windows and doors.

Manuel kissed my other cheek and said, "*Linda preciosa*."

Beautiful, precious.

And then he walked away. I stood there for a moment, and backed up into my house, hyper-aware that the seat of my pink dress was covered in diarrhea, that my white lace bloomers were now loaded down with liquid poo. "See, I told you he loved you," I said to my own image in the bathroom mirror before peeling the shitty clothes off with trembling hands. One thing was for sure: no one could ever accuse me of being cynical. Or pessimistic.

Experienced love bug that I was by age six, I gave Mario the San Francisco garbageman the drawing and he kissed me on the cheek too. It was clear as day that they both loved me: Manuel hadn't cared that I'd shit my pants during my declaration, and Mario could give a shit that I was now Deaf-Mute Pee-Pee Girl in this country where adults threw rocks at brown children on yellow buses, black people were forced to take up arms against the police, and men and women came from all over the world to reinvent themselves.

Shortly after the coup, when the military raided our house, it was scientifically proven that Manuel was unequivocally a god. My father being a physicist, I had always known about the superlative importance of irrefutable scientific proof, that indeed people only took you seriously if you were able to provide it, usually in the form of a foreign language referred to as "formu-las." These filled Papi's notebooks, but even he had to admit:

"I don't believe in ghosts, but they do exist."

Science had proven that the force of gravity existed, that there was no end to numbers, that the earth was beholden to the sun. This time, science—the molecules in the atmosphere, the oxygen in the air, the dark clouds that hung above, the cells of every body in that lane that bore witness—proved that a fourteen-year-old pots-and-pans vendor with holes in his shoes was veritably a god. The god of courage.

Science and its proven theories mattered, but of equal impor-tance was that ephemeral notion, love. Although, according to my mother, love was not airy-fairy at all and could only exist in the material world, proven not with test tubes and formulas but through everyday gestures, displays, and sacrifices, what she called "actions." The heart could overflow with all the love it wanted, but if deeds weren't done to prove it, it meant nothing and for all intents and purposes didn't exist, said Mami. She'd explained it after my declaration, as she'd soaked my shitty dress in the sink, when I'd asked her about love and its meanings. I hadn't let on that I'd shit my pants due to that earth-shattering, pelvis-rocking force. Mami had explained about the abstract and the concrete, her hands grasping at the thin air like someone trying to catch a mosquito to illustrate the former and knocking on the top of the bathroom counter to drive the latter point home.

On the day the military raided our house, a year later, Manuel proved scientifically, in the material world, just how much he loved me.

They ransacked the house in search of my parents, who were not home, and any incriminating documents they might have stashed in the back of closets or under mattresses. In the kitchen, our babysitter was being interrogated with a machine gun to her head by two soldiers, while the rest of them turned the house upside down. I watched one tear my favourite doll's head off and wondered where Ale had gone to. I was finally escorted outside at gunpoint, where she stood waiting. We were placed next to each other, turned around to face the front of the house, and ordered to put our hands up. The soldiers had decided to conduct a firing squad with us in our yard. The head military man started to count. Ten soldiers aimed their rifles at the backs of our heads. Our pink rose bush opened its petals and my spirit leapt into one rose's stamen. Nose itching from the overwhelming perfume of roses, arms still raised in the air, prepared to become a human strainer with blood gushing from dozens of firing-squad holes, I heard Manuel's toe-curling tenor from across the way.

"Cowardly motherfuckers! Go back to your mothers' cunts!"

The head military man had just finished counting to ten, the onslaught of bullets about to ensue. Killing themselves laughing, the soldiers emitted guffaws that let on this was really only a *mock* firing squad. Amused no end by their joke, my sister's and my shaking knees offered them continuing entertainment of the highest order. Who knew that if one pretended to shoot a preschooler and a kindergartener, hilarity would ensue? But the coup and its aftermath were proving that in the decidedly concrete, material world, human cruelty knew no bounds.

"Cowardly motherfuckers!" the unmistakable tenor taunted again.

Out of the corner of my eye, I saw him running across the way. The rest of the barrio—the children, the hard-working women and men—trembled on their bathroom floors, some curled up in the fetal position, the adults' bodies over their children, hands spread over the crowns of their heads. That is how I imagined them. The military had already raided Jana's house. The men in her family were fishermen and sold their catches at the Calle-Calle market, on the shores of the river that bore the same name. Her dad and oldest brother, eighteen years old, now sat blindfolded in the back of a military jeep, hands crossed over their heads. Jana's mother clung to the doorway, a silent cry escaping from her guts, chest collapsed, Jana's fists holding fast on to her skirt.

Manuel goaded again.

"Motherfuckers! Cowards! Come after me instead!" And then he ran to the woods that lay at the end of the lane.

The soldiers turned their heads, abandoned the mock firing squad, and followed. A taut silence overtook us, a suspension. Time, that other notion that science had come up with in order to stop everything from happening at once, stood still and everything went into slow motion. Jana's dad and brother straightened their spines, Jana's and her mami's eyes followed Manuel and the soldiers, Ale and I dropped our hands and turned slowly around, ballerinas inside jewellery boxes when the battery is on its last legs. When time caught up, blows could be heard, boots on flesh and bone, moans and grunts coming from within the small triangle of Patagonian rainforest.

The military left with Jana's father and brother in tow, their white blindfolds a sharp contrast to the green vehicles, the pewter sky, the black shoe polish on the soldiers' faces, applied to avoid being recognized. Despite the gaping black holes at Jana's table, life crept cautiously back into the lane, the men emerging from their doors and, after a moment's pause, running to the woods over the fresh tire tracks in the mud. Our neighbours' house remained shut. Pro-Pinochet, they had probably informed on us and Jana's family, who had supported Allende since the fifties, when he'd first started campaigning.

Manuel was carried back from the woods by the lane men, bloodied and bruised, eyes still hollow with fear, but conscious. Alive.

"Motherfuckers," he said. "They went back to their mothers' cunts."

SIX

We ended up staying in San Francisco for only a month. My parents, thanks to all their new contacts, were accepted as masters students at the University of California in San Diego in January 1974, their tuition paid for with scholarships. During our first week there, while we waited for an apartment in student housing, a professor and his wife put us up in their big, airy La Jolla cul-de-sac home, full of beautiful, expensive things. The four of us slept in one room, even though Ale and I had been offered our own. Quiet as a tomb, the place was less home and more house; it felt devoid of life, even though a cat lived there.

I had never seen a pet up close before. In Chile, dogs and cats in the circles we moved in lived in yards, were fed leftovers, had jobs to do, such as guarding the house or eating mice, and were left to their own devices. Although appreciated by their owners, one could hardly have referred to them as pets. Seeing a cat live inside, with its own bed, bowl, and toys, caused a discomfort in me that I couldn't quite put my finger on, but it had something to do with the knowledge that millions of people in the world had nothing to eat, much less a place to live. In San Francisco I had seen black people living out of shopping carts, and here in San Diego entire Mexican families lived on the streets (my mother had explained that these US cities had Spanish names because we were actually on Mexican land, taken by the United States only a hundred and twenty years ago). The cat had its own little bell necklace and was brushed to a shine. Spoken to like a newborn baby, it was given immunization shots like one too, according to Mami. It spent its days lolling around the furniture and, thankfully, had its claws cut regularly, for it tried to scratch me the one time I tried to pet it.

One day, when the couple was out, we left the bedroom and my parents played a record they had brought from Chile on the living room turntable. It was the first time we'd played it since fleeing, and once the needle hit the vinyl, Violeta Parra singing "Que Pena Siente El Alma" (What Sorrow Feels My Soul) emanated from the speakers. As the record played, our parents took our hands and wept. Once the first side was done, Papi flipped it in silence, and we listened to the other. After placing the record back in its sleeve with the kind of care reserved for rare anthropological finds, we went back to our room when the professor and his wife's wood-panelled station wagon pulled into the driveway.

The day before we left, I caught the wife crying into the kitchen sink. Mami offered comfort in the form of her hand on the woman's back, but was swiftly turned down, the wife stating she wished to be left alone with her grief. We retreated to our room and I wondered what had happened. My mother said that the cat had been hit by a car.

On our first day in student housing, there were endless knocks on our new door, the neighbours offering sheets, towels, kitchenware, food, even some clothes and dolls for Ale and me. Mami hadn't brought any warm-weather wear from Chile, but she found a couple of dresses in the giveaway bin at the laundromat and rotated between the two. We slept on donated mattresses on the floor and, as we had no money for groceries, the cafeteria workers at the students' union smuggled us the day's leftovers.

My parents' new student visas allowed full-time international students to be teaching assistants, and my mother managed to wangle a position a few weeks after we got there. Our trickle of money came from her stipend, as well as under-the-table cleaning work they both did at La Jolla mansions. My mother spent nights correcting first-year English essays, while my father studied his ESL tomes; he was starting to revalidate his physics degree in a language he spoke not a word of. He and I explored the area, listening for rattlesnakes in the tall grass and coming across abandoned barracks with the toilets still intact.

"These are left over from the Second World War," he decided.

I learned about wars that day and how they were different from coups, although both left lots of displaced people, my father explained, hands clasped behind him, eyes fixed on the setting sun.

Grade one in San Diego was another series of humiliating, unfortunate events, although I'd managed to figure out where the bathroom was (as luck would have it, right next to my classroom), so now I was only Deaf-Mute Girl, not Deaf-Mute Pee-Pee Girl. The prettiest girl I'd ever seen was in my class. Every last inch of her was the colour of honey—hair, skin, eyes, freckles. She wore tiny gold hoops in her ears, a Minnie Mouse watch on her wrist, denim bell-bottoms, and Adidas Kegler sneakers. In awe of her beauty and fashion sense, all I could do was admire her from afar.

It was glaringly obvious to me that, unlike in San Francisco, where Latino and black kids were bussed to the white school, here I was the only brown kid in class. I was beginning to grasp the concept of *Latino*. It wasn't only someone from Latin America, it was also someone who was brown. Unbeknownst to me, I had always been brown. Compared with white, which was also a colour. My father had taught me that white and black weren't colours, but simply the abundance or absence of light. But in this country, white was certainly a colour, and it held all the power. Blacks and browns had been fighting that for centuries, according to Mami. The war raged on, what with the yellow buses and the rock throwing. In any case, I was the only brown-slash-Latina in my class, and apparently that also meant I was poor. Because in this country, black and brown meant poor, although we were definitely not poor. We had food, shelter, health, and education. All our basic human needs were met, and then some, for we even had our own phone—a first for us.

Mami had explained that the vast majority of whites in the States were not upper-class, and in fact many were quite poor, and that they too fought for their rights, often side by side with the non-whites. That in the final analysis, oppressed people were defined more by class than by race. The point was that everyone else in my rich, white La Jolla classroom was on the cutting edge of fashion, brought their meals in *Partridge Family* or *Star Trek* lunch boxes, and had light eyes and light hair, while I was the brown-hence-poor, deaf-mute retard with the mismatched hand-me-downs. Clueless as to what the aging teacher was saying, I drew pictures when it seemed as if that's what was required, only to have them snatched in frustration by the soon-to-be retiree. As punishment, she'd make me place my forehead on my desk for an eternity while I held my bladder, praying that I didn't become Deaf-Mute Pee-Pee Girl in San Diego as well.

Every Thursday morning, the children brought something from home that they could share with the class, while we sat cross-legged on the carpet, which was in and of itself the strangest thing ever. In Chile, one never sat on the floor, much less cross-legged, even less so in a classroom. One sat on chairs, with legs politely crossed. In class, one sat at a desk, with fingers interlocked on its surface. After the coup, when Ale and I had been kicked out of school for having Marxist parents—the principal had hurled insults at my father and his daughters on the sidewalk, barring us from ever entering the premises again—we'd been put in a school that apparently took mini-Marxists. All the Marxist kids were held in one classroom, despite our age difference, so Ale and I were in the same class. An armed soldier stood at the door, and whenever you had to go to the bathroom, he would escort you, listening as you tinkled. For recess, the teacher would take us outside, where we'd sit on stumps on the edge of a forest and she'd remark on how sad it was that the trees had been chopped down, but at least what remained of them served as seats for us, while the bored-stiff conscript looked on.

One Thursday, while we all sat cross-legged on the La Jolla carpet, one of the boys showed us his collection of little flags from all over the world. At the end of his presentation, he unfurled a Chilean flag, looked right at me, called my name, smiled, and said:

"Chile."

A lump formed in my throat. It was the first time since I'd arrived in the United States that a peer had really seen me, spoken my name, said where I came from. I wondered why he'd never approached me. It was the first time since leaving Chile that I'd beheld my flag. Before we'd left, I'd seen it every day. My parents had been forced to fly it—everybody had—to show their allegiance to Pinochet. The flag had always been something to scoff at, Mami and Papi staunch anti-nationalists (in the fascist sense, not the national liberation sense), but now I wanted to take that little flag in my hand, bunch it up in my palm, and hold it to my broken heart.

Shortly after that show-and-tell Thursday, I had an interaction with the beautiful honey-coloured girl. We were in the bathroom together and I still hadn't been able to figure out how to flush the toilet, because it was an ultra-modern one. Breaking into a sweat—this wasn't recess and I was expected back in the classroom a minute later—I went through the frantic motions of pushing and pulling every knob that looked like a handle, praying that this time I'd hit the jackpot. But nothing happened. I looked down at the yellow urine, mortified that the honey-coloured girl would now know that I'd been leaving my Latina pee in the toilet of her gleaming white La Jolla school.

I took a deep breath, came out of the stall, and waved and pointed at her. She was washing her hands in the sink while humming Terry Jacks's "Seasons in the Sun." I led her to the toilet and she flushed it just like that. Then she got a huge laugh attack at my ridiculous attempts to thank her, what with all the waving of my arms after hugging her was ruled out (she recoiled as if I was the carrier of an infectious disease). Her laughter was contagious, and soon we were rolling around, smacking the tiled bathroom floor with our palms, pointing at each other. The teacher came in, hands on her hips, and yelled.

Forced to stay after school, we had to put our heads on our desks for a long time. My sentence was longer than hers. When she was released, I was left alone in the classroom forever, forehead resting on my desk, while my father waited outside in the baby-blue Chevrolet Malibu. He'd come into the classroom at bell time and the teacher had ordered him out. Speaking no English, he'd gone beet red and bowed, seeing me with my forehead on the desk.

When I reached the car, I burst into tears, he held back his, and we went to the beach. Ale, full of friends, had gone on a play date. We collected shells and felt the wind in our hair.

Papi stared out at the ocean and said, "I took Jaime to the beach once in La Serena on a day like today. The seaweed was red there, though, and the tide had brought in scores of jellyfish."

My uncle Jaime was my father's best friend in the world. They'd shared a room for five years while studying at Santiago's Pedagogical University, a hotbed of MIR organizing, and where Mami and Papi had met. Although all three came from low-income families, they'd been able to attend, live in residence, and eat three full meals a day free of charge because university education—top-notch in Chile—had always been state funded until it was privatized under Pinochet. During their student days, they'd visit Pablo Neruda at La Chascona, his Bellavista home, always open to young people, and go to La Peña de los Parra, the concert café run by Violeta Parra. A full-blooded Aymara Indian from a family of miners in the north, Jaime had been shot by the firing squad at Chacabuco concentration camp in the Atacama Desert a few months earlier. But first they'd tortured him almost to death. He'd been twenty-nine.

Since the honey-coloured girl was now my comrade in the struggle—we had been punished together, after all—I decided to be her clown. She'd clearly loved my bathroom shenanigans—the pointing, the waving my arms around, the silly gibberish sounds that were my attempt at English—so I'd continue in the same vein. She began to seek me out, even going so far as to pull her desk next to mine and leave it there. I couldn't believe my luck. I was her monkey, for all she had to do at recess was point to me in front of the other kids and I'd do the bathroom spiel she loved so much.

Her name was Lassie, like the gorgeous dog whose mane shone in the sun. Lassie was indeed a pet, the first one I'd ever seen, even if it had only been on Chilean TV. Lassie the dog was so special she glowed like a diamond, so it made perfect sense that the honey-coloured girl was named after her. The first English word I spoke out loud, even before *hello* or *goodbye*, was my new friend's name: *Lassie*. I wrote a letter to my abuelita Carmen and abuelito Armando bragging about how the children in the States were named after the brilliant, radiant dog and that, actually, my best friend was called Lassie. Years later, when my grasp of English was that of a native speaker, I bolted up in bed one night and yelled out, "Leslie!" to the pitch-black room. I wasn't conjuring her memory in deepest, darkest Canadian winter. My utterance was the sound of a penny dropping. Of course her name wasn't Lassie, it was Leslie! I now understood why she'd repeated her name over and over again, making me watch the sounds her mouth was making, which I was sure had amounted to "Lassie."

One day, when my mother came to pick me up, Lassie talked to her for a little while. After the impromptu meeting of their minds, Mami announced with a big smile on her face:

"Leslie wants you to go over to her house!"

My first solo outing in North America was to be to Lassie's abode. Her mother waited in a shiny yellow Mustang convertible, a Virginia Slim between her fingers. Lassie and I got in, and we pulled away from the curb. It was evident that Barbie was modelled after her mom, her waist-length blond hair flying all over her face as we manoeuvred the curves that hugged the La Jolla hills, the Pacific glistening below us, Blue Suede's "Hooked on a Feeling" blasting from the speakers. Enormous gold-rimmed tinted shades covered her eyes, and she bobbed her head to the music. I did the same in my spot in the back seat. Her manicured hand reached for the dial and raised the volume to max, and I smiled wider, for she was my kind of lady.

We pulled up to a house that overlooked the beach. The garage door opened all on its own, and we pulled in. "Hooked on a Feeling" was cut abruptly and the only sound was that of the garage door whirring shut behind us. She got out of the car and I was able to admire her in all her glory. Six feet tall, thin as a rake, she wore platforms and flared lime-green polyester pants with matching halter top. She disappeared through a door into the house and Lassie and I got out of the car.

The house created the illusion of being suspended in the air, commanding an impressive view of the ocean with its vast windows. Entranced with the wraparound white leather couches, white shag rugs, white spiral staircase, and entertainment centre with a big set of headphones hanging from the record player cabinet and the biggest TV set I'd ever laid eyes on, I was shocked to hear a lady's voice greet me in Spanish. I turned around and saw what I now knew was referred to as another Latina. About twenty-five, my mother's age, she was wearing a black dress and white apron.

"*Hola!*" she repeated, a big smile on her lips. "*Soy Adriana.*"

She knelt down, gave me a big hug, and asked me what part of Mexico I was from. I told her I was from Chile. She explained that Lassie had told her all about the new Mexican girl in class and that that was why she had brought me over, so the two of us could meet. (Mami thought she'd arranged a play date with Lassie, not an introduction to the help.) Her assertion levelled me. I was flattened like Wile E. Coyote, mere roadkill for flies to feast on once the gravity of her statement hit me like the ton of bricks it was: I would never be like Lassie. For Lassie and all the others like her, I was a poor brown girl who reminded her of her maid. I swallowed hard, reeling. Everything in me froze— my face, my tongue, my heart, my skin, the tips of my fingers.

She kept talking to me, but I couldn't register any of it. I tried to focus on her, this Mexican. Although I'd met Mexicans since our arrival in the States, most notably in my grade one class in San Francisco (oddly, some of them didn't speak Spanish and referred to themselves as Chicanos), this was the first time I realized that we—we Chileans, we Chicanos, we Mexicans, alas, even we black people, and perhaps even poor white people— were one. Her accent was different, but she touched me, she held me, she smelled me and put her face in mine. I understood that in this new life I would forever have more in common with her than with the Lassies of North America. This fresh consciousness gave me the urge to simultaneously hug Adriana and blow her away with a submachine gun, to remove her and all she stood for from the face of the earth.

She spoke of her faraway children, back in Chihuahua—wasn't that a type of dog? I was only now hearing that it was also a place!—as she caressed my cheeks and the deep freeze took over my core, an iceberg floating in my solar plexus, a painful knot forming in my throat. Hyper-aware of Lassie looking on, pleased as punch with herself, I was embarrassed to have all this Latinoness on display, to have Lassie of all people be witness to my moment of concession, the moment of letting Adriana touch me and see me, recognize me—the moment I swallowed the bitter pill of having much more in common with Adriana than I could ever have with Lassie. We were both uprooted Latinas in a place that rendered us either invisible or, conversely, visible only as the degraded, despised, pitied, exploited, exoticized, feared inferior "other."

Lassie started climbing the spiral staircase. I followed and landed smack in the middle of Barbie's dream townhouse. Lassie's pink room was not only a replica of the famous doll's living quarters—as seen on TV during Saturday morning cartoons—it was filled with Barbie herself. There were dozens of her, all blond. They wore bikinis and lay on their own towels, sported evening gowns with heels on their diminutive arched feet and mini-clutches in their tiny hands, showed off sailor outfits complete with caps, and tailored suits with briefcases. Some of them were stewardesses, others nurses, still others gold-medalist Olympians. There was a Barbie bride holding a bouquet of flowers, and a Miss America Barbie with a sash and tiara. Barbie cars, jeeps, campers, yachts, and airplanes, and a

Barbie swimming pool. A Barbie fashion plaza. Barbie purses, shoes, jackets, and jewellery. These Barbies even had their own makeup kits and bubble baths.

Had I known that the spiral staircase led to heaven, I wouldn't have wasted a single minute talking to Adriana. The knot in my throat dissolved, the iceberg melted. I ran around and grabbed as many Barbies as I could, studying them closely, holding them to my chest, trying to decide which one I would play with first. If we were in Chile or Mexico, or maybe even the brown, black, or poor white parts of the States, my friend would have given me one to keep, but I somehow knew that wouldn't be the case with Lassie.

Adriana served us pink milk and cookies at the glass dining room table, and then Lassie led me downstairs to a rec room, as seen on a Kool cigarette commercial. There was a pool table, a Ping-Pong table, a dart game, and a whole other humongous TV set. Lassie opened the mini-fridge in the small kitchen, stacked with pop. The only other time I'd seen so much pop in one place was at the supermarket. She pointed and talked and I figured she was offering me one, so I opened it and took a sip. It was the worst pop I'd ever tasted, but I kept drinking it out of politeness. She gasped and laughed as I forced myself to down more of the hideous thing, murmuring, "Mmm!" with a fake smile and a thumbs-up between each tiny sip.

My father's voice drifted down the stairs, talking in Spanish to Adriana, punctuating the conversation with his signature word, "*Fantastico!*" He was here to get me.

Years later, I realized I'd tasted my first—and last, because I became a teetotaller—beer.

～

The night before we left San Diego in late June 1974, we dressed in our best and Mami and Papi took us out for dinner in a fancy part of town where restaurants lined the beach. We stood at the door of the first restaurant and were ignored. As we made our way down the row, we continued to be ignored or to be told point-blank that all the tables were taken at restaurants that were half empty. In the end, our one and only outing during our six-month stay in San Diego found us back at home eating homemade burgers, Mami trying to make light of the situation by joking that the little bit of money they'd managed to save for a special occasion would now be for something more useful, not a bourgeois farewell meal.

All our belongings fit easily into the trunk of our Chevrolet Malibu when we began our trip up the coast to Canada the following morning. We camped along the way, stopping at waterfalls and forests of towering redwood trees. Ale and I even petted a fawn at one of our campsites. At the final rest stop south of Blaine, Washington, we pulled over and made ourselves presentable before arriving at the Canadian border. My mother scrubbed our faces clean, re-braided our hair, and changed our clothes. We rid the car of any garbage, and when we pulled up to the border wicket, Mami stated clearly that we were Chileans fleeing the Pinochet dictatorship. An hour later, we were accepted as refugees. Ten months had passed since the coup, Pinochet didn't seem to be stepping down any time soon, and if we had been turned away at the border, we would have found ourselves in deep undocumented shit. My parents' student visas were about to expire, and the United States had refused them work permits.

My uncle Boris, aunt Tita, and cousins Gonzalo and Macarena awaited us in Vancouver. They'd arrived only a few months earlier. Uncle Boris was the first Chilean refugee there, along with family friend David, a survivor of Dawson Island, a concentration camp on a remote island close to Antarctica. David's Hungarian Jewish father had sought refuge in Chile at the start of the Second World War, when Chile had offered asylum to Jews fleeing persecution in Europe. Now his son had been arrested and expelled from the country that had taken him in. Boris and David arrived at the same time and met at the English Bay Apartment Hotel, later christened the Refugee Hotel by the Chilean community. Their families had joined them later.

After my uncle had been freed from jail in Valparaíso with strict orders to make himself scarce, he had approached the Canadian embassy in Santiago when he heard that Trudeau had agreed to open Canada's doors to Chileans needing asylum. A group of Canadians had camped out on Parliament Hill and refused to move until Trudeau, who had voiced support for the coup, agreed to accept refugees. My future stepfather Bob had been at the helm of these efforts. He had been held at Santiago's national soccer stadium, turned into a concentration camp, along with tens of thousands of other prisoners, including foreigners from thirty-eight countries. Bob had been one of three Canadians there, all in Chile to support Allende. After the cultural attaché at the Canadian embassy took it upon himself to convince the dictatorship to release Bob and the other two on condition they never set foot in Chile again, Bob returned to Canada. If it hadn't been for the cultural attaché's intervention, the Canadians would have met the same fate as their American counterparts being held at the stadium; they would have been murdered. Bob made solidarity work his mission when he arrived back home, and he was the first Canadian we met when he showed up at the Refugee Hotel. Thanks to his and many others' tireless work, it was the first time in Canadian history that doors were opened to political refugees from the so-called Third World fleeing a right-wing dictatorship.

We drove down Oak Street on that sunny day in 1974, our first day in Canada. Ale inquired from the back seat what country we now found ourselves in, we turned right on 20th Avenue, parked the car, and got out, I admired the burgundy crowns of the trees, and heard a voice yell out:

"Carmencita's here!"

A tall, dark boy ran towards me. Six months earlier, I would have just seen a boy. Now I knew this was a brown boy. When he reached me, he threw his arms around me and an ancient, familiar smell assaulted my nostrils, the scent of my cousin Gonzalo, so big now, eight years old, I hadn't recognized him. We held on to each other and although he was laughing, I had no idea how to explain—to myself or to anyone else—why all I wanted to do was break down and cry. How to find the words to make plain that in my six years on earth I had always thought that tears were for sad occasions. And this was definitely not a sad one. Our family awaited us at the end of that days-long road trip, only this time we weren't disembarking from our yellow Citroën that took us to Valparaíso every summer to see my uncle, aunt, cousins, and grandparents. This time we were on the opposite end of the Americas, falling into their arms on a day that would mark the beginning of a lifetime of exile to be experienced together.

But that was yet to come, because this day was meant to be the first of only a short visit, after which we would cross Canada in our Chevrolet Malibu to the teaching assistant job that awaited my mother in Montreal, secured by Enrique, her linguistics professor from Santiago's Pedagogical University. Recently released from Chile stadium, built for basketball games and now also turned into a concentration camp, Enrique had got asylum in Canada and been offered a position at Concordia University upon his arrival. He spoke perfect French and English and possessed a stunning resumé that included having been on the faculty with Nobel Prize-nominated poet and physicist Nicanor Parra, renowned author and future international award-winning playwright Ariel Dorfman, and visiting Brazilian professor Paulo Freire, author of *Pedagogy of the Oppressed*, all of whom had taught my parents. Enrique had been tortured and was one of the few living witnesses to legendary singer Víctor Jara's final hours. He, like Victor, had been arrested on the day of the coup, when the universities where they each taught, the Pedagogical and the Technical, had been raided. Both institutions remained shut down.

Next thing I knew, my cousin Macarena, five like my sister, was running down the street towards us all, as were Uncle Boris and Aunt Tita. Mami and her brother embraced for a long while, holding each other's faces and hugging again. We were led to their house, shared with another Chilean family and a single Chilean woman. Later that day we made our way to the nearby Queen Elizabeth Park. We kids rolled down the grassy knolls and our parents talked about the epic journeys that had brought us all here. The last time we'd seen each other was eighteen months earlier, in January 1973, when the coup and its bloodiness seemed far-fetched possibilities. We'd spent that glorious summer together in the house on the Valparaíso hill, watching the Pacific swallow the sun whole every evening, waiting for the stars of the Southern Cone to light up the sky.

On the day that would kick off the second leg of our journey, the week-long trip through the province of British Columbia, over the Rocky Mountains ("Don't worry, they're not as tall as the Andes," Uncle Boris, who had never crossed either range, reassured us), across the Prairies, and into Montreal, the Chevrolet Malibu made a decision that would change our destinies. It refused to start. Much time was spent with the hood up, the men fiddling with the motor while we kids looked on, my cousin Gonzalo under the body. There was nothing to be done. Fixing the thing was out of the question, due to a lack of funds.

Within a few days, it was decided that we would stay in Vancouver. The government moved us from my uncle and aunt's home to the Refugee Hotel, until housing and work could be found for us. Once there, we met new Chileans arriving every day, some mere skin and bones from the concentration camps, wearing ponchos, a few with guitars or charangos over their shoulders, sharing gruesome stories of torture. They, the Chilean community in exile, became my new family, bestowed with the titles of Uncle, Aunt, and Cousin.

A few weeks later, we moved to the courts at UBC student housing. As soon as I found Cedar, I climbed him every day, always on the lookout for the witch and the beautiful stranger who had fed me the peanut butter and banana sandwich. One day, I saw her. I climbed down as quickly as I could and stood in her way as she rounded one of the corners of Salmo Court. Moments later, I was over at her house. Miracle of miracles, it happened to be directly across the way from ours, and I wondered why I hadn't seen her sooner. Elton John's "Crocodile Rock" was blaring from the turntable and her older sister, as glamorous as a screen goddess with her long, shiny, light-brown hair, sparkling eyes, enormous smile, and golden aura—I now understood why in Chile the Virgin Mary was depicted with a halo of light around her head, to denote that she was a goddess, just like this older sister—danced all out to the beat. She wore rolled-up jeans, striped knee-high toe socks, and a turtleneck. Taking up the whole living room, she kickball-changed her way around the floor, snapping her fingers, spinning around in the white plastic swivel chairs, flinging her hair in all directions while singing along to the full-blast music.

Once the sandwich-feeder slowed down the breakneck speed of her speech, I grasped that she was called Arabella, was six years old like me, also going into grade two, and that her older sister Gia was eight and going into grade four. Although I understood English now, I was still too shy to speak it, *Lassie* still the only word I'd spoken out loud in this new language, hence still Deaf-Mute Girl in the mainstream world. Both the sisters wore gold crosses on thick chains. Their immaculate house featured minimalist decor and avocado-green, geometrically patterned wallpaper. I recognized the word *Italia* when Arabella pointed to herself. She took me upstairs to the children's bedroom, shared with their younger brother Luigi, and after I admired the tulle bedspreads in mint hues, I saw the witch's costume hanging in the closet. Not only was Gia my first goddess, she was my first witch! For some reason, that combination made perfect sense to me. I caressed the mask and took the cape for a little spin.

By the time, a year later, I hit grade three at age seven, I was talking English as if I'd been born speaking it. It came out in a rush, a cascading waterfall during spring thaw, and my teacher, the beloved Miss Bouchard, was overjoyed when it happened. When it did, Deaf-Mute Girl spoke in perfect conjugations, forming even the most difficult sounds like a Royal Shakespeare Company actor reciting Hamlet's famous monologue. I'd kept it to myself, taking it all in, even though I'd got gold stars on my spelling tests and written stories in this language that I would later find out lived in my throat, chest, and head but not in my heart, guts, and bones. One of my favourite words in the English language was *fucker*.

For many years, whenever I tried to explain Chilean politics to Arabella, my first non-Chilean friend in Canada, I would talk about witches and demons taking over the country. I thought she'd appreciate my parables, since her sister was half witch. In our adult lives, Arabella confessed that she hadn't understood a thing about Chilean politics from my fables, but had rather concluded that I was a deeply disturbed individual in dire need of help. She had decided to keep me as a best friend out of empathy and because of all the fun we had playing rich ladies with the discarded nighties we found in the laundromat and dancing disco to Walter Murphy's "A Fifth of Beethoven." My storytelling skills had needed some honing, and the needing-help part turned out to be true.

Not only was Arabella my first friend in Canada, she was also my first co-actor. We spent all our time playing dress-up and putting on skits. Our most famous play, performed at the height of our collaboration, when we were nine, was a movement piece based on *Romeo and Juliet*. Arabella was lovesick for Dylan, a teenaged boy she swore looked just like Shaun Cassidy from *The Hardy Boys*. Dylan lived in our court, so it made perfect sense to perform our piece in the middle of the cul-de-sac so that the object of her affection could watch us from his window. All the front windows looked out on our impromptu amphitheatre. I went along with the crush, even though I had yet to get a glimpse of the boy. He was fourteen and reportedly had blond feathered hair kept in flawless condition thanks to an orange comb that lived in the back pocket of his Lee jeans. According to Arabella, watching Dylan pull said comb through his locks was orgasm-inducing. She would squeal, "I LOOOOOOOVE HIM!" and jump up and down after imitating the combing motion to me. I recognized her passion, even though it had lain dormant in me since Mario the garbageman in San Francisco, and was a willing wingwoman in solidarity with my sister.

Our rendition of *Romeo and Juliet* had us dancing together in a hybrid of styles—disco, tango, flamenco, with a little bit of cueca, the Chilean national dance, thrown in—and ended with the double suicide. Apparently, our only audience member was Pam, Arabella's white, Canadian, single mother. (Her father, Carlo, was a Neapolitan concert pianist. After they'd split up, Pam had returned to Canada with the kids.) She watched our melodrama from her window while she worked on her master's degree in French farce. When she finished her studies a couple of years later, she would get a teaching post in Port Hardy, Vancouver Island, and the family would leave the courts behind.

My best friend in school was Dewi. She was from Berkeley,

California, and her father was a renowned photographer and musician. Dewi and I also spent all of our time putting on plays, and we were given ample time and space to do that at University Hill Elementary School. Every day at two o'clock, we'd be released to the lunchroom so we could create a play to be presented to the class at ten to three. Our peers relished our performances, what with their slapstick comedy and variety-show feel, which I later realized was a type of vaudeville. Dewi and her older sister Andrea, both geeky hippie kids, were often bullied by the cool element, and that is when my adored word *fucker* came in handy. Once, during recess, I spied a group of grade seven boys from Chancellor Boulevard, one of the richest parts of town, surrounding Andrea, who was paralyzed with fear, her crazy, curly mane of hair sticking out in all directions. I ran over, yelled, "You leave her alone, fuckers!", punched the future frat boys in the chest, and watched them recoil in fear at this brown grade three girl with fuzzy braids. As I grew older, *fucker* morphed into *motherfucker*, much to the dismay of my radical feminist mother.

A few times a year, the police would visit our school to warn us about dangerous men—strange men who might pull over in their vans or sedans, who might offer rides or candy or even money, who might look nice and sweet and clean-cut but were to be immediately reported to the police. We were warned about dangerous men in the woods, who might wait behind a tree and attack unsuspecting children. We were told never to talk to strangers, to always run away and tell our parents at once if a suspicious-looking man came near us.

My gaggle of girls at school—Dewi, and girls from Bermuda, China, Japan, Jamaica, as well as First Nations, some of whom lived in the courts—took it upon ourselves to hunt these men down and turn them in to the police. They had all read Nancy Drew, and although I had no idea who that was, I caught on quickly that she was some kind of detective. We formed our own clue club and would sprint to the woods surrounding the school as soon as the recess bell rang. Once there, we'd examine broken twigs, decide they'd been stepped on by the bad men, and gasp in horror when we saw a scratched rock that the evil men had sharpened their knives on. Candy wrappers had been discarded by said men, and they'd probably crossed the ravine so that police dogs would lose their scent.

We'd finish our hard work by chewing on Indian gum, taken from the trees, or, if it was early September, huckleberries from the many bushes in the area. Sometimes we'd sit on a circle of rocks, probably set up by First Nations people long ago for meetings, the librarian, Ms. Singh, had explained. Julie, our First Nations friend, had shrugged at this observation. She'd been adopted by a white family during the infamous Sixties Scoop, when First Nations children had been taken from their homes and handed over to middle-class white families to be raised in a "safer" environment, and hence had no knowledge of her roots' cultural practices.

One Saturday in 1976, a new Chilean family, consisting of a single mother with four kids, showed up at one of our solidarity fundraisers at a preschool next to Salmo Court, rented often by my parents for these events. My cousins Gonzalo and Macarena were there, as always. They lived on the other side of town, just off Kingsway in East Vancouver. Uncle Boris did the janitorial night shift at a steel mill, Aunt Tita worked the assembly line of a fish cannery, and my cousins fled from school every day and waited on the steps of their house until she got home because they were mistreated by the teachers and bullied by the kids.

After the latest documentary on the situation in Chile had been shown, speeches made, songs sung, and empanadas eaten, the cumbia dancing got under way. The single mother had introduced herself by saying, in a quivering voice, "There are no words to describe how happy I am to meet you all, but I must admit that I'm working for the enemy: Canadian Pacific Airlines, owned by Noranda." The adults laughed and feigned horror and then forgiveness. Noranda was one of the Canadian multinationals that had helped fund the coup. It had mining interests in Chile and wanted the mines to go back into private hands after they'd been nationalized by Allende.

As the adults drank their wine and danced to "Tiburón a la Vista," I went up to the youngest child, a boy about my age, and said:

"Wanna see a secret?"

He nodded and I took him to Cedar, my refuge and watchtower. I could spy on everyone and observe the planes in the sky from there, while dipping my finger in Tang powder and sucking the delicious orange sprinkles off. Cedar was mine for two years now, and my treasures hung in little plastic bags from his branches. Mostly, these were Aero bars and jawbreakers, but there was also the odd knick-knack, such as Ken Dryden hockey cards from my cousin Gonzalo, or Chilean one-peso coins given by recent arrivals that reminded me of going to the kiosk in Valdivia or Valparaíso to buy *guaguitas*, a delicious type of marshmallow. I also took Hawaiian Barbie there, bought by

Mami after much whining and pleading that had begun two years earlier in San Diego after my first visit to Lassie's. Since then, I'd been given second-hand Salvation Army Barbies. When my mother finally agreed to buy me a new one, she had refused to get me a blond Barbie on the grounds that it perpetuated the very narrow and white-supremacist North American standard of beauty. The brownness of Hawaiian Barbie, in her hula skirt and flower leis, rendered her null in my eyes and therefore invisible to the world. I was so ashamed of her, she was relegated to Cedar's top branches.

I wasn't in the habit of showing Cedar, much less to a complete stranger, but there was something about this boy that made me want to share everything with him. It was close to nine at night but still light out, for it was early summer in Vancouver, and complete darkness wouldn't set in for a while.

"What's your name?" I asked, kicking a pebble along the way.

"Lucho."

Lucho was quite formal, and impeccably turned out, with his perfect hair, clean nails, ironed clothes, and shined shoes. Fresh off the Chilean boat, I thought to myself. In Chile, kids were like this, but not here. I noticed him taking note of my messy braids and tomboy attire of dirty jeans and worn-out North Stars. I blushed and offered him a jawbreaker. He politely refused with a "Thank you very much, but no thank you."

I showed him how to climb the tree, he did so with impressive ease, and when we reached the top, I pointed out the sturdiest branches to sit on, the good ones to swing from, and the one that could be walked on like a tightrope. We discovered we were both eight, and that his family was from Ñuñoa, the middle-class Santiago neighbourhood where I had been born, when my mother was still a student and my father, a recent graduate, taught high school. Lucho and his family had arrived only a couple of months earlier and were finally coming to an MIR event, also known as the Solidarity With Chile Committee, although they'd certainly met many Chilean families at the Refugee Hotel.

"Wanna see another secret now?"

"Okay."

Reaching around Cedar's trunk, I untied a brown plastic bag hanging from one of his branches. Inside was a small tin box. I opened it and pulled out a postcard with the picture of a boy, about five years old, and showed it to him. The boy was wearing a birthday hat and the sun was on his face, giving him squinty eyes. Behind him stood a man, his hands resting on the boy's shoulders. They both looked into the camera, the boy's expression revealing some kind of mischief, the man wearing a Mona Lisa smile.

This was one of hundreds of similar pictures. Each was of a disappeared person in Chile. Each picture had been turned into a postcard. There were hundreds of copies of each postcard. My parents, uncles, and aunts had made them that spring, our dining room table converted into a printing press of sorts. We kids had helped out, just as we did when the monthly newsletter *Venceremos* ("We Will Triumph") was printed. The postcards were addressed to Canada's minister of External Affairs and came with a little paragraph asking that he pressure Pinochet into disclosing the whereabouts of the disappeared person featured on the front. They were also addressed to Chile's minister of the interior, with the same demand. The pictures had been provided by Families of the Disappeared, an organization in Chile. They were of men, women, children, teenagers, couples, families, people as old as my grandparents, lots of people my parents' age, working-class people, middle-class people, some upper-class people, city people, country people, a cross-section of Chilean society, all with one thing in common: they were on the left, or were poor.

Of all the postcards, I had chosen two. One was of a young woman reading a book at a desk. When I had turned the postcard around, it said, "Carmen Bueno Cifuentes, age 24, actress. Disappeared on November 29th, 1974, with her companion Jorge Muller Silva, age 27, filmmaker. Where is she?" My whole body had frozen. I had discovered my calling at the age of three, was already putting on plays in the centre of our court with Arabella and at school with Dewi, and here was this namesake actress who had disappeared. I asked my mother about her. She responded that Carmen Bueno Cifuentes had acted in film and theatre and had been active in the now-outlawed Actors' Union. She had also fought for the rights of poor people, and was probably dead, although she could possibly still be in an underground detention centre. Mami also explained about the importance of putting the word out, of holding the Chilean government accountable, of letting the world know that this was happening, of speaking up.

"Silence will never protect us, Carmencita. Always remember that," my mother had instructed.

I had slipped one of the Carmen Bueno Cifuentes postcards into the back pocket of my jeans and then continued to make little piles of postcards, as per my instructions. Holly Near, one of Mami's favourite singers, along with Mercedes Sosa and Edith Piaf, sang "It Could Have Been Me" on the turntable and I thought about how apropos the lyrics were.

The next postcard that had hit me hard was the one of the birthday-hat boy. I turned it around. It said, "Alejandro Avalos Davidson, age 30, professor and researcher at the Catholic University. Disappeared on November 20th, 1975. Where is he?" It had affected me deeply because the boy in the photo with his father was the age I had been when the coup had happened, because his dad, a university professor like mine, had disappeared, and because I was convinced he'd been picked up on the day the picture was taken, during his son's birthday party. I imagined the festivities in the backyard, the military surrounding the house, blindfolding the father, tying his hands behind him, throwing him into the back of a jeep, and driving away with him, leaving behind overturned juice cups, stomped-on presents, a piñata swaying from the branch of an orange tree. This picture had been taken right before the arrival of the military, I decided, and a terrible lonely feeling gripped me as I thought of the silence, the gaping hole of the immediate aftermath. I pocketed one of these postcards too.

Once the postcard piles had been arranged to the adults' liking, I grabbed a little tin box I'd been keeping in my room for an awaiting treasure, stuffed it into a plastic bag, snuck away, climbed Cedar, and pondered the postcards again. As I studied Carmen Bueno Cifuentes, reading at her desk by a window, I pictured the military breaking down her door while she was lost in the world of the book—had they burned the book after snatching it from her, adding it to the tally of books destroyed in bonfires on the grounds of so many of Chile's universities? I wondered—and taking her away, never to be seen again. Holding both postcards to my heart on that crisp spring day, I said aloud, Cedar my only witness:

"Please, dear God, please, find this boy's Papi, find Carmen Bueno Cifuentes. Please make sure they show up again. Thank you."

I closed my eyes that day and envisaged them dead, their bodies lying peacefully in the fresh earth, and then dreamed them rising up and out, walking into the world of the living again, Alejandro Avalos Davidson reappearing at the birthday party so the celebration could continue, the disappearance a mere blip on that festive day, Carmen Bueno Cifuentes picking up her book—I decided it was Eduardo Galeano's *Open Veins of Latin America*, often quoted in our house, burnt, flushed, or buried in many Chilean homes after the coup—and resuming her reading by the light of her window, entering the world of Latin America's history through its pages.

Next, I'd opened the little tin box, kissed both postcards, said, "You'll be safe here, comrades," and placed them carefully inside.

I had put the box in the bag, tied it around the base of one of Cedar's branches, and stayed there for a long time contemplating the sky before climbing back down. That had been only a few months earlier, and now was the first time I was sharing this secret with someone other than Cedar.

"This boy's father disappeared," I told Lucho as I held up the postcard.

He took it gingerly from my hands and said, "That's me. Where did you get this?"

Dead serious, he turned the postcard around, the same little half smile from the picture appearing on his face as he recollected that day, the last birthday party with his Papi. I watched him in silence in that suspended moment, a moment of recognition for us both. We'd found each other, in a tree, in the northern hemisphere. There were no words to say.

We took each other's hand. I explained about the postcards and he nodded as he kept his eye on the picture. Then he said:

"This is my uncle, my mother's brother. He was like a father to me. He was a Communist. And that's why I am one too."

We stayed there until darkness set in. I explained about the little box and the prayer to keep him safe, showed him the Carmen Bueno Cifuentes postcard and told him her story. My namesake's picture spoke to me because I knew I wanted to be an actor, I confessed. Lucho nodded and revealed that acting was his calling too. He became a cousin that day. Years later, while I was running the safe house in Neuquén and doing border runs for the MIR, Lucho started theatre school at the college in South Vancouver.

SEVEN

Performance Lab being a place of experimentation, half-way through theatre school I decided to take another risk. Wearing a nun's habit, I stood at centre stage and recited text from a hard-core porn novel I had purchased at an XXX store. The book was so vile that I'd found myself throwing it across the room between chapters and gulping in air before resuming my reading during late night rehearsals. Being a feminist, I had not only avoided XXX stores like the plague, I had religiously stuck my middle finger out the bus window whenever I passed the stretch of porn shops on Granville Street. As a teenager I had sported a button proclaiming that *Real Men Don't Need Porn*, quoted from Andrea Dworkin's *Pornography: Men Possessing Women*, my anti-porn bible, and had joined marches to shut down Red Hot Video. For all these reasons, I found it logical to plunge headfirst into some hard-core porn text in order to learn how to embrace, embody, and own language that went against every fibre of my being.

Taking a deep breath, I had walked right into one of the stores that offered peep shows, sex toys, and S&M gear and boasted an exhaustive selection of pornography. Confounded as to where to begin looking for the vilest thing in stock, I ended up explaining to the cashier, a scrawny, bald nerd in glasses, that I was looking for the most misogynistic thing he could think of.

"I'm talking teenage girls being raped who scream out 'No' but really mean 'Yes.' No pictures, just text," I clarified.

"Ah, yes. I've got just the thing," he murmured without a pause.

After disappearing into the back, he returned with the novel.

"We don't put these out on the floor," he said in a conspiratorial tone.

"Oh, right," I winked back.

I read the first page on the spot. It introduced a Mother Superior character who ran a convent where men, under her enraptured supervision, raped and tortured the young nuns.

I swallowed hard.

"Perfect. I'll take it."

Pulling my wallet out, I stuttered that I was an acting student about to do a language code exercise that consisted of speaking text that went against your belief system.

He nodded. "Uh-huh."

I placed the book at the bottom of my backpack, emerged from the store with a mix of pride and shame, and gave the finger to the Cecil strip club across the road before making my way down Granville.

For the second time since starting theatre school, I stood on the Performance Lab stage. Playing the Mother Superior in the habit borrowed from the costume room, I spoke in a style referred to as hyper-naturalism, about how my young nuns loved being gang-raped and tortured. I went into graphic, unbearable detail, every single word taken from the novel. In the background, my classmate Andy, sporting a Grim Reaper cloak, face fully covered by the hood, played Harry Dacre's "A Bicycle Built for Two" on the piano. I wanted to see how far one could go, how much I could get into believing and revelling in every word I said while in front of an audience that wouldn't judge me. I knew my experiment in owning the text was working when my peers started to plug their ears, heads dropped in horror. Faces frozen, eyes wide like saucers, the faculty sat in the back row, arms crossed.

Halfway through the piece, the director of the school told me to stop and get off the stage. Shocked that she'd taken over the student-run event, I defied her and continued. She again told me to stop. I kept going. On her third attempt, I paused, numb as an iceberg.

"I'm just trying something," I explained.

She ordered me off again. Some of my peers protested that Performance Lab was a student-run safe space free of censorship and faculty control so us novices could try anything. No staff member had ever stopped a student while they were pushing boundaries on its stage. After some arguing, I told the director I would take my exit even though I disagreed with her demand.

I suspected that was the end of theatre school for me. Disgraced, I waited in the hallway. When the director came out flanked by the co-artistic director and the voice teacher, I debated with them for an hour. But the director stood by her actions, and I stood by my exercise. To my great relief, I wasn't expelled.

The experiment, and the reaction it caused, taught me a valuable lesson. If my first foray into Performance Lab, telling the story of the coup through my five-year-old eyes, had been too personal, this attempt had gone too far in its grisly violence, shock as opposed to insight being its primary value. I still had to learn how to talk about violence onstage without it being too personal or so offensive that it turned people off instead of simply engaging them. It would be a lifelong search in my artistic journey, trying to find that balance, for I knew that the stories I wanted to explore would inevitably include violence. I had failed twice, the second effort being the most humiliating onstage experience of my life to that point, but also worth every minute, precisely because of the lesson learned that could not have been absorbed any other way.

Up until then, my biggest onstage catastrophe had been the time I peed my pants from laughing too hard at my cousin Gonzalo's rendition of Revolutionary Cinderella. Ale and Lucho had been playing the stepsisters, Macarena the clock, the mouse, and the pumpkin, and I had been the evil stepmother. The pee had trickled all the way down the legs of my chair. Said performance had taken place at the rented preschool. We kids would put on shows that I wrote, directed, and acted in that featured Pinochet as mentally challenged, and Cinderella as a revolutionary who took up arms against the stepmother and the rest of the ruling class. My incontinence caused the adults to laugh so hard that my mother and Aunt La Huasa, whose nephews would appear as if by magic at that Buenos Aires rally years later, almost wet their pants as well.

Whether it was an evil stepmother in a slapstick comedy or the vile Mother Superior in a serious drama, what I knew thus far in my short acting life was that playing an oppressor was hard. It was a formidable challenge for me, to embody a torturer, a psychopath. But it wasn't the first time I'd tried to put myself in those shoes. My first attempt at entering the mind, heart, and soul of a person who committed serious crimes against innocent people was a short story I had written at the age of sixteen, three years after I'd been raped.

In it, I visited the rapist in jail and heard him out. He asked for forgiveness after telling me how depressed, lonely, and fucked-up he'd always been, that all he'd ever wanted was love, and then I told him that I would try to get him out of jail so he could be free to pursue love without hurting people. It was a fantastical story in every sense of the word; the man who'd raped me was still at large and assaulting girls around Vancouver's Lower Mainland when I it wrote it in 1984.

Referred to as the Paper Bag Rapist because he covered his victims' heads with a paper bag or with a piece of their own clothing, he was infamous, police sketches of his face appearing on the evening news in the early 1980s on a regular basis. During his reign of terror in the city and its suburbs, girls were instructed by their parents and teachers to walk in large groups, not even in twos or threes. His pattern was to attack a duo, sometimes even a trio, of girls at once. His youngest victims had been two eight-year-old girls, the oldest in their mid-teens. I'd been thirteen, my cousin Macarena twelve.

At the time of my Performance Lab disaster when I was twenty-four, the idea of writing a play about the rape hadn't fully formed, for I was at a loss as to how it could be done.

Infuriated by the depiction of rape on the big and small screens, where the victims were mere victims and the rapists one-dimensional monsters, where the rape was sexualized and therefore titillating, where the story revolved around the rapist as opposed to the victim, I still didn't know how I would approach that story myself, how I would turn it into art, or why I would even want to. But presenting at the Lab what I had lived through by embodying the oppressor in a hard-core porn text was a first step, because I knew that if I were ever to create a play based on the rape, I would have to tackle every angle of that afternoon, which of course featured the rapist himself as a central figure—though in my theatrical take on the subject he'd be the antagonist, not the protagonist. Or would he still be the protagonist? In either case, I needed to inhabit his psyche and soul, to embrace him in all his complexity. If I was going to make art out of that experience, I would not only have to stare the horror in the face, I would also have to explore the beauty of it.

It happened on a sunny late April day in 1981, the first hot Sunday of the season. Ale and I were back from Bolivia, where we'd spent a year with Mami and my stepfather Bob, there to set up a safe house for MIRistas and to do border runs into Chile through the Atacama Desert. They had stayed behind while we returned to be with Papi, now married to Aunt Tita, Macarena and Gonzalo's mother. On that Sunday, Tita was cleaning other people's houses, Ale had ridden her banana-seat bike to her friend Madeline's, my cousin Gonzalo was roller skating around the neighbourhood with his buddy Joel, my father was locked away in his upstairs bedroom working on his PhD, and Macarena and I had spent the morning slouching around the Salmo Court house in our crumpled jammies, sleep still in our eyes. Bored out of our skulls, we'd called my new best friend Amber, who lived in neighbouring Oyama Court, to see if she wanted to hang out, but she hadn't answered.

Eventually, we decided to go for a stroll. A Colombian friend of the family had given me a skirt she'd brought from a trip back home. It was my first wraparound skirt, made of printed white cotton. Yet to be worn, I decided that this first hot, sunny day was the perfect day to sport it. I wore a white cotton button-up shirt to go with it and my new wedge Brazilian brown leather sandals. After some rambling in which nothing of interest happened (in other words, no cute boys were spotted), we made our way to my school grounds, a few minutes away from our house. Surrounded by forest, University Hill Secondary School was right next to the courts.

The week prior, I had attended a lunchtime presentation by Rape Relief. As the women talked about sexual assault, the causes of it—according to them, the patriarchy—and the notion that it was rarely about sex and almost always about power, all I could think was, "That will never happen to me." I shook off the shudders after the talk was through and made my way down the hall to my humanities class, feeling sorry for those faceless rape victims, whoever they were, wherever they cowered. The following day, a Royal Canadian Mounted Police officer came to the school and issued yet another warning about the Paper Bag Rapist, who'd been attacking girls for three years now.

We arrived at the school grounds to find a soccer game about to begin in the field adjacent to the gym. One of the teams was Chilean. Thrilled to see our uncles, aunts, and cousins, we decided to stay awhile.

"Look! There's Uncle Moustache and Uncle Groovy!" Macarena pointed to a couple of the men standing on the sidelines, cigarettes dangling from their mouths.

"Hmm. I guess they're back from the sea," I commented, in reference to their commercial salmon-fishing jobs, a smile forming at the sight of them.

By that time, eight years into exile, the Chileans who had not gone back to join the underground, as my mother, Bob, Aunt La Huasa, and so many others had done, had formed their own little sub-communities, delineated along political lines. There were the MIRista families, which included us, the Communist Party families (the majority), and the Socialist Party families. For those who had put solidarity work aside, the division happened along class lines. The soccer team was made up of the working-class Chileans, those who had come from the Santiago shantytowns, from Valparaíso, and from the northern mining region. Some of the dishy boys were there, and Macarena and I high-fived each other; the dullest afternoon ever had taken a turn for the better.

A cop car turned the corner and we spotted Chris and Mark, the two gorgeous young officers who patrolled the UBC area. Their windows were down, and we waved at each other as they made their way to the school parking lot. Before making our presence felt at the game, we decided to duck into the woods to apply Bonne Bell Lip Smacker and smoke the Benson & Hedges Light cigarette Macarena had stolen from her father, Boris.

We walked into Fairview trail, right off the parking lot. Its entrance faced the front doors of the school. The trail took you through a stretch of woods and spit you out onto University Boulevard, right where the number 10 bus stopped, the one we would take downtown to catch matinees at the Capitol Six on Granville and then grab some fries at McDonald's on the corner of Smithe. Tommy, my first Canadian boyfriend, and I would always sit in the back row and hold hands. Our first movie together had been *Arthur*, featuring Liza Minnelli and Dudley Moore, which was followed by a debate wherein I criticized the movie's message that money makes happiness and he exalted the wonders of the free market that made a millionaire of anyone who worked hard enough, regardless of class, race, or gender. "Ha!" I'd laughed in his face, fists on my waist. He'd walked me to the door of my house and, as usual, I'd made a fool of myself while trying to look sexy, falling through the door when I'd leaned up against it. Ale, Macarena, and Gonzalo had opened it a crack to spy on our goodbye. I'd landed on top of them, got up, closed the door behind me to drown out their laughing fit, and leaned again, hoping Tommy hadn't noticed the glitch.

I'd had my eye on him since the first week of grade eight. He was in grade ten at the same school, lived in a mansion on Chancellor Boulevard, had blond hair, blue eyes, and a freckled face, and hung out with all the other WASPs from one of the wealthiest neighbourhoods in Canada. In short, he was everything I was not. Oblivious to my existence, months had passed and he had never once looked at me, no matter how many times I "bumped" into him in the halls, how close I sat to the bench during his basketball games, or how often I wore my tight jeans from the discount floor at Army & Navy.

Finally, after looking up his number in the white pages, I'd got my cousin Gonzalo to phone him and pretend to be a girl.

For weeks, Gonzalo, calling himself Bo—"Just like Bo Derek"—
in a falsetto, talked to Tommy while Ale, Macarena, and I hovered around the receiver, listening in, hands over our mouths to
stifle the giggles. I would break into spontaneous dancing fits,
kickball-changing my way around the carpet before returning
to my post. After "Bo" quizzed him about his hobbies, favourite movies, and family history, Gonzalo asked him who he
liked. Keeping his privacy intact, Tommy skirted the question.
Then Gonzalo asked him if he was going around with anybody.
Tommy answered no. Using hand signals, I directed Gonzalo
to ask him if he liked me. Tommy said he had no idea who I was.
So Gonzalo recited the speech I had prepared for him.

"Carmen is this really pretty, really intelligent, super-mature
girl in grade eight. Everybody likes her. Like, all these neighbourhood boys and even university guys are after her. Frat boys
chase her down the street. That bitch."

"Oh," was Tommy's response.

The following day, Gonzalo urged me to call him myself.

"These white boys are scared, cousin. And he's so white, he's
like 'let's go hunting' white. So you gotta do all the work yourself, cuz."

As I inserted my index finger into the rotary dial on the tele-
phone, my knees shook so hard they knocked into each other.

"Hi, this is Carmen from grade eight," I said.

"Oh."

I dived right in.

"Wanna go around?"

There was a pause, then a succession of *uhs* that threatened
to stretch into eternity, and then an utterance.

"Yes."

"Okay," I said, and hung up.

Gonzalo, Ale, and Macarena had surrounded the receiver and I bowled them over with my outburst of disco moves.

"He said YES! He said YES! He said YES!"

Grabbing Gonzalo by the shoulders, I shook him so hard while screaming in his face that it was a wonder I didn't give him whiplash, what with his head flopping all over the place. I ran up and down the stairs, pounding the air with my fists, blasted Diana Ross's "Upside Down" on the stereo, and danced like a maniac while continuing to yell, "He said YES!" Ale crossed her arms and rolled her eyes, Gonzalo, in shock, stated the obvious—"Jesus, Carmencita, you're fucking boy crazy!"— and Macarena lit up a cigarette and gave me a high-five, saying, "All right!"

She was a diminutive yet badass twelve-year-old who wore a T-shirt that proclaimed *This body runs on beer and bullshit.* Later, at the age of fifteen, she would buy the most popular white T-shirt of the time, worn by WHAM!'s George Michael in the "Wake Me Up Before You Go-Go" music video; *Choose Life* was printed on the front in massive black letters. Macarena bought it in extra large, crossing out the statement with a black marker once she got home. She sported this T-shirt while we elbowed our way through anti-abortionist crowds blocking the doors to a talk we attended by Henry Morgentaler, the renowned abortion doctor. Once, at the age of eight, Uncle Boris had sat her down and asked, in the sternest voice he could muster, "Macarena, have you been stealing my cigarettes?" to which she responded, "No, Papi. I quit a while back." At twelve, she already wore heavy black eyeliner and loved to rock out to Led Zeppelin, the Who, and the Rolling Stones.

As for me, disco was the love of my dancing life. On weekends, we'd attend the Latino fundraisers, now not only for Chile but also for Nicaragua and El Salvador. There, we'd dance the cumbia we'd been born into, pump our left fists in the air and chant, "*Que Viva Nicaragua Sandinista!*," and make Miguel Enríquez Rebel Youth Brigade speeches (the MIR's youth group we were part of, the local chapter run by Boris), crossing from the Latino-exile world into the mainstream one like the bicultural children we were, so adept in both that we were monocultural in each.

Now, in the woods by the school, knees wobbly from the cigarette, I let her have the last drag. We had entered the familiar Fairview trail, gone over the initial little mound, and stopped at the bottom of it. This afforded us the luxury of still being able to see the parking lot through the trees and spy which cute Chilean boys were getting out of their cars. Chilean slang reached our ears as families arrived with coolers, blankets, and ghetto blasters that would play La Sonora Dinamita cumbias at the game.

"Oh my God, Javier is here—this is gonna be good," I announced to Macarena.

She was facing me and had her back to the parking lot.

"Just make sure you don't break out in hives or shit your pants, Carmencita," she warned, alluding to Javier being a darker-skinned version of Scott Baio, my *Happy Days* crush. A *Tiger Beat* magazine centrefold featuring him in an unbuttoned shirt with a gold crucifix around his neck hung on the wall right next to my bed, the mouth disintegrated from all the times I'd kissed it.

Javier, eighteen years old and way out of my league (he dated bottle-blond twenty-year-old rocker chicks who lived in deep

East Van like him), was the oldest of four sexy brothers, and they too belonged to the Miguel Enríquez Rebel Youth Brigade. They had just arrived in their van, along with their MIRista janitor parents, whom they helped after school and on weekends. Coming from one of Santiago's biggest shantytowns, baptized New Havana under Allende, the father had helped build barricades and burn tires to keep the military at bay on the day of the coup. He'd been arrested, along with many others. Once released, the family found refuge in Canada.

On this day, they made their way over to the field amidst foul-mouthed jokes told in slang so specific to Santiago's poorest quarters that no other Latino stood a chance of deciphering what it meant. The other team was working-class white Canadian, and its supporters also spilled out of their cars, the women in feathered hair, the men with their bushy moustaches, AC/DC T-shirts, and sleeveless jean jackets. Chris and Mark, the two gorgeous cops, climbed out of their cruiser and started walking towards the field, Trident gum in their mouths, Ray-Bans covering their eyes, probably there to monitor who had booze in their coolers.

Out of nowhere, a cold feeling seized my gut. I knew this feeling well: fear. It had gripped me many times in my life, most recently the year before, when I was twelve and living in Bolivia. I had endured two coups there. The first had seen me facing a plainclothes cop who had waved his gun in my face and threatened to shoot me if I didn't go straight back home. There had also been a spine-chilling underground border crossing into Chile, accompanying one of the MIR's central committee members on a train across the highlands.

Watch out, my intuitive inner voice told me.

I looked around.

"Everything okay?" Macarena asked, a final stream of smoke escaping her nostrils.

A twig snapped behind her. The hairs on the back of my neck stood up.

This is your instinct, my wise voice asserted. *This is your instinct telling you there is danger ahead. Get out. Get out now.*

The other voice, the head-voice of reason that made a mockery of my ancient, wise gut-voice, took over.

It's the cigarette, dummy. It makes you wobbly, tickles your tummy, and gives you goosebumps. That's all.

A sparrow flew up from where the twig had snapped.

See? It's just a bird, the pompous voice of reason argued.

The cold, sick feeling in my gut intensified, chills ran up my spine, like a snake slithering its way from my sacrum to the base of my skull, every hair on my body stood on end. The Terror was here, and it wasn't going away.

Run. Now. While you still can. Run, the knowing gut-voice boomed inside me.

Don't be silly and paranoid, the voice of reason scoffed.

I let the voice of reason win and made a split-second decision to stay put.

"Yeah. Everything's fine."

Macarena dropped the butt on the trail. My adrenalin kicked in full force, a door flung open by a fierce gust of wind. Just as I was about to grab her arm, a male voice spoke calmly from behind a cottonwood tree in front of me and behind her, where the twig had snapped.

"Put your hands on your head, turn around, and don't look back."

Focused on crushing the butt with the ball of her foot, Macarena's head snapped up, jack popping out of his box, eyes wide like a Cabbage Patch doll. I took her forearm so we could make a break for it.

"Don't try to run. I have a gun and I will shoot you. Do as I say. Put your hands on your head, turn around, and don't look back. Now."

The tone was eerily unperturbed, taking its time.

Macarena asked me in a low voice, "Is this a joke?"

The inquiry wasn't entirely unfounded. Three years earlier, when I was ten and she nine, we'd found ourselves in a similar situation that had turned out to be a prank.

Locked in the bathroom of the Salmo Court house, applying discarded makeup we'd found in the laundromat, we heard a stranger's voice threaten us from the other side.

"Hey! I have a gun and I'm gonna kill you!"

It had been a young male voice and he'd tormented us for a solid fifteen minutes, pounding on the door, telling us that once we came out, he was going to murder us. We'd wept with terror on the bathroom floor. He told us he'd already assassinated our family and it was only a matter of time before we gave up, came out, and surrendered to him, he of the sinister laugh, he of the infinite patience who could wait for eternity. Recoiling, we balled ourselves into the fetal position in the corner of the bathroom when he finally threatened to kick down the door.

We'd waited and waited for the imminent door destruction, but it never came. Only silence lived on the other side. Holding hands, heads held high, we'd mustered every last bit of courage we possessed and opened the door, surrendering with dignity to whatever awaited us—the man with the gun or the freedom to behold the aftermath of our family's bloodied bodies strewn about the halls and at the bottom of the stairs of our home. But it was Gia, Arabella's half-goddess/half-witch sister, who was standing there, hands on her hips, a big smile on her face, mischief in her eyes.

"Just joking, you two."

That had also been on a Sunday afternoon, and we'd run across the way to tell on her. Our parents were visiting with her mother, Pam, sipping tea from green mugs that asked in gold letters *Your pad or mine?* We collapsed amidst sobs into their arms.

As Macarena and I stood suspended on that trail, I remembered the history behind her "Is this a joke?"

"No. This is not a joke," I whispered back, for by that time I had had enough experience with men with guns to know that this was a real live man with an actual working gun.

"Hands on your head. Turn around. Now," he ordered again, the tightness in his voice now betraying a hint of urgency.

The Terror was beyond any I had experienced, for I was hit with the certainty that this time I would not escape bodily harm, that there were only a limited number of occasions that one could be tyrannized by men with guns and escape intact. I imagined a savage beating and then a shot to the head. Rape did not cross my mind, because rape happened to other people. Or did it?

Swallowing hard, I thought of my wraparound skirt hugging my hips, my fully developed body—the body of a woman, not a girl. I grappled with what the Rape Relief women had said:

it doesn't matter what you wear. But surely it did. Surely my clothes had lured this man into the woods with us. Macarena, deer in the headlights, stood frozen, eyes on mine.

There was nothing we could do. He was placed between the entrance to the trail and us. If we ran in the other direction, towards the bus stop, he would catch us. A quick tally of the situation told me that trying to pound on him would get us killed. Resistance was out of the question. I made note again of why I believed in arming the oppressed. He had all the power precisely because he had a gun and we didn't. Given our circumstances, obedience was the only option. If we bowed our heads and did everything he asked, we might make it out alive.

So I said to Macarena, "Put your hands on your head," and pulled her towards me.

I turned around, placed her in front of me with her back to me, and crossed my hands on the top of my head, as I'd seen my best friend Jana's father and older brother do on the day of the raid. It hit me that Macarena had no idea what lay behind her. She didn't know that the voice was disembodied, faceless. There was the sound of running and within a moment the barrel of a gun at the base of my skull. He grabbed the back of my blouse, bunching the cloth in his fist.

Kicking my calves, he ordered, "Put your hands on her shoulders and walk. If either of you turn around, I'll shoot. You!" he growled at Macarena through clenched teeth. "Walk! I have the gun to your sister's head and I'll shoot her if you don't walk. Off the trail, into the bush. Now."

EIGHT

"You don't have what it takes to be an actor. We're letting you go."

I had lived in angst about hearing those words, and now here they were. I was twenty-five years old, and my lifelong dream was flattened. Having already failed my third term at theatre school, I had taken two terms off to work on myself, and then returned to repeat it. It was December 1992, the end of my second time around, and in my final talks the dreaded axe came down. Hit by a truck, I could barely take in my teachers' assessment: you are out of your body onstage, you are not on your voice, you are not taking risks, you are freezing up, you are so uncomfortable onstage that you are painful to watch.

Although I had spent time away from school going to the therapist, evidently it still hadn't "done the trick." Once a week I saw her, delving into my family history without mentioning my involvement in the Chilean resistance and barely touching on the rape, even though that's what I was supposed to be working on with her. Fear kept me from exploring the experiences that were holding me hostage: the rape and the Terror of my MIR times. I did body work, lying on a massage table for my weekly polarity therapy appointments, my healer a cross between Cat Stevens and Jesus Christ, with his long dark hair, beard, and tie-dyed attire. I attended a group therapy session at theatre school for rape and sexual abuse survivors, and read self-help books. I visualized myself onstage as an embodied, whole human being, accessing the endless pool of emotions that lay in my gut, hip sockets, and cells, and giving them all away with a fully centred voice, my resonators giving it the shape it needed. I envisaged doing all of this while interpreting other people's texts. I imagined myself being a professional stage actor.

In my four terms of class work at theatre school, I'd played Lady Macbeth, Juliet, and Gertrude. I'd done Chekhov, Shepard, Beckett, and Williams. All to no avail. As the axe continued to come down, I heard them say through my numb face that there were times when I was definitely on, and when I was, the work was fine. But there was very little repeatability. I did not have a handle on my creative process, and that's what they were there to teach: how to graduate with a tried-and-true process that could get you through a three-week rehearsal period and take you to opening night with an honest, dependable performance. Having no repeatability meant I was not ready for a rehearsal process, much less for a paying audience or the critics, some of whom revelled in slamming actors. In the second half of theatre school one acted in plays that were attended by Vancouver's reviewers as well as artistic directors, producers, and agents scouting new talent. Did I really want to suffer that level of public humiliation?

I emerged from the office as a newly kicked-out acting student, went home, and lay down and sobbed for two days straight. There was nothing else I could do with my life besides acting. This was my calling. Nothing could or would replace it.

And then the phone rang. The director of the school wished to see me. Once again I found myself in the office, facing the three faculty members, who wanted to know how I was taking the news. I broke down and wept, and they offered a compromise.

"You will not act in our plays because we do not believe that you are an actor. But we do believe that you are a theatre artist. So we would like to offer you the opportunity to stay and learn the art of playwriting and directing. You will be our only student doing that, so you will have access to one-on-one instruction with us for the next eighteen months."

I had mixed feelings about their offer. On the one hand I was grateful and relieved, on the other I saw it as an affront and felt reluctant to continue. Years would pass before I understood the magnitude of the gift that it was.

It was the first day of rehearsals for a piece of musical theatre entitled *The Kat Who Would Be Kool*. I swallowed my pride and, instead of joining my peers onstage, script in hand, pencil behind ear, I took a seat in the house next to the director flown in from Stratford, pulled out a fresh notebook, and said:

"Hi. I'm Carmen. I'll be your assistant."

For the rest of my time at theatre school, I coached my peers on acting, did research for the directors I assisted, filled countless notebooks during rehearsals with ideas on the art of moving bodies around onstage, finding the arc of a scene and communicating that to the actors, working with designers on a common vision; I constructed a thesis on how I would direct Chekhov's *Three Sisters*, and wrote my first play under the tutelage of the award-winning playwriting teacher. Although playwriting, considered an essential part of acting training, was taught to all students for the first three terms, I continued one-on-one with him until I graduated.

Entitled *In a Land Called I Don't Remember*, my play, produced by the theatre school, took place on a bus crossing the Andes mountains from Argentina into Chile. In it, I explored my dual identities, personified by two female characters who were exactly the same age and sat next to each other. One lived in Chile, the other was the daughter of exiles returning from Canada for the first time. The young Chilean woman was carrying documents into Chile for the resistance, and the bus was intercepted by the secret police. The remaining characters represented a cross-section of Chilean working-class society.

I found that taking a risk on the page was not difficult for me. When the instrument was written text, I was able to overcome my fears with exceptional ease. It was only when I myself was the vessel that the Berlin Wall came up. The page as conduit brought out the warrior in me, as I smashed through whatever barriers dared to stand in the story's way.

During my last year at theatre school, thanks to Puente Theatre, a Victoria company that hired me to participate in workshops during summer vacation, I discovered Augusto Boal's Theatre of the Oppressed. Plays were created based on the experiences of marginalized communities, whose non-actor members also performed in them.

I had been introduced to popular theatre when I was four years old and living in Huacho Copihue, Valdivia. The socialist government's literacy campaign and agrarian reform were under way, and my parents participated by going to rural areas and teaching illiterate adults how to read and write. Chile was also experiencing a cultural boom, thanks to Allende's generous funding of the arts. Musicians travelled with him, theatre groups moved into shantytowns and created plays based on the dwellers' experiences, and visual artists painted colourful murals on hundreds of walls across the country with the participation of community members. When the coup happened, Víctor Jara would be murdered, many of the theatre troupes arrested—only to re-form in the concentration camps, most notably Chacabuco—and every last mural covered with black paint.

One afternoon in 1972, a VW van had pulled up to our house. The side door had slid open, revealing half a dozen people in their early twenties, my mother's age. Wearing ponchos, the men sported beards and long hair, while lapis lazuli-encrusted handmade copper jewellery hung from the women's ears and necks. They strummed guitars and sang Violeta Parra's "To Be Seventeen Again," joking and laughing between verses. Some of the women sat on the men's laps, the men's hands caressing their thighs. I had been skipping rope in front of our house and stood in awe at the scene, the van's open door a proscenium. The singing continued as the driver beeped the horn in rhythm.

"Oh my God! Are you Carmencita? Are you?" the people asked.

One of the women jumped out and kissed me all over.

"Oh my God! You're so cute! And you look just like your Mami!"

They all smiled at me and continued singing.

My mother came running out of the house wearing her Mapuche poncho, guitar slung over her shoulder, Chilote woven bag in her hand.

"Oh my God, Carmen, you never told us Carmencita looks just like you!" they all yelled.

Their hands pulled my mother into the idling van.

"Carmencita," my mother said, "these are the people I'm going away with for a week. Remember I told you I was going to work for Chile?"

I nodded, mouth down-turned.

"What will you be doing?" I managed to ask.

It was as if the vehicle was vibrating, as if these people had their own personal spotlights, and there was no way I wasn't going to find out exactly who they were and what they did, for future reference.

"Theatre, Carmencita. Theatre. We're going to put on a play around the countryside that explains to people what the agrarian reform is, and what comrade Allende is up to. Theatre!"

The door slid closed and the van took off with a series of minor explosions, leaving me behind in the dust, tears of rage and impotence running down my face for not having been invited to join them, the only evidence that they'd been there the tire marks on the dirt road. Years later, I realized they were doing agitprop theatre. Those who didn't get away were arrested after the coup, one for the simple crime of wearing long hair and a beard when Pinochet had outlawed these on men (he said they symbolized an allegiance to Fidel Castro) and trousers on women ("From now on, *men* will wear the pants in this country").

"So Mami's friends are actors?" I asked my father that afternoon.

"Yes."

"And Mami is an actor?"

"No, but she'll sing and play the guitar. Did you know she studied twelve years of piano and guitar at the musical conservatory when she was growing up? And she acted once in a play at the Pedagogical University, directed by her professor Enrique. She was nine months pregnant with you, and she was Juliet in *Romeo and Juliet*. The play was set during a street protest, so she held placards and banners for the whole thing," he explained.

He pulled a picture out of a shoebox of my mother at the age of nineteen, wearing cat's eyeglasses, her hair in a beehive, heavily pregnant, holding up a protest sign.

I put it all together then: the mesmerizing circus woman standing on the galloping white horse I had seen when I was three, the van full of people who radiated a light as strong as the sun, and now this picture of Mami onstage while pregnant with me. It all gave me butterflies of excitement and a little bit of fear. Performing, acting, theatre. Yes, this was it. This was my calling! I was going to be an actor, and nobody and nothing would ever stop me.

"And look, here's Mami's uncle and aunt," Papi said.

The sepia photograph featured two young acrobats in impossible positions, with the caption *The Rubber Couple* at the top.

"They spent years travelling the northern mining towns with a small circus."

My stomach flipped, my heart skipped a beat. I dashed to my room, put on my favourite necklace made with the buttons from my abuelita Carmen's sewing kit, and ran outside, skipping rope in tow. Jumping in front of my house, I beamed and beamed, full of the pictures, full of the actors from the van, full of the woman and the white horse, and a spontaneous internal voice boomed in every chamber of my skull:

"Welcome to the theatre. It will never let you go."

I surrendered, whooping as I jumped and jumped with my skip rope in the lane of Huacho Copihue, willing my friends to come out and ask what was up so that I could answer with pride, shining button necklace a crest on my chest:

"I will be an actor."

One of the things that always jarred me about theatre school was its apolitical nature. We were taught everything one needed to know to be a Shakespearean actor and worked like mules until we got it (or didn't), but nothing was ever said in regards to the *purpose* of being an actor. Having just come from Argentina, Chile, Peru, and Bolivia, where art-making was a political act and being an artist came with a huge responsibility to the community, I had crumpled with dismay upon realizing that no one at school—not the teachers, not the students—connected art and politics. Not only that, it was looked down upon to mix the two, which was mind-boggling to me. In contrast to the theatre I had experienced in South America, most notably the Lima curfew players in 1986, in Canada acting seemed to be entirely about fulfilling an individual dream, as opposed to a skill developed in order to serve others. The closest thing to a political statement that I ever heard at theatre school, from peers and the powers that be alike, was the inalienable right to freedom of expression, the right to one's individuality. This right ignited passionate opinions, although it was always the furthest thing from my mind, as it had never been, and never would be, my bottom line.

I left my political being at the door when I entered theatre school, compartmentalizing my life for the millionth time, and in so doing inadvertently shut off access to the wealth of emotional material I could have drawn from. It was no wonder I couldn't stay connected onstage: the compartmentalization was so air-tight that my very identity was absent from my acting classes. On closing night of my play *In a Land Called I Don't Remember*, in 1995, some of the actors admitted to me that they had not believed me when I had talked to them about torture in Chile. They'd been certain that torture only existed in Shakespeare's plays and that the Nazis were the last to have held people in concentration camps. As part of their research, the director had had me do a presentation and I had produced books, movies, and testimonials. They had considered me a liar—until they read about it in Amnesty International files.

The irony was that the Guatemalan janitor family who cleaned the very floor they rehearsed on were survivors of tor-ture. Mainstream Canadian theatre presented overwhelmingly white, middle-class stories—which almost always dealt with the personal crises of the protagonists, more often than not with no social, political, or historical context—without examining its own privilege. The story my play told, although common to thousands of immigrant Canadians, was so absent from Canadian stages that it was met with incredulity from the very artists presenting it, who could not integrate it until they knew it was backed up by a middle-class, white, liberal organization such as Amnesty International. I decided that one of the reasons I was acquiring theatre skills was to tell the stories of my silenced, isolated, and disbelieved community, the Latino community in exile.

Discovering Augusto Boal's Theatre of the Oppressed was such a relief, I likened it to what a desert traveller must feel when coming upon an oasis. I toured the province with the Victoria troupe, even going to Rio de Janeiro, where I performed in a two-hander about family violence with my beloved friend Lucho at Boal's International Festival of Theatre of the Oppressed. In 1994, six months after graduating from theatre school, I started facilitating Theatre of the Oppressed workshops around Greater Vancouver with a local company, Headlines Theatre. With their support and backing I formed the Latino Theatre Group, made up of anyone from the Latino community who wanted to join, as Theatre of the Oppressed was not for actors but for non-actor community members. The group, meant to be a two-month workshop, endured for eight years. We created and presented twenty-five short plays on issues of concern to the participants, who were almost all political refugees, some of them survivors of torture, others whose parents had disappeared, some who were members of infamous street gangs, and still others who had arrived in Canada on foot from Central America. Our plays were presented on the street, at community centres, at festivals, on the radio, on local TV, at solidarity fundraisers, even in my home to private audiences. Two full-length plays were created. They received runs at the Firehall Arts Centre, a Downtown Eastside theatre, part of whose mission statement is to produce work that reflects the cultural pluralism of Canada.

—

Although I was learning a great deal about directing non-actors, coaching, and writing through the Latino Theatre Group and the other workshops I facilitated, I still wanted to act in the professional theatre world, no matter the discouraging comments from my mentors. So, in 1995, a few months after the *In a Land Called I Don't Remember* production, I wrote a one-woman show entitled *Chile Con Carne*. It was dramaturged and directed by Governor General's Award–winning Argentinian-Canadian theatre artist Guillermo Verdecchia, whom I latched on to like a lobster once we met. He was, along with Lucho, the only other professional Latino theatre artist in town.

Chile Con Carne was a dark comedy about the trials and tribulations of an eight-year-old Chilean refugee in Canada in the seventies. The seed for the play had been planted in my first term at theatre school, when I had told the story of the coup on the Performance Lab stage and learned that it had been too personal. I now understood why: the telling of it had been

about catharsis. I had been working through trauma onstage. Now I knew that simply recounting a story as part of a healing process was not art, but therapy. Transforming a personal story into universal experience involved a long, gruelling process where one looked for themes, ideas, and form. Once those were found, one chose the content to support them, so that one was not in dialogue with one's own private pain onstage, but rather presenting a piece of art. That kind of distance from the story could only happen after healing.

Chile Con Carne was a hit and has been produced many times in cities across Canada, as well as Venezuela and Chile in translation, over the years. I was able to bring all the acting skills learned in school and take a risk. I was grounded, embodied, and whole onstage, while holding the audience's attention for eighty non-stop minutes. My next acting challenge would be to do the same thing while interpreting someone else's text, hopefully in a non-stereotypical role. In Vancouver, casts were typically all white, and the roles open to actors of colour were often racist.

All my years of training—including my acting classes since the age of eight—had finally paid off. I was learning to trust myself and my art, and it had brought so much joy to the audience that I was rendered speechless every night. After the show, immigrant Canadians from every corner of the globe waited to tell me in broken voices how much they identified with the character and her story. It was one of the rare times that a refugee story had been told on a professional Vancouver stage in the English language. It was an honour to be a pioneer of sorts. And it was shameful that in a city housing thousands of refugees, its theatre artists had not figured out a way to tell the story more often.

~

"You have two choices," he said. "Either you make love to me or I kill you."

"First of all, it's not making love, it's rape. Second of all, if you're asking me to choose between rape and death, I choose death," I answered.

"It's not rape. You were hooking. I fell into your trap. Only a hooker would wear a skirt like that and be sneaking a cigarette in the woods."

I was silent. Macarena lay face down, hands behind her head, dirt in her mouth and nostrils. He had pulled me away from her, after getting each of us to whisper our name, last name, phone number, and address in his ear ("If either of you changes a detail, I'll kill you"). He would always know where to find us now, where to look for our family. They'd be murdered at his hand if we ever told anyone about this afternoon, he warned. Now he was brokering the deal with me, away from her ears.

"You're sure you want to die?"

"I'm positive."

"Okay. Here's the thing. I only have one bullet left. So here's what's gonna happen. I'll chop up your cousin into pieces, starting at her feet, moving my way up. I have an axe to do that. Then I'll put the pieces in a plastic garbage bag and bury her in the forest. This will happen in front of you. Then I'll shoot you. Actually, maybe I'll chop you up too. Save the bullet for someone in your family. Maybe your mother. I have your address now, so I can find her."

"My mother's in Bolivia."

"Well, your father then. It's all the same to me."

I thought of Papi, locked in his bedroom right now, working on his doctoral thesis in a language he'd only learned a few years ago.

The gun was held to my temple during the negotiations, while I lay face down, fingers interlocked at the base of my skull, his breath hot and sour against my cheek.

"So. What's your answer?"

"Just kill us. Really. Just kill us."

He grabbed me by the shirt, dragged me back to Macarena, and dropped me face-down next to her. A sigh of relief broke her silence. I was back.

~

In the early spring of 1985, when I was seventeen, I got a phone call. After four years, Macarena and I were being contacted by the Royal Canadian Mounted Police, requesting our presence at a Burnaby police station. Macarena, the shortest sixteen-year-old girl I knew, barely made it on that Sunday at noon, stumbling out of her friend's car after a night of carousing. No one else in the world knew exactly what we'd been through, only she and I, and so we took care of each other. I went to parties with her and made sure she made it out unscathed, and she never judged my unwavering commitment to being a teetotaller, honour roll student, and imminent MIR militant, preparing for my return to South America so that I could join the underground there. Unable to reach her the night before, I had prayed she'd got the message about the police station.

She arrived with her two best friends, blue-collar white girls from Canadian Communist Party families, regular fixtures at pro-choice and anti-nuke rallies who loved revelry as much as she did. Mami, my four-year-old brother Lalito (the son my mother had with Bob), and my husband-to-be Alejandro accompanied me. He had come to Canada to wait out my final high school year so we could go back south and join the MIR together. I'd met him when I was sixteen and living in Bariloche, Argentina. The MIR had transferred my mother and Bob there from Bolivia to run a safe house and do border runs into Chile through Patagonia. After five years of underground work, the whole family had come back to Canada in 1984, and my mother and Bob had separated shortly thereafter. We'd come close to falling into the hands of the enemy, but that was not deterring me from going back and joining the movement myself.

"You okay?" I whispered in Macarena's ear after everyone had greeted each other in the parking lot.

She nodded, black eyeliner smudged around her bloodshot eyes. We walked through the police station doors, not knowing what to expect. Inside were about fifty women and girls, sitting and standing in the waiting area, some with parents, others with husbands and babes in arms. I noticed they were all white. A police officer informed us that we were to wait our turn to look at a lineup.

"A lineup?" I asked.

"Yes, you will be asked to identify the Paper Bag Rapist."

Macarena and I stared at each other.

"You mean you caught him?"

"I'm not at liberty to say."

It had been four years since the rape, and although I had never seen him, he lived in me. His voice, his smell, the taste of his saliva, the texture of his skin were imprinted in me, the way one's first love might be, only that in this case they caused a repulsion so visceral that nausea came up when I conjured his memory with my senses. And yet there was no denying that there was an intimacy to rape, that to be attacked with someone else's naked body, their sex a weapon, was intimate. To have the opening at your centre split open, to lie in a pool of your vaginal blood, to sweat, to shed tears, to beg the stranger who holds your life in his hands to spare you, to spare your family, to spare your cousin lying next to you, weeping almost inaudibly, while he shoots his semen into your core, was unquestionably intimate.

There was also a beauty in transcending the horror by inhabiting every moment of what I thought was my last afternoon on earth. It was as if I heard birds chirping for the first time on that warm, sunny spring day. The moss against my cheek, the pine needles beneath my calves, the rays of sunshine penetrating through the cedar trees and landing on my skin were wondrous discoveries. There had been enough time to say goodbye to life, to all my loved ones, to the beloved planet Earth, because the attack lasted three hours. I had no idea that having machine guns pointed at me at the age of five would in some ways pale in comparison with the up-close-and-personal, full-frontal assault of a rape, with having the coldest human I'd ever come across put a pistol to my temple with a steady hand and whisper, "Don't move, or I'll shoot," in a mechanical voice. Passion had driven the machine gun–wielding, following-orders soldiers, political purpose behind their actions. Being in the hands of an emotionless man who attacked for no apparent reason was somehow far more chilling. Political violence was a concept that I got; senseless violence left me with nothing to excuse him with.

When he'd entered me with the force of a knife plunging into warm flesh, my spirit had shot like a laser out of my body through the crown of my head, landing near the top of a cedar tree. Caught in the branches, it had looked down at the white back of a grown man moving rhythmically over a brown girl, her face covered with her white cotton blouse, another brown girl lying amongst the ferns, face buried in the earth, hair covered in moss and twigs, fingers locked behind her head, body shaking like the tremors in Chile. A robin had perched next to my spirit hanging from those branches, a sheet blowing in the breeze. Its song sent my spirit soaring into the blue sky, where a bald eagle coasted on the wind. My spirit, white shroud, had landed on the back of that eagle, and had gone for the ride of its life, the white houses of the courts below, the brick-coloured diagonal roofs of the dwellings a Lego set, the Pacific Ocean licking the land, the snow-capped mountains, the Lions Gate Bridge a hologram of the Golden Gate, the canopy of the trees protecting the rapist and his victims, imperceptible now from this great height, the domain of absolute silence. I'd wanted to stay there forever, but I knew I had to go back. I had to return for Macarena, for my family who would die of grief and guilt if I didn't enter my body again.

The eagle flew higher and higher in a large circle and I hung on to its neck with all my might. Far away, I could hear moaning. It wasn't sexual, it was the kind of moaning one hears when someone is in agony. A dull, low scream through clenched teeth. In the infinite distance I could feel a pain so brutal, it was impossible to stay present for it. Did he have a knife? Was that what he was using? It hurt like a blade reaching up between my legs, tearing through my axis, hacking at my insides, splitting me in two. It was so far away now, that torment, but I could still feel it, across the realms that I had crossed to escape it, I could still hear the moaning, in spite of the silent kingdom that I was now queen of, flying with that eagle, my arms spread out over his wings now, trying to ignore the murmur in my ear that kept telling me to moan sexily, that it was embarrassing to mewl like a calf being slaughtered. What would he think, this man with the gun? I tried to blot out that voice by yelling, "Woo-hoo!" into the imperturbable sky, the eagle diving now while I tried to hang on to its feathers, but losing my grip, slipping from its back and clinging to the tip of one of its wings, the knife a pestle now, my pelvic basin the mortar where my womb was being ground up, shredded, no mysterious corner or virtuous crevice left untouched.

The eagle changed directions as it dove, and I hung on with my teeth now, my jaw clamping down with all its might, the wind filling my spirit, a sail on the open ocean. "You wanna go for another spin?" the eagle asked me. And I tried to answer yes, yes, let's go for a spin again, but I couldn't because my teeth and jaw needed to clamp on to the tip of its wing. It spread its wings farther, and I fell.

No longer soaring, my spirit plummeted back to terra firma, a bird shot by a hunter, back through the canopy of the rain-forest trees, landing with a resounding crash in my split-open, hollowed-out carcass of a limp body. I jumped a foot off the ground and my mouth emitted a shout, like one sometimes does when about to fall into a deep sleep. But where was he? Where? Impossible to know if he was lying next to me now, or standing, or tearing through the woods, clothes back on, gun in his jacket, leaving us behind. There was a ringing so loud I feared my eardrums would explode, and then, two feet away, Macarena's weeping.

Every seat, wall, and inch of the floor was taken, the women and girls with their supporters talking in hushed tones or staring into space. We stayed by the door, discussing this third chapter of the thread of our lives entitled *Rape*. The first had been the rape itself, the second the aftermath, his being caught the third. The key question was, how could we identify him if we'd never seen him? Throughout the three-hour ordeal, Macarena and I had either faced forward while he held the gun to the back of my head or lain face down while he held the gun to our lower backs, or I had had my head covered with my own shirt during the rape itself.

In the weeks after the rape, we had spent countless hours with two undercover detectives. They had taken us to a hypnotist to see if we could get a description. The sessions revealed that I had caught a glimpse of the rapist's face while I tied the shirt around my head, the look lasting only a millisecond. The image was stored in my subconscious mind, they explained. Once I'd been able to provide my hypnosis-induced description, the detectives had taken us to soccer games to see if we might see someone there who looked like the rapist, had us pore over twenty-five hundred mug shots at the police station and retrace step-by-possible-step in the forest, and had gone back to different parts of our account in order to look for a new angle every time—anything that might lead to the Paper Bag Rapist, who at that time continued to terrorize the city, always attacking groups of two or three, always getting the victims to cover their heads with a piece of their own clothing or a paper bag. During the hypnosis, a clear picture of his hand and then his face had surfaced, a silent ship materializing through the fog. The hypnotist, the best in the business, had swung a crystal back and forth in his Gastown loft while I sat on a leather chair, feet resting on a tiger skin, trying to divert my eyes from a life-sized black-and-white picture that hung behind him. In it, he was naked on a Santorini beach, a lotus flower held up to his privates.

In my suppressed memory, the rapist's hand was white, freckled, and covered with reddish hair. The face was white, the hair brownish red, and there was a moustache. He was in his thirties, about six feet tall, and had a medium build. He looked like half the white men in Vancouver.

I stood at a window and looked at the lineup. We had waited for two hours, watching the women and girls emerge, the colour drained from their faces, whispering to their parents, husbands, and children in shaky voices. We'd been the lone group left sitting in the emptied-out waiting room, the only evidence of the victims' presence their fingerprints on the seats and vending machines. The very last to go in, I now faced twelve men, each with a number pinned to his chest. They wore the exact same attire: jeans, a white T-shirt, and bare feet. They were medium-built, six-feet-tall white men in their thirties with light-brown hair and moustaches. It was a hopeless situation. Holding the pencil to the sheet of paper I'd been given, I was at a total loss.

Each man, starting with Number One, walked up to the mirrored window he could not see through, stood about three feet away, and stared right at me. A male voice barked out orders in a drill-sergeant timbre. At each order, the man would turn to the left, then to the right, and then present his back to me. I studied each face, each body, each set of eyes with as much objectivity as I could muster, trying to decipher any hint of a clue.

I had thrown in the towel when Number Twelve arrived at the window. Up until then I had been grounded, present, focused with every filament of my being on the task at hand. One could even say I was relaxed. Number Twelve changed all that. From the second he reached me, goosebumps erupted on my skin, the hairs on the back of my neck stood on end, my knees shook, and my stomach got queasy. Grinding his jaw, his palms formed fists, then opened, formed fists, then opened. My heart galloped at top speed, cold sweat covered my body. I wrote 12 on my piece of paper. I wanted to smell him, though. Sick as that would make me, if I could smell him, I would be one hundred percent sure. I wondered why they didn't make them talk, for surely if he spoke, I would recognize his voice.

He walked away and joined the lineup again. I handed my sheet to the cop outside and joined Macarena, chain-smoking with the others in the waiting room.

"Give me one of those," I said, demanding a cigarette.

After lighting up my du Maurier, I asked, "What number did you write down?"

"Ten."

"Oh." I exhaled, my stomach sinking. "I wrote down twelve."

"I wrote down the one with the hands that kept making fists."

"That's the one I wrote down. How did you know it was him?"

"Gut instinct."

She exhaled through her nostrils, a tremor in her hand.

Years later I'd learn that between each victim they would change the numbers on the men's chests.

On the way back home that day, a small smile graced my lips. They'd got him. They had finally got him. I didn't wish him dead. I wished him cured. I didn't know then that he would be diagnosed as a psychopath, a condition for which there is apparently no cure.

A month later, Mami appeared at my school and pulled me out of my grade twelve class. Holding the *Province* newspaper, she took me to a nearby café and unrolled it. On the front page was a photograph of Number Twelve. Below it, a list of victims. Not by name, by location and date. Our attack was there: University Endowment Lands, April 26, 1981.

On that day in 1985, the *Province* newspaper proclaimed that the Paper Bag Rapist had been caught. His name figured prominently on the front page: John Horace Oughton. My mother and I sat in stunned silence. I could breathe easy now. For the four years he'd been at large, I'd walked around Vancouver wondering if he was watching me, sat on buses asking myself if the man next to me was him, made my way home with my heart in my mouth when I'd heard sirens in the neighbourhood, distressed that my family might be dead at his hands, for I had defied his orders and told about the rape. Macarena and I had told in the immediate aftermath.

One morning in May 1995, my mother phoned me. I was at my computer writing on deadline for *Chile Con Carne*, set to receive its world premiere that fall.

"Go get the *Vancouver Sun*," she instructed.

When I did, I saw on its front page a story regarding John Horace Oughton. One of his victims was calling on fellow survivors to join her at his upcoming parole hearing. In the extensive interview, she explained that she'd been going to all his hearings, which happened every two years, as mandated by Canadian law. She had always wondered why she was the only victim there, and had come to realize that most victims didn't know he was eligible for parole, or that we were allowed to attend his hearings. I decided on the spot that I would go.

In the fourteen years since I'd been raped, I had only seen him through the window at the lineup, though a part of me still wondered if it was really him. During the trial in 1986, there had only been enough evidence for eighteen victims to bring their cases forward. They were the ones who had seen him during the attack and could thus point him out from the witness stand. In the end, he had been convicted on fourteen counts of rape and assault. Bob, still very close to me, had collected all the newspaper clippings covering the sensational case and mailed them to me in Neuquén, when I was still with Alejandro and working for the underground.

Sent in a large manila envelope, a note accompanied the cut-outs:

"Carmencita, I don't know if you're interested in looking at these. You may just want to burn them. But here they are if you want to read. I love you."

I had devoured all the articles, featuring titillating headlines such as PAPER BAG RAPIST ADMITS HE RAPED 180 CHILDREN, alongside a mug shot of John Horace Oughton, and THE CHAMELEON: THREE FACES OF J.H.O.; HOW THE PAPER BAG RAPIST CHANGED HIS APPEARANCE, with a sketch of him. He'd begun using a paper bag or a piece of the victim's clothing as a blindfold once he'd refined his procedure to make sure his face was never seen, and before he used a gun, he'd lured his victims with a story about a lost puppy. At the beginning of his eight-year reign of terror, in the late 1970s, he'd dressed as a police officer or letter carrier, and had dyed his hair on a regular basis, changing his facial hair as well. I read that two of the victims at the trial were boys. I pored over the stories at my kitchen table, going numb, shaking my head at the irony of ironies: My mother and Bob had sent Ale and me back to Canada in 1980 in order to keep us safe from the perils of life in the underground in Bolivia. Within nine months of our return, I'd been raped.

"Okay, so here's what's gonna happen. I just had a really interesting chat with your cousin Carmen here. And she told me she wants to see you die. She wants to see me chop you up into pieces with an axe and bury you in the forest here where your parents will never find you. Okay, so I'm gonna be honest with you. Your cousin brought you here on purpose. She's a hooker, you know. Bet ya didn't know that, Macarena. Well, she is. She's a hooker, and she made a date with me here in the woods. That's why she brought you here, that's why she was smoking with you. This is all on purpose. And she did it 'cause she wants to see you die. She just told me that, whispered it in my ear. She whispered, 'Kill my cousin. In fact, chop her up.' And then she laughed."

Macarena's huge brown eyes darted towards me. I met her gaze with mine and saw terror in hers. Terror and that look of falling into a void when you think you've been betrayed, when the rug has been pulled out from under your feet. She believed him. He'd been psychologically torturing us for hours and he'd broken her, this twelve-year-old girl who looked nine. The crux was here, and it had broken the back of her sanity. He'd spent the afternoon wondering out loud what he was going to do to us, and had several times decided to abandon us, walking away, twigs cracking under his feet. When he'd done that, we'd waited for eternal moments before starting to get up. Then he'd pushed us down onto the forest floor again, placed the gun to the backs of our heads, and asked:

"Whatchu doin'? Tryin' to run away from me? Why? Dontchu like me? I don't like ingrates. I don't like brats. I don't like being left, you fuckin' little cunts."

Now I knew the end was near.

"So. Your cousin's such a fuckin' little liar that now she doesn't want to make love to me, even though that's what I'm paying her for. 'Cause she's a hooker and she gets paid for what she does. Dontchu, Carmen? I'm paying her good money, and now the slutty little brat's changed her mind. She'd rather see you die than hold up her end of the bargain. But here's what we're gonna do. I'm a good, understanding guy. So I'm gonna give her one more chance. I'm gonna give her ten more seconds to decide. I'm gonna count to ten and when I reach ten, it'll be her last chance. Either she makes love to me or I chop you up into pieces."

It wasn't the first time I'd been sexually assaulted. The first time had been on a bus sixteen months earlier, when I was twelve years old and eleven-year-old Ale was sleeping in the seat next to mine. Ale and I had arrived in Chile from Bolivia via rail, accompanying Trinidad, an MIR member who was on the central committee and on the most-wanted list in Chile. She'd crossed the border with us under an assumed identity, put us on a bus that would take us from Arica, the northernmost city, to Santiago, and waved her hand from the curb as the bus pulled out of the station and started the journey through the Atacama Desert and on to the capital, twenty-four hours away. The three drivers had been given strict orders to keep their eyes on us and to hand us over intact to my abuelita Carmen, waiting at the Santiago station. It was our first time back in Chile.

In the middle of the night, I'd been woken up by one of the drivers. He was bald and in his forties. One hand between my legs, the other on my budding new breast, he'd forced his tongue into my mouth. Petrified, I'd swallowed the vomit that came up and sat still as a statue as his fingers and tongue probed, my heart pounding out of control, his hands hurting me with their force until he stopped, begged for forgiveness, and retreated. I'd sat like a stone for the rest of the night, my sister's deep breathing soothing me, my heart a withered prune, holding my breath as I kept my eye on the Southern Cone constellations, shining diamonds in the pitch-black sky, chest caved in, crotch and breast sore, the Southern Cross framed by the window pointing to my destiny, the city of my birth, the final destination, the return to the homeland that lived in every cell of my body, now marred by the stink of the bald man, the sour taste of his slug-like tongue in my mouth.

The next day, he ignored me completely, avoiding any possible eye contact, and the other two drivers sat for breakfast with us, patted our heads, and offered us toothpicks and sticks of gum. Again, the irony was that Mami's precious girls hadn't fallen into the hands of the military that guarded the border or the secret police that pulled buses over in the middle of the night, but rather into the grip of a pedophile.

I never told anyone about that assault, for I was convinced it was all my fault and did not wish to get into trouble. I also knew that it would break my abuelita's heart. That twelfth year, 1979, I was learning a great deal about the adult world, where things were rarely what they seemed, where one plus one did not equal two, and where one needed to stay alert to find the hidden meaning behind words, offers, and behaviours. In La Paz, Bolivia, Ale and I had been given free admission to the Sunday matinees at the Miraflores cinema. The invitation had come from the ticket tearer, and I had quickly learned that in exchange for the complimentary tickets he wanted to grope me. He was in his twenties, I was twelve. When we arrived for *Every Which Way But Loose*, our first matinee, he placed his hand on my butt, squeezed, and pressed his erect penis against my thigh while Ale fetched the two "free" Fantas from the concession stand and salivated at the caramelized peanuts wrapped in Cellophane. We never returned.

Unbeknownst to Ale, who labelled me a spoilsport, my mother, and Bob, it was because I was terrified of the ticket tearer in his tight jeans and mod boots, feathered black bangs falling into his eyes. I knew it was my fault, for failing to decipher the illicit meaning in the offer, for not understanding it was to be paid for with sex. The whole incident had left me with an upset stomach and a humongous knot in my throat, so tight it was painful to swallow, my sunken solar plexus a quivering, freshly hatched bird, surrounded by broken eggshell, wet and cold in the air of the ruthless planet Earth.

Now here I sat at my kitchen table in Vancouver in 1995, at the age of twenty-seven, reading a newspaper with the words *Paper Bag Rapist* in the headline for the umpteenth time in my life. As far as my experience with pedophiles went, he took the cake. And now I would be able to see him. The parole hearing was at Mountain Institution, a medium-security jail in Agassiz, a small town in British Columbia's Fraser Valley.

I got up at the crack of dawn and drove the ninety minutes in silence, watching the sun come up over the mountain in front of me, golden raptors gliding over the fields. The jail, with its tower and guards, lodged in a narrow crevice of the lush valley, emerald on this late spring morning, came into view. When I pulled into the parking lot, there were news vans and reporters standing around, and groups of people waiting at the front doors. A lone bald eagle circled above. It was no surprise that he watched over me on this day, the day I would be in the same room as the man who'd invaded my most intimate spaces more than half a lifetime ago, and still inhabited them.

NINE

The Native reserve was so isolated that in the winter the sole way in or out was by train. When summer rolled around, only those with halfway decent four-by-fours dared tackle the gravelly road that clung to the sides of this stretch of British Columbia's Coast Mountains. Said highway could either send you rolling down into the raging river below or deliver you in one piece onto the pavement that would lead you to the nearest town. Provisions could be bought there, as well as bumper stickers proclaiming *I Survived the _____ Crossing*. On the rez, deer, the staple diet, were hunted and frozen for winter meals, and the houses were nestled deep in the woods, connected by dirt lanes in such sorry states that it was the norm to spend half your day fixing flat tires.

It was July 1996, a year after I attended Oughton's parole hearing, and I was to spend a week facilitating a Theatre of the Oppressed workshop for the community's youth. My contract stated that five days later, three short plays based on the issues the workshop participants faced were to be presented at the rez hall for the five-hundred-strong community, including the chief and her family.

The train paused in front of the band office at midday, just long enough for me to step off before it continued snaking its way along the shores of the turquoise glacial lake the rez sat on. Hossein, the social worker, an Iranian exile who as a teenager had fought the Shah in the 1978 revolution, whisked me away in the band van to my cabin, hidden in the woods about a ten-minute walk from the road.

"I managed to wangle six kids. All boys. All fourteen years old. None of the girls went for it. One of them thinks I'm a creep because I made the Iranian mistake of trying to hug her once when she was crying. She's the ringleader, so they're boy-cotting anything I organize," he explained.

"Oh. Shit. What convinced the boys to come?"

"The dance party after the performance. With the MuchMusic van driving through from Edmonton with the DJ and music videos. Free pop and junk food, too. If they don't come to the workshop and put on the plays, party's cancelled. The girls will kill them. The boys don't want that, considering some of them are already engaged to be married to the girls."

"So aside from saving their future marriages, they're coming to the workshop because of the MuchMusic van?"

"Yup. It's their only connection to the outside world. And they're coming for the snacks, of course."

"Okay."

I sighed and mentally steeled myself for the gruelling week he had just prepared me for. Working with teenagers was often akin to pulling teeth, and this was going to be no different.

That afternoon we did the rounds, picking up the boys from their modest homes. Bleeding, glassy-eyed deer carcasses hung from the trees, rusted-out vehicles and appliances, some decades old, lay abandoned in the yards, and naked toddlers covered in snot and dirt chased after dogs. A couple of forgotten nineteenth-century wooden chapels stood amongst the tall grass of the valleys, and families of bears rummaged through the garbage dump. It was my first time on a rez, although I'd driven by the ones in Vancouver, wealthy and developed in comparison with this rural one.

Once the boys were loaded into the van, Hossein dropped us all off at the gym, the lone structure on a mountaintop. He pulled out a cooler with juice boxes, sandwiches, and fruit for dinner break, and drove away. Standing in a circle in the wake of the vehicle's dust, the boys nailed me with their black eyes, their faces neutral masks framed by their hoodies. The hairs on the back of my neck rose. I was alone with a group of absolute strangers, six teenaged boys covered in scars, in the middle of nowhere, on the summit of a hill that would swallow the sun by the time the session was over, prey to their predatory eyes. I took a deep breath, levelled their collective stare with my own steady gaze, and said:

"It's time to start."

I broke the circle and strode towards the door, key chain shaking in my hand.

"Someone bring the cooler."

They followed my orders and walked inside.

I spent the entire afternoon and evening trying to get them to open their mouths. Keeping my panic under wraps, I grasped at straws. If I couldn't even get them to make a single utterance, much less stand up after opening circle, in which the only one who had spoken was me, how was I ever going to lure them onto the stage to tell their stories?

After I explained that we were going to create short plays based on moments of oppression in their own lives, they remained steadfastly mum and stone-faced, refusing to play any of the drama games designed to break the ice. At 9 p.m., after five hours of muteness—they'd had their dinner in total silence, without breaking the circle—I managed to coax them onto their feet by modelling an exercise wherein a person took on the role of an oppressor or oppressed person. I demonstrated an inner monologue, voicing my character's secret thoughts and feelings through phrases that expressed fear, pain, shame, and anger. When I was done, I asked,

"Is that clear?"

They just stood there, with their concave chests, fists rammed deep into their pockets, staring at me with blank faces.

Just as I was about to speak again, one of them broke the silence and observed:

"Boy. I never heard nobody talk so much. You talked a lot, eh?"

His mouth broke into a wee smile and his eyes danced with mischief. Repressing the impulse to hug him with all my might, I said,

"Yes, I suppose that was a lot of talking, but that's what the inner monologue is about, it's—"

"Where you from?" he interrupted.

The others cocked their heads. Was the silence-breaker the leader of the pack? When we'd picked him up, Hossein had told me his name was Callum. I'd watched him walk towards our idling van, black baseball cap pulled low under his hoodie-covered head, a pack of dogs barking playfully around him.

"Vancouver," I answered.

"No. Where you really from?" Callum demanded.

"Chile."

"Where's that?"

"South America."

"Where's that?"

Undoubtedly he was pulling my leg.

"South of here. Past the States, past Mexico, past Central America. Way down south."

"You act like an urban Indian." He scowled.

"Oh. Well, one could argue that I'm Metis, what with the Indigenous blood in my family. You know, most Chileans are a mix of Spanish with Mapuche, and my great-grandmother was Diaguita for sure—"

"What kind of a name is Carmen?"

"It's Spanish. It's from Spain. Apparently it means 'house.' But who knows if that's accurate. Although in Granada there are houses called Carmens that—"

"You talk too much."

"Oh. Okay. I'll stop now."

The ice was broken, so I pushed my luck and introduced the exercise designed to pull the stories out of them, presenting a tableau of a moment of oppression in my own life. I always shared a banal, generic sketch that reeked of generalizations. In other words, it lacked truth. Usually I sat on the ground, head dropped, while I shaped other members of the workshop into oppressors pointing their fingers at me, evil grins on their diabolical faces. A grotesque, one-dimensional illustration of bullying that had never really happened to me. I did this because I knew that the facilitator could not engage emotionally with the group, that emotional involvement voided the entire process, as no one would be present to hold the space and keep the room safe.

I had only ever taken the risk of revealing a real moment of oppression in my life—the rape—when I had co-facilitated a workshop at the women's jail in Burnaby. And by doing so, I had let the double doors of possibility swing open so wide that the harrowing and disturbing images the prisoners subsequently created were like a hurricane blasting through rooms that had been padlocked for decades. Each impression was so honest, so rich and vulnerable, that the risk I had taken had proven to be worthwhile. I had exposed myself yet still managed to keep the facilitator–participant boundary intact. And when I opened myself to those women, they in turn had dropped their guard, their images so real and complex that the plays presented at the end were some of the best I'd facilitated.

Since then, I had returned to the generic bullying cartoon, out of simple fear. I hadn't felt safe enough while facilitating other groups, which included male offenders at halfway homes and reform schools, to display the rape vignette. This made me a hypocrite. Who was I to ask them to unveil their most vulnerable moments if I wasn't able to do the same with them? Whether they knew this consciously or not, I was positive it was something they could sense. And so I took the risk with Callum and the rest of the boys, and I constructed a detailed, no-holds-barred depiction of the rape. Unbeknownst to them, the act of hiking through their woods twice in one day to get to and from the road was the first time I'd walked alone through dense foliage since the attack, fifteen years earlier.

I wasn't afraid of rapists in that remote area, and yet the symbol of trekking solo under the canopy of the temperate rainforest was a powerful one for me, the strength of that picture propelling me in the construction of my piece. One of the boys, playing Macarena, lay face down on the gym floor, fingers woven behind his head, while another was a jogger on the trail nearby. Callum, standing on a chair, spread his arms, the bald eagle flying above, and the final boy was shaped into a pose that echoed the downward-facing dog. I placed myself underneath this boy, eye on the eagle, my face and body a lifeless Raggedy Ann doll. From that position, I instructed everyone to breathe, those who were in the image as well as the two who were witnessing, our collective lungs filling with breath and exhaling over and over again, the act of wilful breathing an exercise in and of itself.

The floodgates opened when each boy galvanized my still life with his inner monologue, spoken out loud, and flew off their hinges when we left my rendition behind and they constructed their own, each placing himself as the central oppressed person in the impression he offered. By the end of the week, we had three dramas based on the many scenes explored during those five days.

Drummers from Kamloops opened the event. After their welcome song, the plays were presented. The boys embodied versions of themselves, their parents, sisters, brothers, grandparents, uncles, and cousins. In the opening number, Callum, playing a raging father, delivered the following speech while his young son cowered in the corner:

"I went to residential school. I was raped, I was beaten, I was starved. I had dust thrown in my eyes."

The residential boarding school system was designed by the federal government to "beat the Indian out of the child." The goal was assimilation, because an Indian who identified with the white man would not fight for his or her land. The schools, run by the Christian churches, which were offered five dollars per head for every Indian they converted to Christianity when the system first began in the 1870s, operated for over a hundred years. The last one had shut down only one month before this play was performed. Attendance at the schools was compulsory, and over 150,000 Indian, Inuit, and Métis children were sent to them, some forcibly removed from their homes by the Royal Canadian Mounted Police. Once there, beatings, sexual abuse, neglect, medical experiments, malnutrition, disease, and even death were not out of the ordinary.

In the second play, Keith, master of the smoky eye, red lipstick, and green-and-blue-hued hair, played a boy being sexually abused by a group of male relatives during a house party. In the third, half the boys played a group of parents off on a bender, while the remaining three were small children left behind to fend for themselves for days on end, in the dead of winter, with no food or heat.

A loaded hush came over the audience once the plays were shown, the kind of alert quiet that befalls one when face to face with an unpredictable wild animal. After a few moments, I broke the charged silence by asking the audience, some of whom had come from neighbouring reserves, others white people from the nearby town, if they recognized the stories the six boys had told. They nodded. For the next two hours, the audience took turns going on the stage, taking the place of the person they believed was being oppressed, and trying different things so that the outcome wouldn't lead to violence, abuse, and neglect. When one of the elders took the stage, I noticed she had scars around her lips. She told that her mouth had been sewn shut at the age of five for speaking her language at residential school.

Hossein, ecstatic with the evening's success, was too busy with social work to take me to the train the following day. So Aunt Tiny, who probably weighed three hundred pounds, picked me up in a 1970s wood-panelled burgundy station wagon. All the seats were missing, except for hers. Callum, Keith, and the other boys sat on wooden crates or leaned against the station wagon's walls. They had come to see me off. A couple of runny-nosed two-year-olds rolled around the floor (so rusty that if one looked down, one could see, through its holes, the dirt road passing by), their tangled black hair halos around their brown moon faces.

I took a seat on a crate next to Callum, who was propped up against one of the walls. Aunt Tiny gunned it, and I lived in terror that one of the toddlers would smash their head. But the little ones squealed with glee, and Callum, the most nonchalant person I'd ever met, asked in his admirable deadpan,

"Got a gun?"

"No. Why would I need one?"

"Cougars. Bears."

I deduced this was in reference to my twice-daily hikes through the bush.

"You mean to say that you've been letting me walk that trail for a week completely unprotected?"

"Urban Indian," he muttered with his poker face, shaking his head, palms flat on the floor, pushing his weight back into the wall of the car as Aunt Tiny took a dangerous corner. My crate was of no use, so I abandoned it and followed his lead. Earlier in the week, when being driven to the workshop, Callum had looked out the window at the green mountain range and told me that centuries earlier their nation had been ten thousand strong. Disease had wiped out most of them. Now there were only five hundred, and everyone was everyone else's cousin, aunt, or uncle.

Keith, leaning right next to me, studied his black-painted nails and sang along to the tape blasting from the speakers, "Waterfalls" by TLC. He wore his usual uniform of black nylon tracksuit with two parallel white lines down the sides, and knew every last word to the song.

"I'm gonna make it to Vancouver someday," he promised me now.

"Well, you better look me up when you do," I ordered.

His uncles had taken him to Las Vegas once on the Greyhound bus. And he'd gone to Kamloops and to the town over the next set of mountains, where the bumper stickers were sold. But he knew all about the world thanks to the satellite dishes found all over the rez, where the TV was kept on day and night and the young ones lived for MuchMusic.

"I'm gonna do drag at Celebrities," he continued, referring to the largest gay bar on Davie Street.

"Will you lip-synch to 'Waterfalls'?" I asked.

"Oh, yeah, baby," and he kept on singing, swaying back and forth to the music.

"T-Boz?"

"Left Eye."

"Of course."

We arrived at the spot where the train stopped. The boys stood by the tracks with me, the seven of us in a circle again, their chests full, eyes shining, faces open and smiling.

I would return over the next two years to facilitate workshops with the rest of the youth and the elders, and this would lead to work at other reserves around the province. I would come in the dead of the twenty-five-below winter, at the height of the forty-plus summer, and in every season in between. Always staying at the same cabin, with its windows that looked out onto the frozen lake during the frigid temperatures, the same lake that invited me for daily swims when the Weather Channel deemed this one of the hottest places in the country. On the train, I would be treated to bear and deer crossings, to the ruthless salmon run when the tracks paralleled the river, the blood and guts of the many casualties washing over the rocks, to flocks of eagles circling above in the expansive blue sky.

On this July day, the last day of my first visit to that rez, I hugged the boys when the train arrived, thanked them for their courage, and let the tracks take me back to Vancouver, vowing to share the rape image in every workshop I facilitated from then on.

When I embraced Callum, he confessed, "I don't feel like I'm hiding anything anymore."

Ever since I'd started pursuing my own selfish impulses, now all about theatre creation and the facilitation of storytelling, as opposed to the selflessness of being a teenaged revolutionary, I'd also given free rein to the romantic infatuations that rendered me certifiably insane. Estéban's appearance on that faraway basketball court had set my Antarctic loins on fire and burnt my house-of-cards marriage to the ground. Since his return to Argentina and our subsequent breakup, the flames fanned by our fucking-and-fighting relationship had continued to lick the sky. I was on a roll, and my crushes often had me cursing the gods above with "Go fuck yourselves, Aphrodite, Eros, and Cupid!" There was a married British rock star, an Australian cokehead TV actor two decades my senior, and an endless parade of other unavailable men who ranged from an American acrobat with a girl in every port, to a South African musician who suddenly took a vow of celibacy when he became an evangelical Christian, to a Canadian mime who couldn't consummate our love due to a long-distance girlfriend whose imminent arrival never happened, to an Italian art teacher who still lived with his mother and who I suspected was a straight woman born in a man's body.

In my late twenties, one of these obsessions led to a serious relationship with a Canadian playwright and actor, a man I loved to pieces and who vowed to love me until death did us part. He was an upper-middle-class rugby-playing, British-boarding-school-attending WASP raised in West Vancouver's British Properties, and had displeased his parents when he'd announced he'd be going to acting school instead of following in his judge father's foot steps. When we started dating, he was shocked when his mother expressed dismay at the fact that I was Latina, and this led him down a path of re-thinking his assumptions about race in Canada—namely, that racism didn't exist. Everything came together. There was sustained emotional, sexual, spiritual, and intellectual intimacy. The immense love I felt for him filled me with equal parts joy and fear, because I had never felt so naked in a relationship, so out of control. Putty in his hands, I was terrified he'd abandon me once he saw the ugly girl who hid within me. A girl so vile she'd deserved to be raped, deserved to have guns pointed at her since she was small, a girl unworthy of the love he was offering. Once I surrendered my vulnerability to him, that ugly, wounded, furious girl took over. She was ultra-controlling, insanely jealous, verbally violent, testing him, seeing how far she could go, letting him know that she wasn't worth staying for, praying he'd prove her wrong. She ultimately succeeded in pushing him away. My fear of being left to my own devices after experiencing true intimacy became a self-fulfilling prophecy.

The separation was so excruciating, it was as if the entire front of my body was gone, like I was walking around with all my organs exposed. Friends later told me it was akin to watching me go through a war, while others described it as like witnessing someone try to heal from a near-fatal disease, yet others as a heroin addict going cold turkey. At that time, between 1997 and 1999, I lived with three roommates in a large apartment above a restaurant on Commercial Drive, my East Vancouver neighbourhood. I could be found sobbing at all hours of the day and night in different areas of our abode. When not in the house, I could be spotted blubbering in my car to *The Miseducation of Lauryn Hill*, in cafés and restaurants, walking down the street, strolling through the Musqueam house posts, Haida House and totem poles behind UBC's Museum of Anthropology, the sacred place where I connected to the spirit of my late abuelita Carmen, who passed away in 1993, eagles coasting above. I wept sitting at my computer hammering out the first draft of my play *The Refugee Hotel*, during rehearsals for plays I was working on, in trailers of TV shows I was acting in.

I hadn't cried for hours and hours and hours on a daily basis for months on end since my self-imposed Santa Fe exile a decade earlier, when I'd followed Estéban into a new identity in the hope it would keep me from confronting my loss-of-revolution grief, my traumas, and, ultimately, myself. I'd been running from singleness all my life. This time, though, I was falling apart outside a relationship, no new lover in sight to witness my breakdown, blame, or take it out on. I decided to stop chasing men, stay put, look the void in the eye, and let it rip. One of my roommates had broken her back and she'd lie on the kitchen floor next to me. We'd wail together, her pain physical, mine emotional. We christened our apartment the House of Pain.

The loss of that relationship had taken me on the most terrifying journey yet: confronting my fear of being abandoned, of being alone. If the conscious peeling back of layers had begun in theatre school almost ten years earlier, then that devastating breakup forced me finally to face the self-destructive, petrified young girl who lived inside me, the girl who'd been clamouring for my attention my entire life and whom I was now ready, in my aloneness, to face and embrace. I had always equated solitude with abandonment and various living nightmares that fell under the heading of the Terror, such as being left to fend for myself as a child after my parents were killed in a concentration camp, being murdered by firing squad right after the coup, being dragged away in the middle of the night and thrown into a car by four armed secret policemen, being tortured and made to disappear without a trace when I was in the MIR, being chopped up and buried in the bottom of the forest in a large black plastic garbage bag while my parents spent the rest of their lives looking for me.

I started weekly therapy sessions with a straight, male, middle-class, Buddhist WASP and began confronting the Terror head-on. I had stopped seeing the Birkenstock-wearing lesbian counsellor during my last year at theatre school, after I'd been told I wasn't an actor, but she had paved the way for the rape to now elbow its way front and centre, where it stayed. I'd been turning the kaleidoscope intermittently for years but had yet to focus on its nucleus: the rape itself and the effect it had had on me and my intimate relationships.

Over the next decade, each terror took its turn in the spotlight, and my therapist guided me on my demon-facing journey with the compassion and assurance of a master who'd been counselling survivors of trauma for twenty-five years. I allowed myself to fall apart during those two House of Pain years, and would later refer to that part of my life as my Saturn Return Nervous Breakdown, because the relationship had begun when I was twenty-eight, ended when I was thirty, and had me crying until I was thirty-two.

In the fall of 1999, I got a part on a TV show playing a devout Catholic mother of two East LA gangbangers. All I had to do was fall to my knees a lot in front of my Guadalupe shrine while sporting fake grey in my hair and painted-on wrinkles. When the actor flown in from Los Angeles to play my older son walked into the makeup trailer (at thirty-two, I was only five years older than him) and turned out to be the most beautiful man I'd ever seen, I was hit by the recognizable fever that had frequently consumed me since the age of four. I also recognized him in the literal sense: he was a California Chicano, and thus reminded me of the place just down the coast where I'd first experienced exile.

At the end of our week on the North Vancouver set, we got it on at the Sutton Place Hotel, where LA actors were put up. After two years of celibacy and soul-searching, the stakes were extraordinarily high. The man who'd played my son and been romancing me all week was now making love to me, the first to touch me in those twenty-four months of raw pain. I'd been spit out the other side of the rape-confronting period of my therapy back into the light in a state of such innocence that it was like being reborn, like being a virgin, as though the rape had never happened. I could start over by opening my legs to a lover of my choosing: a North American Latino, the male embodiment of my own dual identity.

Two months after our Vancouver night together, I found myself on an LA-bound flight, going to spend a week with this man whose Chicano-ness had me remembering my first encounter with North America, when I was six years old and spoke no English; and California, the original exile-home, was where I discovered what brown was, what poor was, what Latina was.

He picked me up at the airport and drove like a maniac along the 405 freeway. We passed a mint-condition baby-blue 1970 Chevrolet Malibu, the same colour, make, and model that my family and I had driven to Canada lifetimes before. Its bumper sticker asked,

If not for love, then why?

Inexplicably yelling all the way to West Hollywood about how busy he was and how this was a really bad time (no mention was made of the fact that he'd been the one to invite me), he went to a baptism after dropping me off at his apartment with a promise to return that evening. He was the only person I knew in that vast city. I took a lonesome stroll along Sunset Boulevard, a block away, and was approached by a nineteen-year-old, nine-month-pregnant Romanian fortune teller who pulled me up a flight of spiral stairs, sat me down in front of a crystal ball, and assured me that he was The One. After twenty-four hours of waiting for him to materialize while his roommate loudly masturbated to phone sex lines in the other room, I went back to the airport and boarded a return flight to Vancouver, sobbing into my journal the whole way home. Litanies and laments filled its tear-stained pages, and this entry was no exception:

All the work you've done over the last two years on your core belief that you do not deserve to be loved has been for nothing. You've just thrown it all away. You must keep digging deep, you must keep confronting your fear of being alone, you must stop chasing men who are unavailable, you must stop looking for love in all the wrong places, you must stop working for love, you must stop looking for love outside yourself, you must stop being a fucking addict.

Insight into my self-destructive patterns hadn't meant I was ready to break them. Chasing a man so unavailable that he'd disappeared upon my arrival had proven that.

My best friend, Jamila, a queer first-generation Egyptian-Canadian refugee counsellor and reiki healer, waited for me at the airport and shook her head with fury all the way to her place, where she played her CD of oming Tibetan monks and cursed the ground he walked on.

"That man is so pathetically dark, kinda like a limp dick, that I don't worry too much about all the damage he'll do in the world, you know?" she'd noted while pouring me a cup of Tension Tamer tea.

A few days later, she gave me one of her beetle paintings and ordered me to hang it over my bed, for protection.

That twenty-four-hour passage through Los Angeles had sealed the deal for me. I would never EVER return there, what with its twenty million cars, endless sea of hundred-foot bill-boards, charlatans, and despicable men.

Two months later, in February 2000, I found myself at LAX again, visiting another Chicano actor who was part of a renowned Chicano theatre troupe. I had met him in Seattle, where Jamila and I had gone to see one of their touring plays. We'd waited around after the show, and had all gone for drinks. During his run, he'd come to Vancouver for a visit and had invited me to LA. When I landed at LAX this time, I wasn't met by a mind-blowingly self-centred boy in a man's body, but by a little red carpet leading to the door of a gold 1970s Cadillac, against which Chicano Actor #2 leaned, white wife-beater showing off the Virgin of Guadalupe and *chola* tattoos on his brown arms. Upon seeing me emerge from the automatic airport doors, he yelled out, "You're a fuckin' queen, baby!", a bouquet of red roses in his fist.

We laughed all the way to his downtown loft, Santana's *Supernatural* album blaring from the ghetto blaster resting on the back seat of his vintage vehicle, also reminiscent of my fam-ily's baby-blue Chevrolet Malibu, passing a car with a *Powered by Mexican Huevos* bumper sticker. We stopped at a *botánica* in Echo Park so he could buy a votive candle to burn for his recently deceased uncle. One glimpse of that east-side-of-LA neighbour-hood, with its murals of Mexican screen icons Fernando Soler and María Félix, Aztec serpents, Quinceañeras, and a brown boy holding planet Earth in his hands, streets with names like Alvarado, Quintero, and Laguna, mariachi bands tuning their instruments outside the many Mexican restaurants, avocado, *champurrado*, and ice cream vendors with carts displaying names such as *Delicias de Michoacán*, not to mention its majority population of working-class brown people from Mexico and Central America, and I knew I'd arrived home.

This Chicano theatre artist came from a line of farm workers, and his father had been one of the founders of the United Farm Workers union, alongside César Chávez. A massive United Farm Workers banner hung on one of his edge-of-downtown loft walls, while a mural of La Lupe, Frida Kahlo, and Che Guevara took up another. Visitors from the Chicano arts community, be they rappers, visual artists, or actors, dropped by nightly. Days were spent at diners, burrito stands, Olvera Street, and driving the gold Cadillac down Sunset Boulevard and César Chávez Avenue, all while discussing ideas for plays, taking notes on napkins and the tops of our hands. Evenings took us to the theatre, where Chicano stories were told, he always knew the players involved, and discussions with fellow North American Latino artists took place. On my last day there, the space shuttle took off from a Southern California air base, the earth shaking so hard I was sure disaster had hit in the form of a major quake. As serendipity would have it, the takeoff happened at the moment of climax during a passionate morning embrace.

The trip was orgasmic in the metaphorical sense as well, and I wept with relief. Full circle, my Saturn Return had brought me right back to where I'd started, the state of my first exile-home. I belonged in a city in the United States, the last place on earth I'd expected to find roots. A place where over 50 percent of the population was Latino, a metropolis that was a haven for my dual identity. Although he was emotionally unavailable and juggling a dozen women across the country I would be forever thankful to Chicano Actor #2 for swinging open the doors of LA's east side and its Latino artists to me.

No words could do justice to what I felt when I discovered that just down the coast there was a thriving community of Latino artists creating the kind of content I had been exploring in complete isolation as the sole Latina in the Vancouver professional theatre scene (both Lucho and my Argentinian mentor had moved to Toronto). In Vancouver, the closest I'd come to working with fellow Latino actors in recent times was playing Chicano Actor #1's saintly mother, and pretending to suck off a renowned East LA stand-up comedian in a straight-to-video movie. I had worn red polyester lingerie; he'd been in animal-print Lycra bikini briefs, a fake hard-on made by the props department stuffed inside. My only line as Mexican Hooker #1 had been "Ay, señor," my only blocking that of being on my knees, my face an inch away from his crotch.

The role had been vaguely reminiscent of what I considered to be one of my first paid acting gigs in the mid-nineties, a phone sex operator for an illegal call centre on Vancouver's East Hastings Street. Although it operated out of Canada, the sex line serviced the States, including its military bases around the world. It was a sweatshop: forty booths stuck together under fluorescent lighting in an airless room and a boss who listened in on your calls and fired you if you failed to keep a customer on the line for at least five minutes. I had got the job shortly after graduating from theatre school, as an alternative to waiting on tables.

Questions about the integrity of prostituting my voice quickly turned to outrage when I realized they charged five dollars a minute and we got eight bucks an hour. I worked forty hours a week, sometimes took two calls at a time (there were two phones in each booth), told the callers my name was Miranda del Amor (double Ds, long wavy hair), heard up to 120 men come per day, and suffered from neck and jaw problems. I also worried that my saliva glands would give out as I spent an average of six hours out of the eight-hour shift sucking on a soother. When I wasn't sucking on the soother, I was tickling the inside of my cheek with my index finger while keeping my upper teeth touching my bottom teeth. This sounded like pussy being eaten.

Some of my co-workers had no papers. They were Guatemalans, Mexicans, and Salvadorans, there to speak Spanish to the Latino callers who wanted service in the mother tongue, the men working the phones pretending to be women. There were a few punk rockers, an old lady who crocheted baby blankets, and an ex–football player whose persona was Candy (four foot nine, blond hair down to her bum). He was goal-oriented:

"Hey everyone! Ten minutes says I get this one to stick a frozen wiener up his ass!"

When I got a call, I immediately asked the caller's name, wrote it down on my list, and then said his name over and over again. It was called intimacy. Every booth contained a mirror in which you could see the reflection of your own face eight hours a day. This was to make sure you were always smiling. So you sucked on the soother, whipped the phone, and finger-fucked the inside of your cheek to your own image, which was about a foot away from your face. After twenty-two minutes the call was automatically cut off so you wouldn't develop any real intimacy with the clients.

I learned a great deal about what men really wanted during that stint. More often than not it wasn't sex, but love and intimacy. I had gone in prepared to listen to and follow commands; we had to say yes to absolutely anything the client requested. But instead of the callers issuing horrific, degrading, misogynistic orders, I'd been directed to say "I love you" almost every other time. Sometimes the men and boys, for there were teenaged boys who called as well, wept as the *I love yous* fell out of my mouth, always followed by their name. It was overwhelming, eye-opening, and heartbreaking, and revealed so much to me about the human condition and the state of the North American heart, the North being a place where so many people live in isolation.

Although I had come a long way since the phone-sex operator job of my mid-twenties, writing and acting in my own plays, facilitating Theatre of the Oppressed workshops, running the Latino Theatre Group for eight years, it wasn't until the spring of 2002, post–Saturn Return, that I finally accepted the title of writer. At that time, I was playwright-in-residence at the Vancouver Playhouse, British Columbia's regional theatre, and I'd written or co-written ten plays. All had been professionally produced, three had been nominated for awards, and two had been published, but I still felt that labelling myself a writer was self-congratulatory and putting on airs. The same went for calling myself an actor. I'd always felt uncomfortable with it, as I had so much respect for both those crafts that I'd decided I would only refer to myself as a professional when someone who was a master in the form bestowed that honour on me. It happened during the Banff Playwrights Colony, where I was working on the third draft of *The Refugee Hotel.* An autobiographical piece about the Chileans I'd met at the Refugee Hotel, it featured a main character based on my adored uncle Boris. I'd written the first draft during my House of Pain years, inspired by Pinochet's 1998 arrest in England and as homage to my uncle, who'd drunk himself to death in 1995.

During the Colony, the great playwright Tomson Highway came to one of the readings and paid me the highest compliment from an artist of his calibre:

"Thank you. I learned so much from your writing that it's cured me of my writer's block. Oh, and I do have one note for you. The end of your play is sappy and sentimental. That's all."

I skipped through the cemetery at the bottom of the arts centre as I made my way to town to buy condoms for the looming lay with one of the actors, a sexy nerd who tended to brood. Clapping to myself, I finally admitted what I'd been working towards since my days in theatre school: I really was a storyteller. With that title came a responsibility so great I'd better brace myself for what was to come.

Miranda del Amor, gangbanger's Devout Catholic Mother, numerous maid roles, and Mexican Hooker #1 had helped pay the bills, but now that I'd discovered a robust Latino theatre scene a mere freeway ride away, that June 2002 I drove down the coast to Los Angeles. The plan was to spend the summer there, checking out the lay of the theatre land for a possible move to the City of Angels. Now that I'd decided not only to embrace my calling but to take responsibility for it, the realm of possibilities was endless. Life had taught me that anything could happen and did, and ever since deciding to follow the dream of being an actor, and now a writer, I was committed to going wherever that dream took me. In the summer of 2002, it pointed south.

Stevie Wonder's *Musiquarium* album blasted from my stereo as I drove through Washington, Oregon, and California. A brand new chapter was about to begin, the tears of the House of Pain left behind, along with the exile-country of the far north, the one that had taken me in, educated me, held its doors open time and time again. A country that I loved but which, alas, did not live in my marrow, now a mere image in the rear-view mirror. I drove south for three days along the west coast of the Americas, towards my place on planet Earth, the mountains a spine to my east, the potent Pacific the blood that rushed through the veins and arteries pumped by my ever-expansive heart.

I let the memories of driving north along this very coast in 1974 in a baby-blue Chevrolet Malibu bombard me, tears falling at the recollection of my devastated parents—at the thought of their youth, their courage and terror, their superhuman effort to give my sister and me a good life no matter what the cost. "You Are the Sunshine of My Life" played at full volume as I mourned the loss of my original plan: to return to Chile or Argentina right after theatre school and leave the North behind, forever, for good, a project abandoned because I went wherever my calling took me and it hadn't taken me back there. I confronted, foot flooring the accelerator, eyes on the freeway that stretched into the horizon, the booming voice in my head that still told me I did not deserve to follow a selfish dream, to do something only for myself, to do the opposite of what a revolutionary would do.

My ongoing therapy had taught me that the only barriers that had ever held me back on my artistic journey were psychological.

Nothing was stopping me except myself. I was middle-class, I was privileged, hence I had options. When I was young, I'd opted to join the MIR so that everyone would have access to basic human rights. Now I was choosing to follow my artistic calling, and with that decision came the same ruthlessness of the earlier choice: what are you willing to do, how far are you willing to go, what are you willing to give up for something you believe in this much? And although I struggled with going to the United States, the heart of the empire, to pursue my calling even further, I was actually doing it, and not only that, I was doing it by myself, for myself, with no one to answer to, no one to consider but me.

I drove the 101 freeway through California and remembered the books of John Steinbeck, gasping at the superlative beauty of this place. When I turned off the freeway to check out a sea-side town, I inadvertently joined a pageant. Cholos showed off their art-piece cars. Elaborate paintings of Aztec warriors holding maidens in their arms, adorned skulls, roses and thorns, the words *La Raza* and *Lowrider*, juxtapositions of Emiliano Zapata with Guadalupe, Queen of the Americas, took up the entire hoods of vehicles from every era, bouncing up and down, chrome motors on full display. Unable to find a way out of the car show, I blasted Stevie Wonder's "Do I Do" and waved at the crowds that lined the sidewalks, my Virgin of Copacabana pendant, a gift from my grade seven classmates in Bolivia, swinging from my rear-view mirror, until I saw the freeway entrance and continued south.

Upon my arrival in LA, I went for dinner at La Parrilla, a Mexican restaurant on César Chávez Avenue, in Brooklyn Heights, Eastside Los Angeles. There, two Salvadoran crooners of a certain age with Elvis pompadours, Elvis sideburns, and white polyester seventies suits with matching white patent-leather shoes, serenaded the tables with the classic boleros "Perfidia" and "Sabor a Mi," and the undocumented waiters served the undocumented families on the land they had lost a mere century and a half before. I was home.

Within two days, I found a summer room rental in a rundown building just off the intersection of Hollywood Boulevard and Highland Avenue—the dead centre of Hollywood. My roommates were two undocumented Mexicans; they slept in the living room, I in the bedroom. One was a bartender at the Gaucho Grill on Santa Monica's Third Street Promenade, the other a massage therapist who moonlighted as a conga drummer. The building was inhabited by some of the Mexican and Central American families who made up the millions-strong invisible brown workforce of LA—gardeners, janitors, car washers, mechanics, sweatshop workers, construction workers, truck drivers, parking lot attendants, groundskeepers, pool cleaners, vendors, maids, and nannies. Everyone looked out for each other, as it was evident that almost no one in the building had papers. When there was a dispute in an adjoining apartment, instead of calling the police, the men in the building, including my roommates, went to the door of the home where the yelling was coming from armed with baseball bats. Phoning 911 was out of the question.

My bartender roommate had already been picked up once and put in jail due to his undocumented status. While he was there, the tattooed Latino gangsters who protected their countrymen no matter what their reason for being inside had taken him under their wing. After a few months in jail, the judge had given him two options: immediate deportation or community service. It was not clear what would happen to his status when the community service was over, but he chose the latter. For six months, a white van picked him up at seven every morning. Inside were others who had been caught, people of all ages, even entire families, small children in tow. They were driven to South Central Los Angeles, where, armed with large plastic garbage bags, they cleaned up the alleys in one of the region's twenty-five neighbourhoods for eight hours straight. Under no circumstances could a day be missed, and, this being community service, there was no remuneration for the work. Once it was over, the van simply stopped picking them up and the state turned a blind eye, releasing them back to their undocumented, precarious lives in a land their Aztec ancestors had named Aztlán.

The people in the building had come to the States looking for work. As for my two roommates, they were from middle-class families and were fleeing traumatic childhoods. The three of us stayed up all night on a regular basis, discussing the history of our tortured continent, admiring the Cuban revolution, always a beacon, philosophizing about the imminent defeat of neo-liberalism in Latin America. Evo Morales in Bolivia was yet to come, as were José Mujica in Uruguay and Rafael Correa in Ecuador, but Hugo Chávez in Venezuela brought a smile to our faces, our hopes pinned on the Bolivarian Revolution. We discussed the United States' history of slavery of Africans and genocide of its Indigenous people and the social movements that had marked the preceding century. Silvio Rodríguez played on the stereo, hard-working families rested above and next door, while a regular red carpet unfurled religiously a mere block away, where movie premieres happened and celebrities posed for a hundred flashing bulbs on the star-encrusted boulevard, the Hollywood Walk of Fame.

That summer, I fell even more head over heels in love with the Latino Los Angeles. The Latino arts community welcomed me with open arms. I went to plays, concerts, art openings, parties, and spent afternoons writing at one of the many Latino cafés, Espresso Mi Cultura, in East Hollywood, also known as Little Armenia. A Chicana scholar who had written about *¿QUE PASA with LA RAZA, eh?*, one of the plays I had co-written with the Latino Theatre Group, not only introduced me to the Chicano playwrights, producers, and actors at the Center Theatre Group, California's regional theatre, she invited me to a family gathering in Southgate. A whole roasted pig with an apple in its mouth was the centrepiece of the outdoor dining room table, mariachis played, tequila was drunk, and a marriage proposal happened, sending the future bride into a near fainting fit. Candles burned around a statue of the miraculous Our Lady of San Juan de los Lagos, in whose honour the party was being held. The hostess had prayed for a top-secret favour and it had been granted.

By the end of that 2002 summer of love with a capital L, I knew I had to move to this city where South and North clashed, converged, and gave birth to the kind of plays that spoke to me and moved me, that reminded me and reassured me why I had chosen to follow my calling after the terrible defeat of the 1980s revolution.

TEN

In May 1995, ten years after Oughton was caught, we were in Mountain Institution, the first time that a group of victims were attending a parole hearing in the pedophile wing there. The guards who dealt with us were born-again Christians, the prison smack in the middle of one of Canada's many Bible belts. Some were elderly and had tears in their eyes. Our presence caused a stir amongst the guards who worked with Oughton day in and day out. Seeing so many of his victims was hard for them because it made the abstract concrete.

We were taken to a waiting room, where coffee and cookies were served. There were eight of us, all female, most with our parents, one with a girlfriend, another with a husband, as well as a woman about my age, twenty-seven, who, like me, was alone. While the hearing went on, my mother and Ale had organized a protest outside the BC Legislature, demanding that Oughton's eligibility for parole not even be a possibility. A woman from the parole board walked us through procedure and then answered questions. Elizabeth Aird, a *Vancouver Sun* reporter, was present, interviewing us with the utmost care and respect.

I learned that three of the women, Barb, Laura, and Jean, had seen Oughton during the attack. They had been part of the case against him and hence had been in court with him for months. Barb, the woman there with her husband, was the oldest of us; it was she who had gone to the *Sun* inviting fellow victims to come to the hearings she'd been attending alone. Barb was the only known adult victim, and was also the final one, her attack leading to Oughton's arrest. He'd been blindfolding his victims for years, but after almost a decade of evading capture, in his cockiness he hadn't done so with her. She was raped in Burnaby's Central Park while she held her little one in her arms, gun held to the back of her infant's head.

"My baby was so scared, he scratched my neck to shreds," she told us.

Laura, the other lone woman, a star witness at the trial, was attacked at eight years old, along with a friend the same age, in the early days of Oughton's rampage. He'd walked through their west-side school in a policeman's uniform, found them playing in the playground after last bell, and lured them into the adjoining woods by claiming to have lost his puppy.

"I had to sleep with my parents for years," Laura confessed.

Jean, there with her parents, was raped at age ten with her friend while at a Fraser Valley sports day event. Also one of his earlier victims, he hadn't blindfolded her.

"I have nightmares to this day," she said in a quiet voice.

Like me, the remaining four had been blindfolded or had a paper bag put over their head. They had gone to the lineup and hadn't attended the trial. For these four too, this would mark the first time they'd be in the same space with him since being attacked.

Laura's and Jean's friends, like Macarena, had chosen not to come. We realized that all eight of us were the ones in the duo who had been raped, while the ones made to witness were absent. In Barb's case, the reason was obvious; she would not bring her son, now ten years old, to a hearing. The stories, never shared in detail during the trial, flew out the way one exhales after holding one's breath for a scary amount of time. Overlapping, leaning in, we heard the penny drop: he'd done the same thing to all of us.

The woman there with her girlfriend said, "I was with my friend when it happened. We were being kids, that's all."

Her words and the tiny stuffed bunny she caressed for comfort were jolting for me, because in them was an empathy I'd never had for myself.

We were being kids, that's all.

We were being kids. Right. That's what Macarena and I had been doing. Being kids. Yet as far as I had always been concerned, I had brought the rape on myself. For being physically developed at the age of thirteen, for wanting to check out guys on the day it happened, for smoking a forbidden cigarette in the woods, for not being a little blond girl skipping rope in a frilly pink summer dress, the way I imagined these women (with the exception of Barb) to have been at the time of their attacks. For being from the dirty refugee class that scrubbed the toilets of the privileged, for wearing Salvation Army clothes my whole immigrant life and having the mouth of a truck driver since elementary school. For being brown.

But being in that room of blond women confirmed one thing in flashing neon words: *it wasn't my fault.* Not only that, it wasn't personal. The more detail I got from the others, the more I understood what a modus operandi was. It was something he did to everyone, exactly the same way, regardless of who the victim was. To hear that every single thing he'd done to Macarena and me had also been inflicted on them filled me with an immense sense of relief. Not only was I free of blame, there was nothing I could have done to stop it, to control the outcome. Following the impulses of a lazy Sunday afternoon all those years before did not get me raped, did not give me "what I deserved," did not land me in the hands of a psychopath. If it hadn't been me and Macarena, it would have been two other girls—or boys—and so it might as well have been us, because in the end, the experience had led me to this room of sisters, converged in the pedophile wing of Mountain Institution, connecting on a level so deep that it cut through all social protocols. It made us speak the unspeakable, name the unnameable, stare into each other's eyes and read each other's thoughts:

We're alive. We survived. He didn't kill us. We are here.

I had had many communities in my life thus far—the Chilean community in exile, the underground MIR community in South America, the Latino community in Vancouver, the theatre community—but in that room I encountered a tribe that would have verged on the surreal two days earlier. It was the community of the Paper Bag Rapist's victims and their families. Although I had known there were others and had seen them at the lineup a decade earlier, I had lived that defining story in isolation. It had never occurred to me that perhaps I could have reached out before now, formed a sisterhood. Thankfully, Barb had, and now here we were. I listened and listened and couldn't get enough of their words. I sat close and smelled them, wanted to squeeze them. We smiled and laughed together, a palpable sense of consolation hitting us all, the recognition of our shared experience transforming the molecules in the air, while the parents, silent witnesses, sat back, my heart breaking at the sight of their pained faces, the set jaws of the fathers, the wet eyes of the mothers holding their purses to their bosoms, as we held our boisterous conversation.

"He told you he'd kill your family too?"

"Holy shit, that's what he told me!"

"He said you were a hooker who was asking for it by wearing that skirt?"

"Fuck. He said that to me too."

"He told you it was making love and not rape?"

"No way, he said those exact words to me!"

Our subtext was:

I thought I was the only one.

One of the men present was Rick, the RCMP detective who had headed the thirteen-strong investigative team that caught Oughton. He would become a steadfast friend of ours.

When the time came to go into the parole room, over an hour had passed. In those sixty minutes, a group of strangers had formed a clan whose bonds would last forever, and I only wished Macarena hadn't refused to attend. For five of us, it would be the first time since the rape that we'd be breathing the same air as, occupying the same space as, listening to the voice of the man who had changed our lives in ways so profound it would take a lifetime to understand the depth of the wound inflicted by his cruelty.

His mother was there. Sitting by herself. She wore dark glasses and a large white summer hat decorated with fake fruit and flowers. She had on a gauzy white dress cinched at the waist, white pumps, white gloves, and gave the general impression of being dressed for church. Gaze fixed forward, heavily powdered face set in a frown, she refused to turn her head and acknowledge our collective entrance. The victims sat in the first row, our supporters behind us. Members of the parole board faced us from a table on the opposite end of the room.

Once we'd all settled, a door near the table opened. A guard came in, and behind him a man about my mother's age. The man who had graced the covers of so many newspapers over the last decade and a half, who had monopolized the evening news so often, whose moniker, the Paper Bag Rapist, incited the same reaction in Lower Mainland children that "the bogeyman" did in other places, was here now. Dressed in jeans, denim shirt, and cowboy boots, he still sported a moustache.

Watching him walk towards his place at the table, where he would sit with his back to us, I was grateful that I was seated. My knees had shaken when we'd entered the room, and now my stomach flipped at the sight of his hands making fists and opening. It was Number Twelve. I took note of how fear and excitement caused the same sensations in my body. I had no idea if I was shaking and flipping out of fear, which would have been irrational, what with his being in jail, or with excitement at finally confirming that it was him. Or both. I would spend my entire life trying to distinguish between the two, most notably in the romantic realm, which was indeed driven by fear, or excitement. Or both.

And now here I sat with my new-found sisterhood, seeing the man whose loaded gun was still at my temple, his finger on the trigger, pulling it whenever a worthy romantic companion got too close. This man who still held my life in his hands was in the room now. He was always present in my bedrooms of love and sex, in the four chambers of my heart, my guts, my womb, in the childhood forest I hadn't returned to since the rape, present in the booming recital hall of my skull. He was here. Touchable, smellable, audible, present inside these four walls that contained him, contained us, contained our supporters, contained those who would decide his fate, contained his mother, whose down-turned painted pink mouth spoke of misery, of shame, and yet of strength, the determination to be there for her son, no matter what. The Paper Bag Rapist was loved by his mother. Air filled my lungs when that realization hit me, and I took her in, my peripheral vision heightened to the nth degree.

He sat down and I wondered if the eagle still flew above, outside the jail, where the camera crews and reporters waited, circling the sky, watching, protecting. The tips of my lungs' branches swelled with my every inhalation, and my spirit did not shoot out of my crown, ricocheting off the ceiling and walls, seeking a way out of the prison and onto the wings of that loyal bird. It clung to my bones instead, stayed with my vital body, with my deep and steady breath.

The hearing lasted all of one minute, because as soon as the parole officer started his welcome speech, John Horace Oughton interrupted by yelling, "They wanted it!" He then leapt up, ran towards us, brushed by our knees, and dashed through the door we had come in from, two guards in hot pursuit.

Parole was denied, and the request was made that he be cuffed at the wrists and ankles at subsequent hearings.

‿

"I'm not the rapist. I'm not him."

Phrases spoken by my husband, Alejandro, in moments that threatened too much intimacy. The drawbridge would come up, the crocodiles would snap their jaws, and the cannons would get their order to launch. Outwardly, my fight against intimacy with him was the opposite of violent; rather, it was the defence that only a corpse can offer, the resistance of lifelessness. The words would be spoken when my spirit had left, my body in a state of general anaesthesia, ready to be cut, entered, consumed, chopped into pieces.

Sex was not the problem; intimacy was. I was good at giving during sex, putting my focus on him and being beyond generous. Receiving was the issue, because in that position I was vulnerable. Giving put me in control, receiving was loss of control. When I felt safe enough with him to receive, a sense of nausea so unbearable hit me that he was never able to touch me again. A repulsion so great seized me that our marriage ended. Being as defenseless as a newborn baby in the presence of an unwavering, loving man had made me so ill that not only did I have to swallow my own puke, I lost twenty pounds. With Alejandro I had yet to learn that what lay at the bottom of the repulsion was self-loathing, for surely I was unworthy of receiving the unconditional love he was offering. The rapist had come into my life to prove that.

He started counting. For the second time in my short life, I had ten seconds to say goodbye to the world, the first having been before the mock firing squad in Chile. I thought it wouldn't be enough, but it was, proving yet again that time and space are human constructs that exist on planet Earth only for measuring the immeasurable, for making finite that which is infinite.

When I was a child, my father asked me, "If there is an end to space and time, then what comes after?"

Infinity did indeed exist, and the proof lay in those ten seconds. Suspended in eternity, my entire life came into sharp focus. Flesh and bones fell away, and my spirit, free of all anchors, soared into the realm of memory. I conjured things that had happened, and things that were still to happen and now never would. I invoked my father's Paihuano childhood stories, my first carnival in that enchanted valley of his birth, my mother and Bob in Bolivia right now, hiding MIRistas in their house, my baby brother Lalito, whom I would never see grow up for he had been born there the September before, after Ale and I had returned to Canada. I envisioned my uncle Boris, chain-smoking his Benson & Hedges and drinking his trusty Havana Club as he sat in front of the TV, gathering his energy to do his Sunday night janitor work. I visited my sister Ale, riding her purple banana-seat bike to the Lucky Dollar, just up the street from where we now lay, where she would buy Life Savers and her first Revello of the season; my cousin Gonzalo, roller skating in his blue-and-yellow-striped skates around the courts. Now I visited my abuelita Carmen in her house in Limache, Chile, where fall had just begun, snoring during the climax of *Den of Wolves*, the most popular soap opera on the air, my abuelito Armando gathering the eggs from the chicken coop, checking the ripeness of the avocados on the tree, their long bloodline of malnutrition and disease, both survivors of large broods of siblings who had not made it past childhood.

My spirit landed in the place where the then and now meet, where the here and there converge, and I imagined a young woman, me, who would join the MIR and fight to the end, taking Santiago in the back of a truck, rifle in right hand, left fist pumping the air on the day of the triumph. She would participate in the reconstruction of a socialist Chile, picking up where Allende had left off, but armed this time, armed in order to defend the hard-won achievements of the revolution. My spirit blasted through clocks and calendars, walls disintegrated, ceilings opened, and it entered the life of that future me, now a doctor, in a relationship with a fellow revolutionary (I still didn't believe in marriage, but rather in companionship), offering my services all over the so-called Third World, giving my grain of sand so that no child would die of a curable disease, of hunger, ever again.

As the number ten grabbed my spirit by the nape and brought it back to my body lying next to Macarena's, the here and now landed with the impact of a meteorite and my last thoughts were with someone a few blocks away, almost touchable, almost audible, almost smellable. Tommy, my Chancellor Boulevard boyfriend, wearing ironic polyester bowling pants bought at the Salvation Army ("They're tacky!"), sitting in his white-shag-carpet rec room, practising the Rolling Stones' "Start Me Up" on his brand new drum set, facing the trampoline on the back of the lawn where fellow rich white boys who shopped at thrift stores as a fashion choice jumped in their bare feet. It was, after all, the first hot, sunny day of the year.

In the spring of 1995, one month after the parole hearing, I performed a five-minute playlet at a new works festival on

Granville Island, Vancouver's theatre hub. In the piece, part of a larger series of vignettes entitled *Women and Fear*, I recounted being wheeled through white corridors on a hospital gurney, the fluorescent lights flying by as a nurse held my hand and a police officer gave a plainclothes detective the location of the crime scene. This was my first attempt at creating a play about it, and as far as I was concerned, it was a failure, if only because the form was boring and the work was lacking in complexity. In it, I was a one-dimensional victim. The only salvageable thing about it was the structure: I did not disclose that I was at Emergency after being raped until the last beat of the play, and that realization elicited a gasp from the audience. Years would pass before my full-length play about the attack crystallized, after I'd chewed over ideas and images forever. I had discovered that I didn't want to tell the story in a literal way, and had yet to learn how to create a piece of theatre, like the unforgettable Lima curfew play, that would do so through movement and non-linear text.

By the time I moved to Los Angeles in late 2002, I had a concept. After a decade of pondering concepts and themes, it materialized. A young tree lay on the stage. A man swung an axe over his head and brought it down, full force, right into the middle of the trunk. Every time the man brought the axe down, a young girl in a harness twirled in circles above his head, like water draining when the stopper is pulled, the laws of gravity reversed, the girl being swallowed *up* into a black hole of sorts, as opposed to *down*. The sound of the axe cutting through the air and landing on its mark, the grunt of the man every time he brought it down, the girl in the twirling harness, and the iambic pentameter of a heartbeat constituted the sound design.

The lines "Don't move. Don't speak. Don't breathe," uttered by both the man and the girl, would echo throughout the play. The theme would be self-destruction, the title *The Trigger*.

"Don't move. Don't speak. Don't breathe."

Words spoken by the Paper Bag Rapist. Or had they boomed in my own head, my inner voice speaking them? Impossible to know. Impossible to remember. Yet those are the words that had always stayed with me when it came to the rape itself.

The endless ten seconds, a portal to the dimension where past, present, and future meet, had provided me with a framework to say goodbye to my bodily existence on earth. As he'd counted, I'd believed with every fibre of my mortal being that ten seconds later I'd be dead, and had hence taken the time to breathe in and taste the moist dirt that my face was jammed against, finding comfort in the certainty that my flesh, bones, brown skin, white skull, and green heart would join that earth, a universe all its own made up of the remains of millions of creatures that had lived and breathed full lives before me. A deafening roar like a wasps' nest boomed in my ears when the counting was done, the ringing stretching through five more seconds of silence.

He let out an impatient sigh.

"I have one bullet left. I'm going to chop up your cousin now in front of you, starting from the feet. Then you'll help me put the pieces in a plastic bag. Then I'll shoot you."

He kicked me in the calves to punctuate his last assertion. My young, vigorous heart imploded, as if the axe he spoke of had chopped right through my chest bone.

Macarena turned her face towards me. It was covered in snot, soil, and tears.

"Please. Do it for me."

She mouthed the words. There was no breath behind them. Her eyes akin to the eyes in a photograph I'd seen of Jewish prisoners looking out from behind the barbed wire of a Nazi concentration camp. Nobody had ever looked at me that way, and I hope nobody ever does again.

"Okay. I'll do it," I informed the rapist.

My voice hadn't trembled. It had not caught in my throat.

My surrender was absolute, as had been my conviction ten seconds earlier that I would be murdered rather than raped. I looked the horror in the eye, even as he held the gun inches from my temple while I tied my white blouse around my face.

"How long will this take?" I asked him.

"Thirty seconds."

He had just counted to ten. I decided I'd count to thirty. Not out loud, to myself.

It had occurred to me that I'd never thought much about the actual act of sex. At thirteen, I was too young for that, wrapped up in more abstract ideas of love. Penetration was never a part of my fantasies, nor was having my naked body grabbed and fondled. My daydreams revolved around kissing and hugging, staring into my beloved's eyes, caressing each other's hair, whispering sweet nothings into each other's ears, *a la* Sandy and Danny during their summer of love in *Grease*. I'd heard about lovemaking, and understood that it was the most pleasurable, intimate act that two human beings could experience with each other. But I'd never *really* thought about the nuts and bolts of the situation, the which-part-goes-where aspect of the act. And yet I was aware that the opposite of lovemaking—rape—would cause such unfathomable pain that I would rather have died.

Earlier that afternoon, upon meeting the Paper Bag Rapist, every goosebump on my skin had warned me that this time severe physical harm was inescapable. I steeled myself for it now, whatever it was, however it would feel. The belief that it would be worse than a bullet to the back of the head sent my body into a tailspin. I started to shake so hard he had to pin me down, the chattering of my teeth reverberating in my ears along with my galloping heart, the wasps' nest full blast now.

"Don't move. Don't speak. Don't breathe. Don't move. Don't speak. Don't breathe. Don't move. Don't speak. Don't breathe."

The mantra reached me from afar, whispered as if by butterfly wings. He pulled the shirt off my mouth and stuck his tongue deep inside it. The force of the incantation matched the violence of his probing tongue.

I could hear my own voice now, pleading, despite my resolve to face the beast with head held high, to never beg this cruel human who now made a sport of pulling my trembling legs apart.

"Please. Please don't. Please don't." I could hear my girl's voice. It cried, it whimpered, it dropped to its knees and begged.

And then he sliced me clean in two, which is why I wondered if he'd used a knife.

My body went limp and my spirit rocketed out of the top of my head. Macarena, face in the dirt, bearing silent witness, stayed behind. Although we were only two feet away from each other, it was one of the loneliest moments of both our lives.

∼

I wrote the first draft of *The Trigger* in Los Angeles in early 2003, as winter rolled in and I sat at the drafting table of my newly rented Los Feliz room. After directing an adaptation of Julio Cortázar's *End of the Game* at my Vancouver alma mater in the autumn of 2002, I'd closed up shop and driven south for the second time in six months, moving to the City of Angels. I'd taken the Mount Shasta curves, in northern California, to the beat of Astor Piazzolla and Nestor Marconi's modern tango and Lito Vitale's virtuosic piano, the score for the play I'd just directed. Within two days of my arrival, my landlord, a flamboyant, closeted, fundamentalist Christian ex–movie director in his fifties who ran a small theatre company in Hollywood, not only rented me a room ten minutes after meeting me, he also cast me in one of the one-acts he was producing.

The dead of night saw me hammering out *The Trigger*, and days had me pounding the pavement for an agent along with a Canadian actor friend. Weekends found me carrying on with a mid-twenties Palestinian jeweller I'd met on Venice Beach who was a survivor of an Israeli prison. Picked up at the age of thirteen for throwing stones at Israeli tanks during the First Intifada, he'd been released at eighteen. He'd been severely tortured, and when he reunited with the girlfriend he hadn't seen for five years, he learned that she too had been in jail and that her nipples had been cut off. A teenaged brother had been shot dead in the street by the Israelis. Like so many oppressed people with zero sense of entitlement, his outlook on life remained inspiringly positive, stating that being a political prisoner for his entire adolescence had in fact been a gift, because he had spent his time reading and discussing books with the Palestinian intelligentsia he was in jail with.

"I couldn't have asked for a better education. And it was free."

When the Second Intifada began in 2000, his parents, fearing that this time he'd be killed, had smuggled him out of Gaza and sent him to live with wealthy relatives in Los Angeles. This intifada was still going strong, and he'd recently learned that another brother had been murdered. Upon his arrival in Los Angeles, his relatives had filled out all the sponsorship papers to get him a work permit and then a green card. It had all been about to go through, but then 9/11 happened in 2001, and hundreds of men were still being arrested across the country for the crime of being brown, Middle Eastern, and Muslim. US immigration denied his papers. Now he was undocumented.

We'd walk the Venice Beach canals together, watch the sun set on the ocean, dance salsa at El Floridita Cuban restaurant in Hollywood, ride the Sea Dragon at the Santa Monica Pier, all while discussing Palestinian, Chilean, and world politics— in all of which, due to his prison education, he was a master. Our short-lived relationship ended when an American woman in solidarity with the Palestinian cause offered to marry him so he could stay in the country, but we remained friends for years.

I forged friendships that would prove to last a lifetime in those first few months in LA. I attended the 100,000-strong marches along Sunset Boulevard against the United States' imminent invasion of Iraq, cheering along with the others when Martin Sheen, who played the president on the popular TV show *The West Wing*, took the stage and yelled, "Make love not war!" More celebrities condemned the looming invasion at subsequent rallies, and seemingly every documented progressive Angeleno took to the streets.

In Vancouver, regular seawall walks had fed my writing. In Los Angeles, when not strolling the Malibu beaches, where I laughed with joy at the jumping pods of dolphins and at the sight of a playful grey whale close to shore once, or people-watching at an outdoor Venice café, I'd walk the Latino quarters, devouring that concrete jungle with all my senses heightened. Santee Alley, in the heart of the downtown garment district, was a favourite, as was Broadway, studded with Latino jewellery stores. Both were within walking distance, and provided for an afternoon of serious sensory overload. Once, I found the entrance to one of Broadway's many old buildings and took the stairs up, desperately seeking a bathroom, and came across sweatshops where Latinos laboured in cramped rooms, hunched over sewing machines next to mountains of clothes, their bosses monitoring their every move.

A skinny teenaged boy with fear and determination in his eyes stood at one of the doorways. He told me he'd just arrived on foot from Guatemala and was hoping to get a job. Someone had also informed him that there might be food on these floors. I handed him a twenty, wished him the best, climbed back down the stairs, held my pee, and continued down Broadway, a knot forming in my throat at the knowledge that I was no longer part of a movement to change all this, a wave of guilt and longing washing through me at the constant reminder that I was perhaps a sellout for not only following my selfish dream but letting it take me to the heart of the empire.

I let the self-loathing wash over me, exhaling as I passed windows displaying kilos of silver, gold, and precious stones in the form of Guadalupes, crosses, Marys, Christs, anchors, nameplates, *quinceañera* rings, rosaries, rope chains, and bamboo hoop earrings of every size. Cumbias blasted from speakers, taco stands proliferated. *Botánica* shops sold sex-life-enhancing phallus candles, "Curse Breaker," "Come to Me," and "Lucky Casino" herbs and potions, 7 African Powers bath salts, red La Santísima Muerte votive candles with images of the Grim Reaper on them, and *Fasten Your Man* candles featuring men wearing only underpants on all fours with chains around their necks, lit by women who wanted to keep their men by their side. Lineups formed under signs reading *We wire money to Mexico, Guatemala, Honduras, and El Salvador for less.* El Salvador's economy would have collapsed if not for the remittances sent from the States, where the vast majority of Latino labourers sent a good portion of their pay back home.

Shortly after my move to LA, a spur-of-the-moment phone call from my Chicano scholar friends found me back in San Diego for the first time since I'd lived there, to watch the Mexican Elvis, El Vez. The concert happened in a bar under a bridge in the seedy part of town, and when El Vez came on with his backup singers Las Elvettes, paid tribute to the Zapatistas, and planted a kiss right on my first-row mouth, I knew I was home yet again. He played all my favourites, such as "Lordy Miss Lupe" and "Never Been to Spain." On our drive back to LA, I was flooded by bittersweet memories of my first North American friend, Lassie, her dying-of-homesickness Mexican maid, my parents' dignity in the face of hardship, the drive away from an undocumented future in the baby-blue Chevrolet Malibu with Barry White's "Love's Theme" playing on the radio, so far north up the coast that we would find our-selves in a temperate rainforest that mirrored the Patagonian one we'd just fled. Now my scholar friends and I passed yellow warning signs featuring drawings of families running across the freeway, with the word *Caution*. I shook my head, El Vez's kiss imprinted on my lips.

Although I found an acting agent and a writing management team who set up meetings with a Paramount producer looking for a Latina to write a romantic comedy (I decided mine would be called *Cojones or Bust* and would feature a strong, powerful Latina who comes undone for the wrong man), and I was meeting regularly with the folks at the Center Theatre Group (they eventually produced a staged reading of *The Refugee Hotel* as part of their New Works Festival), I ended up moving back to Canada in the late summer of that year, 2003. The reason was the same one that had had us driving away at the beginning of exile: I had no papers. Upon my arrival I had hired an immigration lawyer to start the green card process, and had even found a sponsor. A work permit would be ready within nine months. But three months after my arrival, the US invaded Iraq and my lawyer informed me that the process could be delayed by up to two years. I'd come with savings to take me through the first six months, and prayed that a work permit would be expedited once I was offered a part or a writing job. A pipe dream, perhaps, but many foreign actors and screenwriters in Los Angeles had got their permits that way, including some I knew. Paramount's interest in my screenplay held promise, but it had not led to a concrete offer in the short time I was there. I was disappointed, but the friendships and work relationships I forged would remain strong, and I would return for visits, and even work, on a regular basis.

I drove back north blasting *NoElVezSí*, El Vez's latest album, first drafts of *Cojones or Bust* and *The Trigger* in my laptop, bursting with gratitude for how much Los Angeles had fed my soul and my art. Wildfires burned on both sides of the Interstate 5 freeway, and I gunned it through the smoke.

ELEVEN

"You're still a virgin," my best friend Amber told me in the girls' washroom the day after the rape.

"You will be a virgin until you do it with someone you want, because you want to, because you love them."

Sage words spoken by a grade eight girl labelled white trash by the more privileged sectors of University Hill Secondary School society.

My father had ordered me to stay in bed for a week, and I had responded with:

"I'm not sick."

Shoulders hunched, Adam's apple quivering, my shell-shocked Papi had shrugged and gone to his gardening job at UBC's botanical garden. The rapist hadn't killed me, he'd made me stronger, so I'd walked to school by myself, books held tight against my chest, humming Sheena Easton's "Morning Train" along the way. The song had been playing on LG73 when my clock radio went off that morning at 7 a.m. I'd placed Air Supply's

"Lost in Love" on the turntable during breakfast, swallowing hard, flanked by posters of Che Guevara ("Until the Final Victory Always"), Fidel Castro ("A Revolution is a Struggle to the Death between the Future and the Past"), Salvador Allende on the day of the coup holding the AK-47 given to him by Fidel, and Miguel Enríquez, the leader of the MIR who had died in combat a year after the coup ("Only Revolution Will Free Us"). If they were brave enough to do what each of them had done, then I was strong enough to go to school. I'd thought of Bob, held prisoner at the National Stadium, of Uncle Boris, arrested in Valparaíso, of all my aunts and uncles in the Chilean community who had survived imprisonment, torture, assassinations and disappearances of loved ones, exile. If they were able to get up every morning and go scrub floors, then I could face this new day without crumbling. I imagined Macarena, also alone, en route to University Hill Elementary School down the way, where she was in grade six.

I filed Amber's wise words for later contemplation. Hailing from Trail, BC, she was a rocker chick who loved to swear as much as I did. She and her single dad had moved to the courts after her father enrolled at UBC. In charge of housework, Amber kept their place spotless, was a straight-A student, and went to Bible study on Sundays. On Friday and Saturday nights she partied.

Many afternoons were spent swimming at UBC's aquatic centre, dancing in her living room to Blondie's "Call Me" and Donna Summers' "Bad Girls," and walking around the courts singing. Rough Trade's "High School Confidential" was our top choice, Santana's "Winning" and Juice Newton's "Angel of the Morning" close contenders for second place. Whenever we walked by Cedar, I wondered if the postcards of Lucho's uncle Alejandro Avalos Davidson and Carmen Bueno Cifuentes, the disappeared actress, still hung from his branch. I hadn't climbed Cedar since becoming a teenager, and this filled me with loneliness and yearning. He was still my secret tree. I hadn't told Amber about him, for fear she wouldn't understand the extent of what his refuge had meant to me. Amber, like most of my school and neighbourhood friends, was in the dark about the details of my parallel life, the one led in the Chilean exile community.

When Kim Carnes came to UBC's Thunderbird Stadium, Amber and I were in the stands, in heels (mine bought at Zellers with my paper route wages, hers shoplifted from Eaton's), full makeup and crimped hair, singing along to "Bette Davis Eyes," another one of our chart toppers. Amber was warm, funny, and smart, and knew how to embrace suffering.

"So if anybody asks, you'll tell them you're a virgin," she said now.

Holding my shoulders against the washroom wall, she nailed me with her fierce green gaze, her determined eyes lit up by the sun pouring through the window directly above my head.

"You hear me? You hear me?" she demanded.

I nodded. Although it had only occurred the previous afternoon, the story was already on the front page of the paper, the school on alert. It was 8:45 in the morning, and five minutes later, when the bell went off for second block, the classrooms would belch hundreds of students into the hallway.

"Besides, it's nobody's fuckin' business, and you'll keep your head up and walk these brutal halls like the Chilean queen you are, you hear?"

She took my hand in hers and sang the "Winning" lyrics under her breath as we emerged together from the bathroom.

She was preparing me for the aftermath, which I was yet to understand would never end, for I didn't know one doesn't get over childhood rape, one simply learns how to integrate it.

She guided my dismantled bag of bones through the treacherous hallways, the pain between my noodle legs so great I had to widen my gait, the front layer of my body disintegrated, innards exposed, organs on display, heart floating in front of me, a Chinese lantern in the night, breath shallow in my chopped-open chest, the axe now lodged in my sternum, the contents of my womb scooped out and discarded like the pulp and seeds of a pumpkin, the knife still inserted in my pubis, my disembodied head, a balloon floating above me, trying to make sense of it all, a knot the size of a peach pit in my throat.

We passed the biology and chemistry teachers, ex–frat boys in their late twenties. They stopped in their tracks and looked at me, forced smiles on their faces.

"Carmen! How *are* you?" asked the chemistry teacher.

His hands, a magician's doves, escaped from the pockets of his lab coat, as if to caress my arm, and he plunged them straight back in, nipping his tender impulse in the bud. My lantern heart contracted, the aftermath hitting me like a block of cement dropped from a great height.

"I'm fine, thank you," I answered.

Amber, a Parthenon pillar, stood next to me.

"We just wanted to say that if you need *any*thing, we are here for you, okay?" stammered the biology teacher, his eyes wide behind his John Lennon specs.

"Okay."

The conversation came to a crashing halt and they moved on.

The school had been informed by the police first thing in the morning that the Paper Bag Rapist had attacked one of its students in the adjacent woods, and my father had phoned to let the principal know I was the victim referred to in the paper and to ask if the counsellor could please talk to me. She called me into her office when she saw me standing on the front steps, facing the head of Fairview trail, Tommy by my side. Sitting across from me, she'd spoken of experiences that life sends us so that we can learn something. Five years later, when I took the MIR oath in a Lima café while bombs went off around me, the Terror sending me into a shaking fit, my superior, Juan, would take my arm and reassure me with a similar statement:

"Any experience is good, comrade. Any experience is good."

The counsellor spoke about the death of her husband, how that experience had taught her something, and said that the rape experience would teach me something too. After a long silence, she'd asked:

"How do you feel?"

"It hurts," was all I was able to come up with.

I had meant it in the literal sense, for sitting down was painful.

As I'd imagined the previous afternoon, Tommy had been practising on his new drum set during the attack. I'd called him late on Sunday night and asked him to meet me at eight the following morning at the school.

"I have a class," he'd said.

"Skip it. I'm calling from the police station."

"Seriously?"

"Don't worry, I didn't commit a crime. But I have to tell you something."

"All right."

Degradations had competed against each other that Sunday night. First off, when the trail had spit Macarena and I out onto University Boulevard, none of the cars we flagged had stopped. This was the beginning of the aftermath. The possibility that no one would come to our aid had never crossed my mind, the prospect that a crime of this magnitude would be ignored inconceivable to me. As far as I was concerned, when two young girls covered in dirt, tears pouring down their filthy, distorted faces, one of them with bloodstains in the crotch area of her white skirt, waved at you to stop, you stopped. But no one did.

"Let's run," I finally said to Macarena.

I'd managed to get my shirt back on, haphazardly doing up the buttons with my shaking fingers. Time being of the essence, I'd grabbed my sandals and run without putting them on. I held them in my trembling hands now. Barefoot, we ran west, panting and wailing, the cars still whizzing by. Neither of us knew where we were running to, only what we were running from: the rapist, wherever he hid. Free from him now, out in the open, those indifferent cars were also our unwitting saviours, for surely he wouldn't careen out of the woods and pull us back in full sight of the vehicles, apathetic but witnesses all the same.

After the rape, during which I had not counted to thirty, as I'd promised myself, but had instead gone for a precarious spin on the black wing of that eagle, I'd come crashing down into my body with the force of a grand piano dropped from the balcony of a penthouse suite. Lying there, ivory keys dislodged, spring-steel strings cut and flailing, ebony rim split as if by a deranged axe, I'd reached for breath through my blouse-turned-blindfold. No longer pinned down by his weight, I was free to shake now. And so I'd shaken as if my naked body were lying on the tundra permafrost in the dead of winter, not the bed of the temperate rainforest on the first hot day of the year.

"I'm still gonna kill you both. I don't trust ya. You're gonna tell everyone, 'cause girls have big mouths. So I'm gonna kill you anyway."

The shaking had grown in intensity. I wondered if I looked as though I were having an epileptic fit.

After interminable moments, he'd said:

"You're gonna count to two hundred. Out loud. Both of you."

We could hear him tearing through the forest as we counted. Dead silence followed when we were done. Lying there for an eternity, we didn't dare move, for fear he'd jump out from behind a tree again, demanding to know where we were going, gun in one hand, axe in the other. Sounds reached me from afar: the singing of the robin perched on the cedar branch above, the susurrus of the leaves of the birch trees, the number 10 bus's door flapping open, the jogger panting on the trail nearby (or was it him?), the sound of the bullet that would never be shot ringing in my eardrums.

"Are you there?" Macarena asked in a small voice.

"Yes."

"What should we do?" she asked in Spanish, the language of rebellion. When we'd spoken it at the beginning of the attack, he'd threatened to kill us because he couldn't understand what we were saying.

"Run. Run for it."

I yanked the shirt off my face, my pupils contracting when the sun pouring through the trees reached my eyes at the speed of light, my chest expanding to the rhythm of my first inhalation, oxygen filling every lobe of my lungs. I scrambled to my knees and pulled on my crumpled clothes as Macarena unbraided her fingers from the back of her head, placed her palms on the forest floor, and looked up. Our eyes met for a brief moment, a tidal wave of love crashed onto the shores of my broken heart, flooding all its vacant chambers, and fresh tears poured down both our faces. I placed my hands on her shoulders and said:

"We're going to run. Towards the sound of the bus. It means we're closer to University Boulevard. So we're going to run. As fast as we can."

I led the way, through spiderwebs and ferns, salmonberry and holly bushes, the sound of the traffic my magnetic north, heart at full gallop, listening for that shot aiming at the backs of our heads, whizzing through the cottonwoods, elders, firs, birches, and cedars.

Now we were running along University Boulevard in the opposite direction of the impervious cars, and through the tears, through the horror and terror, I started to laugh. I laughed and laughed and laughed while the blood trickled down my inner thighs, and I didn't care if I peed.

"This is no laughing matter!" yelled Macarena.

To which I answered:

"Macarena, we're alive! We're alive! *We're alive!*"

To feel the warm cement slapping the bottoms of my bare feet, to see the light of day again, to know that our parents would not have to spend the rest of their lives looking for us while we lay in pieces at the bottom of the forest, to understand that death, though inevitable, had not come for us yet, filled me with elation.

"Excuse me, sir, we've just been raped and we need to use your phone," I told the poor man who watered his plants outside his modest brick house on Presidents Row, now watering his shoes.

I'd left bloodstains on their white couch after he and his wife invited us in. She'd offered us water as he called the police station. Then they'd driven us there. Chris and Mark, the same cops we'd seen when we'd come upon the soccer game, were waiting for us at the door to the station, around the corner from the Lucky Dollar. I was filled with shame that they were seeing me like this.

While one of them pounded out our answers to his questions ("Where did this happen? What did he look like?") on a typewriter, the other one phoned our parents. Meanwhile, the couple left, pale as ghosts, eyes wide like the moon that would rise in the sky later that night.

I answered the questions ("Fairview trail. We never saw him") as best I could, though the shaking that had begun during the attack grew even worse now, as though I were being electrocuted. Minutes later, my father, my sister, and Macarena's mother and brother walked into the station.

"What's happening?" asked my disoriented father.

"Your daughters—" one of the cops started to answer.

"I was raped," I took over in Spanish.

Papi, a soft-spoken man, took a good look at my pulverized face and body, pounded his fist onto the counter, and yelled at the top of his lungs,

"*Mierda!*"

Ale came to me and tried to hug me through my shaking seizure. My cousin Gonzalo stared at the wall with all his might and swallowed, over and over again. Shock immobilized Aunt Tita, a woman known for taking the bull by the horns in any given situation. Macarena cried and cried.

"It's okay, everyone. It's okay," I reassured my family through chattering teeth.

While Macarena stayed behind to answer more questions, I was taken to UBC hospital, where I was laid on a gurney and a nurse took my hand.

"How do you feel?" she asked, the kindness in her eyes so disarming that my solar plexus released and a fountain of fresh tears poured down the sides of my face.

"It hurts down there." My voice broke for the first time.

"I know," she responded, eyes fixed on mine, never letting go of my hand, keeping the safe bubble she'd created intact.

We were in the bustling hallway of Emergency, and she just kept gripping my hand, never diverting her pupils—the axis of the world spinning around us—from mine. A few minutes later, after they found out UBC hospital didn't possess a rape kit, I was put into the back seat of the police car and driven to Vancouver General Hospital. The emergency room was packed when we arrived, and the officer yelled out:

"We've got a rape case here!"

Everyone turned to look at me, with my bloodstained skirt. Still carrying my sandals in my trembling hands, I walked with the cop and my father down a white hallway, the floor cold on the bare soles of my feet, the fluorescent lighting dull on our skin, my stunned father next to me, eyes on the ground. I swallowed down my tears and held my head up high for both of us.

I was placed on my back, naked on a hospital bed, feet in stirrups. An older male doctor wearing a suit, no doctor's coat, placed a clamp in my vagina, to stretch it open, and scooped out the rapist's semen. My spirit clung by its claws to the ceiling, giving me a bird's-eye view of the scene. The doctor put the evidence, which included the rapist's pubic hairs he'd found on my labia, in little containers—the "rape kit"—held up by a nurse. Neither one of them ever acknowledged my existence. They compared notes while they looked at my vagina, talked about my broken hymen. They gave me a shot, handed me a small plastic bag of clothes from the Salvation Army—the police would be keeping my own—and left the room.

The bag contained black polyester bell-bottoms with a broken zipper and a black turtleneck. There were no underpants. I took note that they were seventies clothes, out of fashion, "tacky," as my boyfriend Tommy would say, but not in the ironic way, for I was not a rich white kid playing poor, I was a brown refugee kid who had just been raped, made to wear embarrassingly out-of-style clothing.

I put them on and waited in the room for what felt like an hour. I thought about Mami, in Bolivia. I remembered her smile, her embrace, her benevolent eyes. My abuelita's soft voice filled my ears, my abuelito's proud gaze. The shaking stopped and warmth and calmness set in. I remembered the shafts of sun piercing the branches of the trees when I tore off the blindfold. A sigh escaped my mouth.

When I was finally fetched by a nurse, I was taken to another room, where Papi stood with the plain-clothed doctor and two men in blazers.

"There has definitely been a rape," the doctor was explaining to my father.

My word didn't count. Only this doctor's did. I had been guilty of lying until the rape kit proved the truth. I didn't understand anything, except that I was at the mercy of whatever system I now found myself in. My father nodded at everything these men said, for what else was he to do? They spoke of an investigation, of trying to catch the rapist, of the injection they'd given me to prevent pregnancy. They told my father I'd be nauseous due to the vaccine, as I stood there, invisible to them, underwear-less, pubes poking out of the broken zipper, a non-person. Was it because I was a girl? A child? A brown immigrant? I had no idea.

"Do you have any questions?" they asked Papi.

"Yes," he responded in his thick Chilean accent. "Do you think we should leave this country?"

Having no clue what to respond to this nonsensical question (to them, certainly not to me, probably not to any refugee or immigrant), they simply stated:

"No. We need you here so we can conduct the investigation."

My father was taken home in one car, I was ushered into another and driven back to the scene of the crime. It was cordoned off, surrounded by police cars with their strobe lights on, University Boulevard shut down to traffic. We pulled up, and as soon as I got out of the cruiser, a big German shepherd jumped on me, paws on my chest, almost throwing me to the ground.

"He can smell the rapist on you," one of the detectives explained.

That's right, I thought. I haven't showered. He's still all over me. Everyone can smell him on me.

Macarena had already been taken to the scene of the crime and was back at the police station now, dictating her detailed report of what had happened, they told me. As for me, I was led to the location, found by the dogs, lit up with spotlights now, and asked if this was it. I nodded, though I had no idea if it was. There were all kinds of experts there, all white men, in blazers, suit jackets, trench coats, a few uniformed cops. As I was being taken back to the idling car, one of the two detectives from the hospital approached from the trail.

"Look at this," he said to his partner.

He held the cigarette butt that Macarena and I had been smoking.

"He might have been smoking."

"No. That was us," I said.

Now they knew. They knew it was my fault. For being a bad girl sneaking a cigarette in the woods.

Back at the police station, I told the cop everything I could remember about the rape as he pounded away on his typewriter and tried not to yawn. He asked me if the rapist had hurt me in any way, if I was sure it was rape, if I had been wearing provocative clothing. He asked why I had taken Macarena into the woods. I answered his questions and heard my mother's furious feminist voice booming in my head. I nodded at it, knowing everything that was wrong here, and also understanding that this man was ignorant, that he was doing his job, for he was required to ask these questions by a system that considered a young girl raped at gunpoint guilty until proven innocent. I wondered what the questions would be if I were a boy. I wondered if I'd be laughed at if I were a boy. I wondered if a boy would even tell. To think the aftermath had only just begun.

After buying me a Coke from the vending machine, the officer took me home in the cop car. He offered to turn on the strobe lights and I agreed, for it would be fun. It was well past midnight when we pulled up to my house. A bone-crushing exhaustion unlike any tiredness I'd ever experienced hit me. It was a cement flattener. I walked up to the door alone, legs far apart due to the throbbing pain between my thighs, waved goodbye to the cop, and entered my house.

My entire family was there. Aunt Tita had made me vegetarian *pastel de choclo*, my favourite dish, and it sat waiting for me at the head of the table. When I made my way down the hall, Uncle Boris took a drag of his Benson & Hedges Light and yelled out,

"Well, thank God she's not in a wheelchair!" and let out a long exhalation.

Everyone laughed. A smile spread across my face and I knew all would be fine, for humour was the way Chileans dealt with the worst of tragedies. So, after taking my first bite of food, everyone's eyes fixed on me, I cracked a joke myself.

"Oh, fuck. I just realized I haven't showered or brushed my teeth, and now I'm eating, so I probably swallowed some of the rapist's pubes."

But I was the only one who laughed.

I took my family in, one by one, nodded to myself, and silently thanked the Virgin Copacabana, the patron saint of Bolivia, the one who keeps the roads clear, for bringing me back to them safe and sound.

~

Now it was 8 a.m. the following day and I stood on the front steps of the school with Tommy.

"I was raped in there yesterday afternoon," I said, indicating the woods with my chin.

"What?"

"I was raped."

He searched my face.

"They told me last night that it's the Paper Bag Rapist. Because of his MO. After I told them everything he did to me and my cousin. So they made a big deal about it. They cut off University Boulevard and everything. Anyways, I'm fine. But I wanted to tell you."

He took my hand and asked to hug me and my heart over-flowed with love for the umpteenth time since the rape. I was alive. I was alive. As he rocked me from side to side, I squeezed my eyes shut and breathed in the scent of his neck, like the time we'd slow-danced in his rec room to John Lennon's "Woman" from the *Double Fantasy* album I'd given him for Valentine's Day. I smiled at the memory of his Halloween costume. He'd worn a white and red leotard, tied a Canadian flag around his neck, and called himself Captain Canada. I beamed at the image of him pulling up to school every morning on his red ten-speed, wear-ing his blue windbreaker, dirty-blond hair framing his freck-led face, at our arguments over the Cold War, over El Salvador, over capitalism and imperialism. When I opened my eyes, the culpable forest rose up in front of me in all its green, inviting glory, and I thanked my lucky stars for having met a rapist, not a murderer.

TWELVE

Oughton's corrections officer was a three-hundred-pounds-of-muscle, soft-spoken white guy with a shaved head, gladiator tattoo on one bulging biceps, dragon tattoo snaking around the other, a silver braided Celtic wedding band on his ring finger. There was a large bump on his forehead, as if he'd just finished restraining an out-of-hand prisoner.

"I deal with Oughton," he told Laura and me, stance wide, arms crossed over his chest, as we waited in a small room for our tenth parole hearing to begin.

An Edmonton Oilers dream catcher hung in the window behind his head. St. Patrick's Day stickers of leprechauns, four-leaf clovers, top hats, and pots of gold at the end of rainbows decorated its panes, despite it being October.

The year was 2013, and we were at Bowden Institution, a jail an hour's drive north of Calgary, where Oughton had been transferred from BC's Mountain Institution. We'd attended every hearing over the last two decades, through marriages, divorces, children, heartbreak, depression, disease, bankruptcy, career highs and lows, and, now that we were in our mid-forties, menopause. In short, through our adulthood. Over a dozen victims, on top of the eight who had gone to the original hearing we'd attended in 1995, had come and gone, sadly never a male one. Laura (the other lone woman at the first one, now one of my closest friends) and I were the constants in a whirl of women who came to catch a glimpse of him. So many stories had been swapped, so many details shared, so much recognition of each other, Laura and I always there to offer guidance to the new ones, and now the last ones standing. Rick, head of the investigative team that had caught him after the assault on Barb, loyal friend and unwavering supporter, was there every time.

Eighteen years had passed, and controlling, attention-seeking behaviour on Oughton's part had been intrinsic to every hearing since he'd first yelled and run out of our first one, from refusing to show up at the last minute while we all waited in the next room, to an outburst in which he had been wrestled to the ground by two guards and Rick, to his insistence at the ones he'd attended long enough to speak at that "They wanted it. I am *their* victim," while his mother shot us dirty looks from her seat. When she stopped coming, we learned she had died in a car accident on the Trans-Canada Highway on Mother's Day. She'd been on her way to see him in the stretch limo she had hired.

For years, a few of us had regular dinners and brunches, the bond between us so strong despite our very different lives (from a globe-trotting high-fashion model to a personal trainer to a criminal justice worker to a midwife to a hotel receptionist) that there was nothing to explain when we talked about our issues around sex and relationships (some of us were in difficult marriages, others divorced, others dating, others too jaded to go anywhere near any kind of intimacy). During one of our dinners, held on the back balcony of a Commercial Drive Italian restaurant, we'd dialed 911 when we heard a young girl scream out "Rape!" from the dark alleyway. Laura had kicked off her heels and chased the rapist for ten blocks while I'd run the other way after the victim, a terrified teenaged addict from skid row. Too afraid to talk to law enforcement due to her hard-drug use and the petty crime that came with it, she'd continued on her way after she calmed down, and the rest of us waited for the police to arrive. Laura had managed to keep the would-be rapist in view during her sprint, and arrived with him in the back of a cruiser. When we gave our statements, the young cops, a man and a woman, thought we were pulling their leg when we told them we were all victims of the Paper Bag Rapist. Some people believed he had been a myth that parents used when barring their daughters from leaving the house.

Over the years, we'd got to know each other's parents, relatives, spouses, and friends who came to the hearings to offer support. Afterwards, we'd have lunch at Earl's Restaurant, just off the highway in Chilliwack, and discuss Oughton's latest courtroom antics, and then catch up on each other's lives. I was always alone, for the rape could never be discussed with my father, who left the room whenever I mentioned it. He wasn't even aware that I had continued going to the hearings after the first one. Right after the attack, when we'd been speeding to the general hospital along University Boulevard, he'd said quietly,

"I don't think we can ever speak of this," his voice breaking clean in two.

I'd looked out the back window of the cop car as we passed the entrance to the trail Macarena and I had emerged from just an hour earlier. I nodded, still holding my sandals in my shaky hands, my bare feet covered in the dirt and grime of the forest floor, boulevard cement, police station tiles, and UBC hospital hallways. And I understood that the pain caused by the rape of his child was bigger than the grief of his best friend being shot in the firing squad. Bigger, even, than losing an entire country to exile.

For the next few weeks, he spent all his free time with me, taking me on walks through UBC's botanical and rose gardens, and along Spanish Banks, Locarno, and Jericho beaches, during which he urged me not to tell too many people about what had happened, because the world is a cruel place and I would be blamed and called terrible names, and he philosophized about life. About how one must always stay positive and not focus on the negative. One night, he took me to Martin Scorsese's *The Last Waltz* at the Ridge Theatre. He loved the movie (as did I) and behaved like a teenager through it, bopping his head up and down to the music, clapping, whistling, and cheering, modelling his "focus on the positive" philosophy. For the first time, I saw a new side of Papi in relation to me. Although we could never talk about the rape and its effects on us, he was letting me know he could also be a friend and a peer, not just a father figure.

As for my mother, I'd been forbidden to tell her until the next time I saw her, which was later that year, when I moved back to Bolivia, the logic being that there was nothing she would be able to do from her distant post other than worry sick about my emotional well-being. Strange as it was to keep such a key piece of information from her, especially taking into account that we corresponded on a regular basis, it also made sense. My northern life was compartmentalized from my southern one; the two had never met. The rape was part of my northern narrative and identity, and being barred from telling Mami in the long letters I wrote her kept it that way. So I'd dealt with the immediate impact with the help of my friends, who were always willing to lend an ear when I'd tell them about it, ignoring my father's advice to keep it to myself, the act of repeating the sequence of events in a factual, detached way helping me to process the horror of it.

Word of the rape had spread like wildfire. It was on the cover of the *Vancouver Sun* that I delivered on my paper route the afternoon after it happened, and everyone at school and in the neighbourhood knew that Macarena and I were the victims, much to Papi's dismay. There was no need for her and me to speak of it; we both knew what we'd been through, and that was enough. We were each other's silent witness, and we were bonded for life in the certainty of what we were capable of doing for each other. In this way, I was not alone in my suffering. I had my friends and I had her. I had her knowing look across the dinner table, her gentle elbow in my ribs when breaking news of the Paper Bag Rapist's latest attack appeared on TV and in the headlines of the newspapers I delivered, I had the way she held her breath every time we passed the guilty forest.

She was now a working mother of three children and had no interest in the hearings or in meeting the others. She believed she was not a real victim because she hadn't been raped. She was hard on herself, not only in her certainty that she hadn't been victimized, but also in her core belief that the rape had been her doing, for she had mouthed the words "Do it for me" as a twelve-year-old with a gun to her head. The position he had put her in was his biggest crime, as far as I was concerned, for no matter how the adult Macarena tried to convince the child Macarena that she had been set up to feel responsible, the belief was still there, unshakable. When Laura and I spoke to our fellow survivors, we recognized a pattern in how the witnesses had dealt with the attack: drugs, alcohol, other addictions. In half the cases, the duo was estranged.

I was always alone at the hearings, and would have wanted only Macarena there, for I didn't want to take care of a third party's feelings, a role I fell into seamlessly and that I was most comfortable in. Knowing that I always chose to go unaccompanied, others' support people went out of their way to be there for me, so much so that I felt a blood connection to those parents, there to do for me what Mami and Papi had never been able to. Their pain had been insurmountable, their guilt unbearable. Neither of them could accept that there was nothing they could have done to prevent the rape, that there are things that cannot be controlled. Both knew how to fight for humanity's basic human rights: food, water, shelter, medical care. Figuring out how to provide emotional support for their raped daughter did not propel them into action the way the revolution did. On the contrary, it immobilized them, silenced them, left their lungs devoid of breath. "Don't move, don't speak, don't breathe" had not only been my survival psalm during the rape itself, it became theirs in the aftermath.

My mother had collapsed onto the couch when I'd told her and Bob in Bolivia later that year, a grunt as though she'd been kneed in the gut escaping her mouth. I knew I couldn't go into detail as I watched her double over, arms on her stomach, something I'd never seen her do before. Of all the things we'd been through in my thirteen years of life—persecution, exile, the MIR's Return Plan that had us leading double lives in Bolivia—this was the event that succeeded in pulling the rug out from under her feet.

We hadn't spoken of it after that. Referenced it, but never spoken about the actual attack or its ongoing effect on me. Bob, on the other hand, had asked questions from that day on that were hard to ask. He was brave, confronted the dark head-on, always had. When I was nine and he'd first become my step-father, I'd requested he climb Cedar with me, the only adult ever to receive that invitation. Not only had he accepted, he'd understood what Cedar meant to me and we'd shaken on the secret once we reached the top. Since then, Bob had been a twin soul. I had lacked his courage, though, for I'd never had the guts to ask him what had been done to him when he'd been held prisoner at the stadium in Santiago, what he'd witnessed, how he'd felt, the way he'd asked me. His ability to dig, to inquire over the years, helped to demystify the rape, and took away its power over us.

In 1997, sixteen years after the rape, on my thirtieth birthday and on the cusp of my Saturn Return Nervous Breakdown, Mami and I sat in the Caprice Theatre on Granville Street, waiting to watch the matinee showing of *Autumn Sun*, an Argentinian film featuring two of my all-time favourite actors, Norma Aleandro and Federico Luppi. As the lights went down, she said:

"I went to see a psychic healer the other day. Because I feel pain and I've gone to doctors and they haven't found anything wrong with me. She told me she could see me being attacked and raped when I was thirteen. I told her there was no way. That that wasn't me. She said yes, she could see it, that it was horrible, absolutely horrible. She insisted. I finally realized it was you she was seeing. It was you."

Mami's voice grew thick with emotion.

"So I told her. I said, 'What you're seeing is my daughter.' And she told me what she saw. The man, on top of you, the gun, Macarena with her face in the dirt next to you, the terror he put you through. And I kept saying, 'That's my little girl. That's my daughter. That's my daughter. That happened to my little girl.' And she said, 'That is your pain. That is the pain that lives in your body.'"

The theatre went to black, and we took each other's hands and let the tears cascade down our faces in the dark. We didn't let go, fingers braided together.

That was the first time I cried over the rape. And even then, I wasn't crying for me. I was crying for her. But that matinee brought the rape centre stage and was the catalyst, along with the breakup from the love of my life, for me to make the conscious decision to cry over it. To cry for myself, for the young girl I had been, for my loss of innocence. From then on, for the next few years, I took every month of April, always a trigger for me with its spring smells, to cry for myself, with the guidance of my long-time therapist. There were Aprils in which I wept every day. On the twenty-sixth, the anniversary date, I would drive away, taking the Sea to Sky Highway north from Vancouver, to Britannia Beach, wailing all the way, as my car, wedged between the ocean and the Coast Mountains, wound its way along the coast. Upon arrival, I would stroll around the

tiny hundred-year-old village built for the copper miners working at Britannia Mine, now a museum.

Once, on a late 1970s field trip, I'd entered its tunnels.
Wearing yellow hard hats with little lights at the forehead, all
of us delighted schoolchildren had taken a trolley deep into its
secret places, and I'd thought of the copper miners in Chile,
always on the front lines of the struggle, fighting for their rights,
many now rotting in jail, tortured, murdered, disappeared,
or exiled. Tears had filled my eyes in the dark, unexplainable
to my Canadian peers, hence swallowed down. By then I had
mastered my dual existence of mainstream Canadian life and
Chilean political refugee life. The two rarely met, although
each informed the other. Like train tracks, they ran parallel, my
ten-year-old self the only point of intersection if I lay down and
spread my limbs apart like a snow angel. The mainstream life
inhabited my head and lived on my skin, the refugee life in my
heart, guts, and womb.

Now it was the turn of the millennium and I was in my early
thirties, my solitary Saturn Return taking me back there every
spring, walking across the train tracks that lay next to the sea,
the same ones that led to the rez where I'd facilitated theatre
workshops, taking the path of grief in that mining community
that had triggered covert tears the first time I'd visited it. I was
confronting the primordial story that lived within me, abandoned but never forgotten, once and for all, there with all my
willingness to know it, to really really know it. I was asking my
body to tell it to me like it was, giving it the time and space to
unfold before me in living colour, calling on the blood coursing
through my veins, the oxygen filling my lungs, the cells trans-
mitting messages through my anatomy to bring it forth with all

its mighty force through my brutalized, pumping heart. I was ready to re-member it.

Across the tracks sat an art gallery on the Howe Sound shore, a big white wooden house with blue trimmings where classical music played at full volume. I would walk through the rooms admiring the oil paintings made by the family that ran the gallery and worked in their upstairs studio, Germans who painted the forests of the Pacific Northwest. I would take in the landscapes of yellow and red cedars, Douglas firs, hemlocks, and spruce while Chopin's nocturnes, played by Mami on the piano when I was growing up, or Vivaldi's *Four Seasons*, listened to by Papi throughout my childhood, emitted from the speakers. Coast Salish masks, drums, paintings, and jewellery also covered the walls, ledges, tables, and shelves, and through the windows one could see the ocean, the densely wooded land across the way, the trees that housed families of raccoons and on whose high branches eagles built nests.

After rambling through the gallery, I would go outside and stand under the conifers, letting the wind whip my hair, gulping down the fresh, salty air, and continue to cry for that scared girl, that girl who had had to make a terrible decision, who had been split open, who had not lain down and spread her legs for a boy her age, a boy she loved, a boy who loved her. That warrior girl who still cowered deep within me, who continued to guard my most sacred places—spaces that no longer needed protecting—with the ferocity of Medusa, turning to stone anyone who came too close. I let that girl overtake me every April from 1998 to 2004; I let her sob and wail and weep and rage and heave in pain. I let the knowing, nodding world be her witness, I let the adult me take care of her, until she was satisfied. Until she'd cried herself almost dry.

In 2009, I told the story of the rape to Oughton's brother, Marc. A restorative justice group brokered the conversation, and we met at a Greek restaurant on Commercial Drive. Laura and I were there, as well as Allison, who'd been attacked with her best friend when she was eleven years old during Girl Guide camp in Richmond on a Sunday afternoon. Rick came to the meeting, as did the two restorative justice facilitators. We victims, the three of us close friends, arrived a half-hour early to get our bearings, and once we sat down, an older gentleman who reminded me very much of my late uncle Boris approached us and asked,

"Are you Laura, Allison, and Carmen?"

We nodded.

"I'm Marc Oughton."

His ex-wife arrived a little while later. Still married to Marc when Oughton was arrested in 1985, she was now Marc's best friend. Once the others got there and we ordered our food, the encounter began in earnest. Marc's generosity humbled me. He spent two solid hours answering every single one of our questions—queries about their childhood, their parents, the most intimate, personal details of his flesh and blood. He was forthcoming in telling us how his brother's capture had destroyed his life, and the lives of his children, bullied at school. He'd lost his job and many friends, gone bankrupt, and had to endure dead silence falling over rooms he entered, distasteful pedophile jokes, and anger aimed at him. He'd attended the trial and had shared an elevator once with Laura's mother, both of them staring into space during the silent, loaded ride.

The meeting with him opened us up even more to the scope of Oughton's attacks. We'd known the repercussions on our families and communities, on the domain of our city and its suburbs, but we'd never dwelled too long on the effects on his brother, sister-in-law, nieces, and nephews. Or on his lover, a woman he lived with for the entire time he was terrorizing the Lower Mainland. When Marc and Laura's mother had taken that interminable elevator ride together, neither had been able to reach out to the other as what they both were: Oughton's victims.

At the end of our inquiry, we asked Marc if he needed anything from us. And he stated in no uncertain terms that he wanted to know exactly what his brother had done to us. So much had been alluded to, so much suggested, so much unspoken, so much left to the imagination during the trial, that he really just wanted to know. And he wanted to know from the mouths of the survivors.

I went first. Marc and his ex-wife-turned-best-friend sat across from me and I told them, including specifics of the rape itself, the one and only time in my life I would do so without sparing a single detail. Their jaws trembled as I spoke, the colour draining from their faces.

"Thank you," he said in a hoarse voice after I was done.

They'd had no idea the serial pedophile who dominated the news for so many years was the brother he'd grown up with, playing in the fields and ditches of Port Coquitlam. That the man who would arrive unannounced at their home on late Sunday afternoons, tracking moss and dirt, riding his motorcycle and taking his sister-in-law for a spin across the border to Washington, was the Paper Bag Rapist. Once he'd been captured, they realized the impromptu border crossings were his alibi. When a map taped on his wall with tacks marking the locations of the attacks was shown on the news (he'd insisted they denoted the spots where he'd sold hot tubs, as he was a salesman), as well as the guns hanging from their holsters on his bedpost, and the hair dye and disguises in his cabinets and closets, they wondered how they could have been blind to the obvious.

Allison and Laura told their stories, and when we were done, a respectful, heavy silence, like the silence heard at a wake, took over the table. Marc and his best friend thanked us again, he insisted on paying the bill, and when we hugged goodbye, we did so as fellow survivors.

The demographics of our supporters changed over the years, what with divorces, new spouses, and parents and relatives passing away. And now here Laura and I waited, alone, in October 2013, on an overcast prairie day at this Alberta jail, still standing, till the bitter end.

The hearing was held in the gymnasium, which doubled as the multicultural elders' room. A poster listing the Native American Indian Ten Commandments, a mural of Turtle Island, bear pelts, and bison and deer heads graced the walls, as did beaded dream catchers in an array of animal shapes (buffalo, wolf, eagle, raven) made from wood, feathers, fur, and leather. Bunches of sage, folded-up woven wool blankets, deerskin drums with the four directions painted on them in white, black, red, and yellow, and a lone guitar inhabited the corners. Bowden's Indigenous population stood at 30 percent. In some Canadian jails, it was 50 percent. In others, 70 percent.

Laura had managed to wangle us seats a few feet behind the parole officers. A first, since we had always been seated behind

Oughton, seeing only his profile when he entered the far end of the room, the back of his head once he sat down, a flash of his face when he'd brushed past our knees at our first parole hearing eighteen years before. Once we were all settled, he entered, flanked by three corrections officers. OUGHTON J was written in black block letters on the left pocket of his white shirt, Buddhist beads dangled from his fist, a burgundy Tibetan shawl was draped around his shoulders, and he held a foot-high stack of handwritten papers against his chest. He took his place at the table. His support person, a fellow inmate in his sixties, sat down next to him.

For the first time, we faced him. He was just across from us, close enough for eye contact. I studied his face, the face of Number Twelve from the lineup thirty-two years earlier. The face that had metamorphosed from a rough black-and-white police sketch to a full-frontal Technicolor mug shot splashed across every media outlet when one of the most-wanted men in Canada was finally caught. There he sat, closer than ever before, with his Scotch-taped glasses, wearing a silver stud in his left ear.

One of the parole officers, the only female one, swatted a fly from her face and he warned her about killing the insect, for it could be the reincarnation of his grandmother. As a Buddhist, he explained, he had taken vows against violence. He rambled for the next ninety minutes, covering all manner of topics, from his panic attacks ("I took my medication early today") to his dyslexia ("I only learned to read fifteen, sixteen years ago") to his mental illness ("I'm genetically deficient. I have paranoia and depression. I get a shot every month for paranoia") to his physical ailments ("I have cataracts") to his dental health ("I need to get my teeth fixed at Minimum"), while a young female corrections officer, one of the ones who had escorted him in, rolled her eyes behind him and let out a conspicuous sigh. Placing his hand on the stack of papers he'd brought in, he spoke of the books he'd written, one called *Mountain Thoughts*, the other *Hysterical Darkness*. In the latter's pages, he explained, he apologized to his victims (specifically, the one who had held a Bible to her chest during the attack) and their families. He stated that he had also written several tomes on psychodynamics, had run a rational living centre for ten years, and was a Buddhist teacher.

When the fly-swatting parole officer asked him point-blank about raping children, he became agitated.

He raised his voice. "There is no physical evidence of semen."

I wondered at my rape kit. I had always assumed it hadn't been frozen properly and hence thrown away, but now I made a note to ask Rick about it.

"I am not going to apologize for being mentally ill," he continued.

"I was called Bugsy as a child and everything you can imagine under the sun for having buck teeth. I was beaten and robbed in Hawaii. White females always humiliated me. They said, 'One look at your face and I can tell you're a rapist.' My victims were all in the wrong place at the wrong time. I had no attraction to them. I hated them. I am not a pedophile. I hate children. I hate my nieces and nephews."

We made eye contact. Twice.

The fly-swatting parole officer asked him about reoffending if he was released back into the community.

"I'm already in the community. I talk to people. I'm on the phone. I buy and sell real estate. This is just my office. I use my money to help others. I'm actually a very quiet person. Most Buddhists are. I came to the conclusion that no matter what you do, you can't change the world."

He pulled his meditation beads off his left wrist and put them around his neck.

Then it was his fellow inmate's turn to speak. The inmate accused the parole board of behaving like a bad parent and concluded by giving Laura and me counsel.

"I understand there are victims in the room today. I would advise you to watch the National Film Board movie *Scared of My Own Shadow.*"

We couldn't stay till the end because I had to get back to Calgary to act in a play entitled *The Motherfucker with the Hat*, also featuring my childhood friend Lucho. As we were escorted along the outdoor walkway that led to the prison entrance, we passed a Native elder with a silver braid cascading down his back and a very young Native man. They smiled and nodded at us.

Driving south on Alberta's Highway 2, passing trucks with *Bison Transport* painted on their sides and pickups driven by men in cowboy hats, Laura and I laughed at the darkly comic nature of the hearing, of his words, of his fellow inmate's statement. The land stretched out as far as the eye could see, hawks flew overhead, and magpies rested on cattle ranch fences, revealing their white-tipped accordion wings when taking flight.

As we pulled up to the theatre's stage door in downtown Calgary just in time for my half-hour call (like most actors, I went wherever my calling took me, and that fall it was Calgary for six weeks), we got a text informing us that, for the fifteenth time, Oughton had been denied parole. I walked down the back halls of the EPCOR Centre for the Performing Arts, where three theatres were housed, and greeted the *Great Gatsby* cast, some of whom I'd gone to acting school with twenty years earlier. Thirty minutes later, I stood barefoot in the wings wearing a long black oversized T-shirt with *It's All About Me* written across the front, hair in a tight ponytail, generous amounts of emerald-green eyeshadow on my lids, pointy red rhinestoned gel nails over mine, large gold hoops hanging from my ears. The Commodores' "Brick House" swelled when the house went to dark. I took a deep breath, walked onto the pitch-black stage, and stood on my mark. The lights snapped up, the song went out, and Veronica, a Nuyorican cokehead with a vicious tongue, wicked sense of humour, and heart of gold cleaned her one-room ghetto apartment while talking on the phone with her mother.

I had learned how to interpret other playwrights' text by doing it over and over again, my second language migrating from my northern head and now firmly anchored in the Southern Cone of my anatomy.

THIRTEEN

The super moon was waning, the first new moon of the fall a couple of days away. Thirty-three years had passed since the rape, and I was walking the Bowden Institution grounds again, on the last day of summer, 2014, only eleven months after the last parole hearing. The sun was rising when we got there, lighting up the big blue prairie sky from the edge of the horizon.

"Why do you want to meet him?" almost everyone had asked.

So I had quoted Laura, one of the wisest, most articulate people I've ever known.

"Because I'd like to meet the man I've been in a relationship with for my entire life."

There was also the opportunity to even out the power imbalance between us, to sit across the table on my terms and look into his eyes.

Laura and I had spent the night at the Best Western in Innisfail, the town next to the jail. Wrought iron signs daring you to *Walk on the Wild Side* hung from the main street's tele-phone poles, a red and white revolving restaurant sign offered *Western and Chinese Cuisine*, and farm machinery ads dominated the billboards. A freight train passed by the hotel, and a group of immaculately turned-out west African tar sands workers down from Fort McMurray hung out in the adjacent Boston Pizza lounge, where a young woman with a Ukrainian accent served us dinner. At the booth next to ours, eight fishbowls filled to the brim with a slushy orange cocktail were placed in front of eight young white men, perhaps descendants of the Danes who had settled here a hundred years ago, eyes glued to the Sunday night football game playing on the half-dozen TV screens strategically hung around the joint.

Brad and Abbey, the restorative justice facilitators who had brokered our meeting with Marc Oughton five years earlier, sat with us. They had extensive experience, not only in Canada but also in Rwanda and South Africa during the Truth and Reconciliation trials they had attended there. Abbey, based in Edmonton, had had several talks with Oughton in the last ten months, in preparation for the face-to-face conversation Laura and I had requested with him. He'd been open to it from the beginning, but plans had stalled when he had two heart attacks in June. Now, three months later, he had recovered enough to see us, and the four of us went over protocol as we dug into massive servings of ribs, fries, poutine, and pasta.

Inevitably, I had made the connection between Oughton's double heart attack and the ending of my play *The Trigger*. I'd hammered out the first draft—always the hardest, often likened to childbirth—in the dead of night at that drafting table in my Los Angeles room in 2003. Norah Jones's "Don't Know Why" had played on repeat on my boom box, and the sunrise had sometimes caught me still at the table. While I wrote, a hawk visited during a particularly difficult passage, the one about the rape itself, landing on the edge of the roof of the house next door. It looked right at me through the window, and stayed there for a long time, the flap of its wings when it took flight an echo of the eagle's on the day of the rape. The passage flew out of me, my fingers on the keyboard barely able to keep up with my stream of consciousness, and remained the same in subsequent drafts, needing only minuscule edits.

Victims who'd never gone to the parole hearings came to *The Trigger* when it premiered in February 2005 in Vancouver, and waited to speak to me after the show, along with their parents, friends, and partners. In the end, I had written a non-linear work for five female performers with movement, trapeze, and a live musical score. I played the rapist (referred to as "He" in the play) and the main victim, "Carmen." An actor/dancer played "Macarena," and the remaining three, actors and musicians, were a variety of characters, including other victims, cops, the hypnotist, doctors, nurses, schoolmates, friends, parents. The play ended with "Carmen" delivering the following words directly to the audience:

> As for me, I have this fantasy that all of a sudden, from one day to the next, he starts feeling things. He is no longer a psychopath. Yemaya, patron goddess of the ocean, organizes a tidal wave. And all his feelings of remorse, compassion, sadness, grief, anguish, devastation and bone-crushing pain come up like a flood. And his heart explodes with it all. No, I mean literally. His heart explodes from feeling too much.

A month before the show premiered, the 2004 Indian Ocean earthquake and tsunami caused devastation in Southeast Asia, and beloved Bob died of a heart attack. Now Oughton's heart had stopped. Only he knew whether it was from feeling too much or too little. A week before the face-to-face meeting, a group of theatre students at the University of Montana had staged *The Trigger*; this very monologue had been performed while Oughton sat in need of triple bypass surgery.

A heron flew low in the sky above the farmland on our way to Bowden, round bales of alfalfa and clumps of birch trees, their green summer leaves turning to autumn hues, interrupting the vast golden terrain. Abbey mentioned the Nirvana Outcome, which rarely happened and consisted of the offender offering a heartfelt apology to his victims. Laura and I both laughed and reassured Brad and Abbey that we were expecting no such thing from Oughton.

We walked through the entrance and were greeted by the guard, a female senior citizen, with a gruff:

"Why didn't you leave your purses in the car?"

After we put our notebooks through an X-ray machine, walked through a metal detector, and got frisked for weapons, the four of us made our way to the chapel, where the meeting would be held. We walked by two small cottages, built for prisoners to stay in with their visiting families, and a sad little playground in an abysmal state of abandonment. Several First Nations inmates were gathering stones into a pile at its centre, in preparation for a sweat lodge. Others sat at picnic tables. A stereotypical con, what with his shaved head, homemade tattoos covering his neck and face, and cold look in his probing eyes, passed us. The sun rose over two parallel barbed wire fences to our left, lighting up the willow trees that lined the path to our right. An inmate mowed the lawn underneath them.

"The sound of a lawn mower is a trigger for me," Laura said, swallowing. "My father was mowing the lawn when I got home after the assault."

The white chapel came into view, and we noticed that red police tape with the words *Danger do not enter* written across it blocked its front doors. Laura and I saw the humour in this. A bird's song reached me from a birdhouse hanging from a tree branch.

"The sound of birds is a trigger for me, but in a good sense. There was a robin singing in the branches above me right after the rape, and it brought me so much peace and comfort," I told Laura.

We spoke of how these two triggers that had presented themselves to us were connected to the immediate aftermath, not the assault itself.

We entered the building through the back door, and were greeted by the chaplain, a warm, pleasant, middle-aged man with a firm handshake and gentle eyes. A couple of inmates read on a couch in the office area, and the chaplain escorted us into the chapel itself. A sign on the door said *No entrance during Muslim Prayers*. When we entered, I noticed a painting of the Last Supper next to a poster entitled *Major Jewish Holidays*. Another poster asked, *Celebrate Recovery: When was the last time you did a house cleaning of your soul?*, and a box labelled *Wiccan Group* sat on a shelf next to a wall hanging with the words *Psalm 98:4 Make a joyful noise unto the Lord, all the earth: make a joyful loud noise, and rejoice, and sing praise* embroidered on it. A painting of Jesus behind bars also caught my eye. More than one sign implored: *Do not steal from the chapel.*

We set up the tables and five chairs, placing Oughton, due to arrive any minute, across from Laura and me. Three young corrections officers, two women and a man, walked through the chapel, making no pretence as to what brought them here: they wanted to get a look at Oughton's victims. Inmates took turns looking through a small window at the far end of the room. Moments before Oughton entered, a lone fly landed on the table in front of us. We looked at each other and laughed.

"Maybe it's not his grandmother. Maybe it's mine," Laura offered.

He entered with a cane, the chaplain following with a box. We stood. He offered me his hand.

"I'm John. Nice to meet you."

"I'm Carmen. Nice to meet you again."

It was the oddest thing to say. And yet both parts of the latter statement were true. Oughton had come into my life to teach me what I was made of, and for that, I was grateful. It was also not the first time we'd met.

"May I offer you snacks? Cheezies? Crackers? Orange Crush? Root beer? It's part of my Buddhist practice to make an offering," he clarified.

He wore the beads on his right wrist, a gold-coloured watch on his left, and a red string around his neck. The silver stud still lived in his left ear, and silver-rimmed seventies tinted glasses covered his eyes. His white hair was combed back, his white moustache trimmed. A greying white T-shirt covered his torso, jeans his legs. Once we were all seated again, he talked about the cane he used, which to the naked eye looked like wood but was in fact made of paper. By him.

"How do you do it?" asked Brad.

"I change the molecular structure of paper and cardboard to make a cane that holds me up. I make boxes, briefcases, you name it. I am a master replicator of all Buddhist altars. I'm actually an accomplished artist under a different name. I have showings in galleries in Vancouver. I hate everybody equally. I'm an artist in his cave."

He chuckled, pleased with himself.

We let him talk for the first while, get it out of his system. He rambled about having his pilot's licence but being afraid of heights, of ghosts in his room, of burying the dead birds he found around the institution, of converting to Buddhism the day a nun saw him save a mouse from being mauled by a cat. He seemed much calmer than ever before. He had always been agitated, defensive, unpredictable. Now he sat still, the cane laid out on the table in front of him. I took note of the fact that there were no guards in the room; if he did snap, this wooden object made from paper to hold him up could be a swift, hard weapon.

"I'm still in the nosebleed section of Buddhism, but I'm learning compassion."

The lone fly landed on my open notebook.

We took a break at the two-and-a-half-hour mark. The meeting was to be five hours.

Laura shook her head over lunch. "He didn't just change the molecular structure of paper, he changed *our* molecular structure."

When we walked back, it sounded as though dozens of singing birds had taken over the tree that stood outside the chapel. The sun was hot on our skin, and a ladybug crossed our path.

His Buddhist altar was set up now, and he wore his burgundy sash. We took our seats and he poured some oil into a small wooden cup that sat on the altar, placed a tiny little harp in another cup, and an Oreo cookie in a third.

"I'm offering Buddha liquid, food, and music. Would you like a cookie?"

"So you made everything we're looking at here from paper?" I asked.

It all looked like wood.

"That's right."

"Even the harp and the cups?"

He nodded. "Even my briefcase."

Brad steered the meeting towards a conversation as opposed

to a mere monologue. When Oughton had agreed to the encounter, his only reluctance had centred around my presence. According to him, I was not his victim. He had been charged with eighteen offences and convicted of fourteen. Laura was one of the latter. I was in neither the former nor the latter group. So he stood steadfast by his statement:

"She is not my victim."

I was not his victim. There was some truth to this, for there was so much more to my identity than being the Paper Bag Rapist's victim. I went anyway, of course, aware of my unofficial status. Now that we were back from lunch, Laura talked to him about her attack, and the effect it had on her and her parents. To my surprise, he was visibly affected by her story, his eyes welling up. But he said he remembered none of it.

"I have problems of losing space and time," he explained.

When it was my turn to speak, I told him that I understood that he denied being my attacker, that I nonetheless believed he was my attacker, and that we could agree to disagree on that. And then I spoke to him about the effect the rape had had on Macarena, my parents, my siblings, my friends, my community. And I said that that was what caused me the most pain. I told him I didn't feel comfortable going into my intimate life, and the effect the rape had had on me and my relationships.

"You are not my victim," he challenged, looking me straight in the eye.

I inhaled and kept my pupils on his. Themes of invisibility seemed to weave through my life: to have my immigrant story disbelieved by the mainstream since arriving in Canada, to have hidden my true identity during my underground years in South America, to have the man who had changed the course of my intimate, erotic life deny that he was the antagonist of one of my key narratives.

"You are not my victim because I don't remember you and because you are not white. All my victims are white."

"I remember your voice," I countered firmly.

"What were you wearing?"

"A white wraparound skirt, a white cotton blouse, and brown sandals."

"No. I don't remember. There were hundreds. I don't remember."

He started rocking back and forth a little, shaking his head, breathing hard, beads of sweat forming on his forehead.

I plowed forward. Talked about the axe, the gun, the psychological torture, the threat that he'd kill my family. I omitted the rape itself. And I could see his clogged-up, scar-tissued heart knocking at his chest, his T-shirt trembling, his face flushing, his eyes getting wet again. It was shocking to see him moved. The only other time I'd been this close to him, he had been so cold and calculating that I'd known in my bones from the moment we fell into his hands that we were at the mercy of a psychopath, rendering our situation hopeless. But now I saw him feel. And the foundation of my conviction that he was, when all was said and done, a heartless creature was shaken. I marvelled at the soul's capacity to transform, and wondered at the terrain of the journey the past three decades had taken him on, culminating in his heart attack and this very meeting with Laura, the star witness at his trial, and me, the embodiment of so many of his faceless, nameless victims.

"You say I did that to you?" he asked in a barely audible voice.

"Yes."

"These are stories I hear in group. . . . I blindfolded you with your shirt?"

"Yes."

"Did I ask you to do it or did you do it yourself?"

"You asked me to do it while you held the gun to my head."

"I don't own a gun. I own a rifle."

"You told me it was a gun. It could have been a stick for all I know—that's beside the point. I never saw it."

"And I held it to your head while you tied the shirt around your face?"

"Yes."

"Well, now that rings a bell."

It was more than I ever could have expected from him. I nodded and exhaled.

The meeting had gone well enough—he had actually listened to our stories and been touched by them—that for a fleeting moment the Nirvana Outcome seemed within reach.

"We would like you to apologize for what you did to us," Laura said.

"I can't give you that. I can't because I don't remember any of it. But I understand the concept of compassion for my victims. Not viscerally, but cerebrally."

"There's a need for genuine remorse, John," Brad pushed. "What some might call a godly sorrow."

He became agitated again, rocking harder, shaking his head with more force, his voice tight.

"No. I don't feel that. I can't offer that. How can I feel remorse over something I don't remember? I would have to be a fly on the wall to see it all. But I'm learning compassion."

We nodded and decided that what he was offering was enough.

It was time to leave. In parting, I said my piece.

"John, I have spent many years pondering why you did what you did to me. And I know why. It was to teach me compassion. Even in the moment, during the actual attack, I could feel your pain. I could feel it"—

I patted my heart—

"right here. And so I want to thank you for teaching me compassion."

My heart expanded in my chest, and I thought of the ending of *The Trigger* again. It wasn't his heart that exploded from feeling too much, it was mine. Every chamber opened and filled with blood, with love. His eyes brimmed with tears, and in a broken voice that dark soul that was searching for some semblance of light responded with:

"Well, thank you for saving my life."

His statement was in reference to my show of gratitude, but also alluded to the rapes. He had mentioned that if it hadn't been for the attacks, he would have turned his hatred inward and killed himself.

We shook hands in parting, he invited us to come back any time, and I accepted the package of Cheezies that he offered. On our way to Calgary airport, as I munched on his gift, I remembered the words Marc, John's brother, had spoken all those years before, and realized that that had been our Nirvana Outcome.

"I'm sorry for what my brother did to you," he'd said after hearing our stories.

Now, Laura announced as she read a message on her phone, "Look. Rick wrote back."

She'd asked him why my rape kit hadn't been used to prove that I was indeed Oughton's victim.

"Because we never knew there was one," was the answer.

I let out a laugh and shook my head.

I looked out the car window at the passing farmland, ranches advertising rodeos, and recalled the short story I had written when I was sixteen, only ever shared with Alejandro. In that rudimentary piece of prose, Oughton had apologized profusely and I'd forgiven him. I'd written the Nirvana Outcome before he'd been caught, in the prequel to his having a face and a name.

It had been nine years since I'd been in a relationship, and 90 percent of that time had been spent in celibacy, finally coming home to myself, learning how to love my own company, surrendering to solitude until I'd found a love so immense inside my own heart that there was no more void to fill, no more seeking affirmation outside myself.

I finished off the Cheezies and thought of Robert, dear friend and theatre school classmate who had happened to be on the same flight to Calgary when we were on our way to meet Oughton. I'd told him what Laura and I were about to do and he'd offered his support. He'd been one of the peers in the circle during that pivotal voice class when I'd relived the rape for the first time, when my knowing, crucial body had first told me that it was ready to release it, twenty-four years earlier, almost to the day. Robert's clear blue gaze had met mine when I'd opened my eyes after that catharsis, and after all that time he stood before me at Calgary airport, giving me a bear hug before continuing on his way.

A week later, I would go to Britannia Beach again, a place I hadn't visited for a decade. Walking through the old gallery, admiring the paintings of bison, bears and cubs, birches, the Vancouver skyline, cherry trees in full bloom, a five-foot-long raw wool dream catcher hanging at the entrance, lutes, ukuleles, and accordions leaning in the corners, the big house silent now, the German family no longer there to play the classical music I loved so much, the only sound that of my shoes on the oak hardwood floor, I meditated on how far I'd come since I'd wept my way through these rooms, expelling the remnants of Oughton from my bloodstream, guts, and womb. Upon leaving, I would notice an antique axe propped up against a windowsill, the landscape of a temperate rainforest meticulously painted on its blade. I would shake my head through a smile, stroll down to the dock littered with cigarette butts, and behold hundreds of flies feasting on the pink flesh of a sliced-open salmon laid out on the rock.

During our send-off from the chapel, Oughton had complimented *Something Fierce*.

"My aunt read your book about the underground. She really liked it. Maybe you can write my story someday."

If there was one thing I'd learned from being raped after smoking a stolen cigarette under the canopy of my childhood rainforest—cathedral, playground, witness—on a faraway Sunday afternoon, it was to never say never.

When our plane landed in Vancouver and I walked through the airport's automatic doors, I was met by the sight of hundreds of sparrows flying in and out of the crown of a tree, zooming and diving, all of them chirping, the chorus of their song overpowering the roar of the planes above, the hum of idling cars, the greetings and goodbyes of the travellers coming and going, the pentameter of my own overflowing, embodied heart.

Acknowledgements

I would like to thank my writing group, who heard excerpts of this book throughout the writing process and offered invaluable feedback. In alphabetical order, they are: Leanna Brodie, Lucia Frangione, Meghan Gardiner, Gilles Poulin-Denis, Jovanni Sy, and Marcus Youssef. I would also like to thank fellow writer Dawn Dumont of the Okanese Cree Nation for providing helpful insight into chapter nine. Friend and colleague Quelemia Sparrow, of the Musqueam First Nation, on whose land the University Endowment Lands are located, walked Fairview trail with me and pointed out the names of the flora that surrounded us. An eagle flew above that day, and a humming bird greeted us when we reached the spot where the rape had taken place.

A huge thank you to the Canada Council for the Arts for the individual writing grant, as well as the Writers' Trust and the Woodcock Fund for additional financial support. A week away at Joe Creek Retreat on British Columbia's Sunshine Coast provided for precious writing time. The island of Naxos, Greece, where I completed the final draft, was the ideal location for a four-week writing retreat in the summer of 2015. Thanks to the staff at Prado Cafe and Renzo's Cafe on Commercial Drive in Vancouver for never saying a word when I chained myself for hours to one of their tables and only ordered one cup of tea.

I am associate playwright at The Playwrights' Theatre Centre in Vancouver and am grateful to my fellow associates, Elaine Avila, Dave Deveau, Hiro Kanagawa, Adrienne Wong, and Artistic Director Heidi Taylor and dramaturge Kathleen Flaherty for the animated and informative discussion around the controversial title of this book.

I would like to thank Francisca Rodriguez, Laura Glover, Allison Campbell, Barbara Kelt, Joanne Morgan, Fernando Frangella, Richard Lawrence, Maria Mana, Marc Oughton, Barbara Pulling, Emiko Morita, John Sweet, Mark Bantey, Katey Hoffman, and Warsan Shire.

Gratitude to my family and friends, as always, for their unconditional support during the writing process.

Tremendous gratitude to my brilliant, patient, understanding, wonderful editors Deirdre Molina and Anne Meadows for their keen eye and superlative notes.

And finally to my beloved agent Sally Harding for taking me on, for the endless emails and phone calls, for the support, and for that lunch on the water when the idea for this book crystallized.

CARMEN AGUIRRE is a multiple-award-winning Vancouver-based writer and theatre artist who has worked extensively in North and South America. She has written or co-written twenty-five plays, including *The Refugee Hotel*, which was nominated for a 2010 Dora Mavor Moore Award for best new play. Her most recent one-woman shows are *Blue Box* and *Broken Tailbone*. Aguirre has eighty film, TV, and stage acting credits, including lead roles in the Showcase series *Endgame* and *Quinceañera*, winner of the Grand Jury Prize and the Audience Award at the 2006 Sundance Film Festival. Her memoir *Something Fierce* won Canada Reads in 2012, was a finalist for the Charles Taylor Prize, and was a #1 national bestseller.

Permissions

Grateful acknowledgement is made to flipped eye Publishing Limited for permission to reprint previously published material from Warsan Shire's poem "Conversations About Home (at the Deportation Centre)" from the book *Teaching My Mother How to Give Birth*, published in 2011. Reprinted by permission. Production photo of *The Trigger* by Tim Matheson.